CW00422141

An Autobiography of a
NOBODY

An Autobiography of a
NOBODY

IRENE GOUGH

authorHOUSE®

Chapter 1

From Strange Beginnings

I am, a nobody, nothing special, but somehow over the years, friends and acquaintances have found my life experiences to be both comical and unbelievable at times and on many occasions I have been encouraged to write a book. Maybe I should start at the beginning.

My Maternal Grandmother (Nan), a Londoner, widowed early in life, was left to bring up six children, 3 daughters and 3 sons, one of which sadly died in infancy. There was very little help to hand in those far off days between the two World Wars and as a means of surviving Jessie took a job on Paddington Station—generally sweeping the platforms and keeping them clear of litter.

One day Fate was to take a hand when onto the platform spilled forth a family from 'up North.'
Charlotte (who later became my Paternal Grandmother, known as Gran)) and her brood of six, 3 daughters and 3 sons. They were carrying all their wordly possessions—this was to be a new beginning for them. Tired, almost penniless and with nothing except the dream of a new life, Charlotte gathered 'her tribe' and looked about uncertain of her next move.

Nan, big hearted as she was, went to help and the rest, as the saying goes, is history. Realising the predicament Charlotte was in, with nothing organised, Nan could not see her and her children on the streets. Her shift was almost over, and invited them to go home with her to her 3 bedroom flat. Impossible, you might say, but that was the special kind of person Nan was. The decision was not a popular one with her own children, understandably so, but Nan could be quite formidable at times, and on this occasion her mind was made up.

Sleeping arrangements were quite simple, boys in one room, girls in another, and adults in the third room. Those that could, crammed into beds, those that couldn't, slept on the floor—and even the floor was a much better option than sleeping on the streets.

At first, Nan's children greatly resented the 'ragamuffins from the North' with their scruffy clothes and weird accents, being forced to share their meagre rations, but slowly the children made friends, as only children do. A decision was made for all the children to go out and look for work in order to help out.

My Mother was the eldest of Nan's children and my Father, the youngest of Charlotte's 'tribe'.

My Mother always thought herself above the scruffy, snotty nosed urchin that had been forced upon her and as she always said, "even his hair was uncontrollable and stuck up at the back."

I have to agree with what she said as it still sticks up like that to this very day.

My Father just thought she was stuck up and tried to have as little to do with her as their situation allowed. They hated each other on sight.

These living arrangements lasted for several years and gradually the older children joined up as World War Two loomed. My Mother joined the WAAFs, and my Father, too young to join up legally, lied about his age and went off to join the Royal Navy.

The war with all its' hardships followed and gradually over the years, Mum and Dad put their differences behind them, started to write to one another, and finally had to succumb to the fact, they were in love. A romance and marriage that was to last for over 60 years.

Chapter 2

A Marriage made in Heaven

After the war, housing of course, was very hard to come by. So many properties in London were destroyed in the Blitz and my Parents decided, after their marriage, to set up home with my Nan. By this time there were only two of my Nan's daughters living at home, which allowed Mum and Dad to have a room of their own. It was not an ideal way to start a marriage even though they all got on very well together After my arrival, a couple of years later, my Father made the decision to take up a labouring job at AERE Harwell in the rural countryside of what was then Berkshire. This employment, he hoped, would provide his wife and daughter with a better way of life. Encouraging people to move away from the war damaged cities with their housing shortage, places like AERE Harwell offered employment with housing. This allowed my Father to take up the tenancy of a prefabricated bungalow which was to be our home for the next six years.

My birth in the flat in the White City allowed me to be a fully fledged 'Londoner.' Minutes after my birth my Great Aunt declared, "was it worf it gal, she aint arf ugly?". My Nan counterclaimed, "Ugly in cradle, pretty at table" and I became her pride and joy. My Mother, when she moved to Harwell, missed the hustle and bustle of London, the constant stream of visitors to my Nan's house, but most of all, the comfort and confidence of living with her Mum.

We visited Nan on numerous occasions and I spent all my holidays there until I was quite grown up.
It never ceased to amaze me when I visited with Mum, there was a special whistle which my Mother always did on the approach to Nan's to denote we were in sight of her flat and then the answering whistle from Nan which meant the kettle was on. In those days we did not have the luxury of a car but travelled up by train carrying everything we needed and walked from the local underground station. Nan would always be there to greet us, filling the doorway with her stocky frame as she scooped me up and smothered me in her ample bosom.

Cups of tea were provided in abundance and always a dishful of Quakers Puffed Wheat for me. They never tasted so good—I do not actually like them now that I have grown up but the memory of those Puffed Wheat can still bring tears to my eyes and make my mouth water. I loved being at my Nan's.

When I stayed, as I often did, there was always someone popping in—the teapot on the go permanently—adult chat, aunts and uncles, great aunts and uncles and cousins I hardly knew, all were made welcome. Maybe this constant hive of activity made my Mother the unsociable person she became. She was different from her Mother, they were almost opposite ends of the spectrum. I like to think I have grown up to be more like my Nan, caring, not only for my Family, but anyone who might need my help. I have tried to model myself on her and hope, if she were still alive today, she would still be as proud of me as I was to be her Granddaughter.

When I stayed with Nan we would always go shopping in Shepherds Bush Market and shopping in the Market was something special, especially with my Nan. Nan knew all the costers and could give as good as she got, even if the air was tinged with blue for most of the time. She would show me off to everyone declaring "This is my Bubbles' daughter from the country" and they would tweak my rosy red cheeks.(I have to explain, Bubbles was my Mothers's nickname from childhood when her hair had been very curly!—It stuck with her throughout her life.) It is no wonder my cheeks are red now with broken blood vessels—they damaged me for life with their overzealous tweaking!

My holidays with Nan were a joy to behold—a time of special memories. Memories of playing in the courtyard with my newly found friends and the inevitable raucous yell of "Irene, get your arse in 'ere, you are not to play with those bleeding piccaninnis!" I suppose that was my first encounter with racism. Even in those far off days of my childhood it was almost impossible to find someone to play with who had the same colour skin as I had. It was ironic that the area was called 'White City.'

As I grew older I became more trustworthy and was allowed to play in the park across the road. This park held a special magic for me as Nan had explained that if you followed the path through the park, the BBC Television Studios were immediately behind it. Wow, that was news indeed! I knew famous actors and pop stars must be continually visiting the studios, so armed with my autograph book and pen I set off on many occasions in the hunt for 'Celebrity Monickers.' I found my way easily through the park and out the other side and Lo and Behold there was a sign directing incoming traffic to the studios. I had made it—all I had to do was sit and wait. Every time we visited my Nan from that moment on I would take my leave and take up my vigil on the kerb outside the BBC. I dreamed of catching sight of Cliff Richard, Adam Faith or Marty Wilde but they kept evading me and I was convinced that the continual stream of vans and dustcarts were a clever ploy to whisk my idols away out of sight from the Public eye. I must admit it was a lonely vigil—was I the only fan interested in autograph hunting? Very naïve and probably the least worldly wise girl on this planet, it never once occurred to me to question why I never managed to get one single autograph in all the months and probably years that I sat on that kerb kicking the dust. It was not until many years later after my Nan's death, when we had severed all ties with the 'White City' that I saw the BBC Studios on the television one evening. Suddenly the penny dropped—I had been sat all that time at the service entrance.

Somehow it all fell into place. Electricity vans, plumbers vans, dustcarts and the like—how foolish did I feel, but it did make me chuckle all the same. I am sure the children of today would have cottoned on a lot quicker but as a child I was very innocent and never looked beyond what I was told—the other side of the park was what my Nan had said, so that was where it was!! It was a good job I grew up and widened my horizons or I could still be sitting there to this present day.

Chapter 3

Learning my Place in Society

My Parents move to AERE Harwell was an enormous change of life for them. This was a time for standing on their own without the close knit infrastructure of Family and friends. Our neighbours in the street seemed to have everything—cars, they went on holidays and more aggravating than anything else were their 'posh accents.' I have to admit they all looked down their noses at this new Family of infiltrators, Dad with his broad North Country brogue, and my Mother with her loud, very colourful, London accent. It took a long time before we were accepted and then only on the fringe of Society, we were never included at the heart. Our life was never a social whirl of cocktail parties, afternoon teas or coffee mornings but the occasional nod of the head in passing, that is, if caught unawares, they didn't have time to cross the road and look anywhere but at us. I think we were thought of as social 'misfits.'

I started school from this 'prefab' and can still remember with pride, my red trimmed uniform, my beret at a rakish angle, complete with satchel, compliments of 'Father Christmas.' I had to travel by school bus to Chilton Primary and Anita, a neighbour's daughter attending the same school, was given the job of looking after me on the journey. I remember Anita as a tall, pretty girl, very sophisticated and grown up. The reality of it was that she could not have been any older than 11 years old as it was a Junior School and pupils had to move on to Senior School after their eleventh birthday.

It was here at Chilton Primary that I first encountered bullying. I have always been a bit nondescript, never standing out from the crowd and certainly never wanting to. Showing off was never in my genes and as long as I could blend into the background I was ecstatically happy. At playtimes, I tried to keep out of everybody's way, not making friends easily, and too young to play with Anita's 'cronies.' There was one girl, I never did get to know her name, who would stalk me round the playground giving me 'evil looks.' I would put my head down and try not to make eye contact. She was much bigger than I was and quite menacing looking and every time I looked up, she was there staring back at me. I was terrified of her, even when I was at home my sleep was disturbed with nightmares about her. The only respite I had from her was if Anita allowed me to join in her game. Well, I am sure we have all played this game in our lives. After grass cutting had taken place, collecting up all the newly mown grass and making it into the shape of a house complete with, sitting room, kitchen and bedrooms—oh! and my contribution to the game A KENNEL! I was the dog, kept in a kennel outside the house shape where I stayed tied up until playtime was over. The other girls never played with, fed, or took any notice of their 'dog' but I did not care. Bliss Indeed! Free from fear—I am sure Anita never realised how grateful her 'dog' was to join in the game. If I close my eyes and think about it I can still remember that fear.

How I pity the victims of bullies these days, bullies who are far more vindictive and threatening than that unknown girl from long ago. Over 50 years ago but fundamentally life has not changed much has it?

When I was about 6 years old, my Father left the employ of the AERE and we therefore had to vacate the 'tied prefab.' We then moved to a brand new 3 bedroom house in Didcot, care of the local council. Didcot, when we first moved there, was only the size of a large village. We lived in a cul de sac and soon got to know our neighbours in the nearby nine houses. It was a lovely place to grow up at that time. We had friendly neighbours, other children to play with, schools close at hand and countryside on our doorstep. I have wonderful memories of street games, skipping with a long rope held by a couple of Dads, cricket with the lamp post as the stumps, kite flying, or rather brown paper bags on lengths of wool, we were far too poor to own proper kites.

It was whilst we were living here that I really began to understand that there were different standards of living. We were definitely not rich by any means of the imagination. Dad always worked hard but by now there had been two additions to the Family in the shapes of my two brothers. Dad's wages had not grown in comparison, so our budget was very tight.

Next door, on the other hand, lived a very rich family indeed, or so they seemed by comparison at the time. I was friends with their daughter who was slightly younger than I was. Their house on the outside was identical to ours but inside—it was a haven of ecstacy! Their house had treasures in abundance. They had a television, a studio couch with cushions and proper rugs on the floor—items I had never seen before. I liked playing with my new found friend because she would invite me to stay to tea quite often. They would have bread and real butter, thick enough to make imprints of your teeth in and cream cakes—heaven. My friend always wore shop bought school uniform and when she had a party, can you believe, the jelly came out of a mould and had a proper animal shape—usually a rabbit sat in green jelly grass. They even had a car. How was that for being really rich? It did not take a lot to impress me in those days.

Without any disrespect for my Parents, who did their best with what they could afford—I felt like a pauper alongside my rich neighbour. Our house, always clean and warm could only offer, a wartime suite that my Nan had covered at some time, in brown mock leather, rugs made from cut up stockings and rags and lino instead of carpets. There was no real butter for us—'Stork' margarine was the order of the day and our party jelly came out of a bowl, a dessertspoonful at a time hurled at the dish. My Mother's culinary presentation left a lot to be desired. We never went hungry but Mum's burnt cakes and blackened jam tarts never seemed quite as appetising as the cream cakes next door.

My school uniform was always tenderly made by my Mum. She knitted my jumpers and got the lady next door to help with the tunic or skirt. Mum was never a competent needlewoman but she did try her best. The rest of my uniform which couldn't be made, was always bought with economy in mind, usually two sizes too big. Even my huge apple catcher knickers were bought to grow into. I looked horrendous the first year but by the third year I didn't look too bad, if a little worn round the edges.

I must admit when I passed my 11+ (the only girl in the street to do so) I made my Parents very proud—their daughter was off to Grammar School.

Chapter 4

Unhappy Schooldays

$\mathcal{P}$rior to the start of the new term my Parents were issued with a complete uniform list which was as long as your arm. They did their best and managed to accumulate all the items needed except a pair of hockey boots. Money and patience had run out by then and they scratched their heads thinking how to get round this last obstacle. My Mother had a brainwave and off she went. On her return she had accomplished what she had set out to do and brandished a pair of hockey boots. Where had they come from you might ask? She had remembered there was a local jumble sale being held and had managed to secure the boots for a fraction of their true cost. The only problem was—the size. They were plenty big enough for me to grow into—Yes sir, they were size 8 and I was just in size 2.

I have great memories of hockey games where I would take two steps before the boots would move. Opponents feared my flapping feet much more than a swipe with my hockey stick. Do you know something? I never did grow into those boots, but funnily enough neither did they ever wear out.

I can honestly say my schooldays were dreadful—I was only an average student except for English. I loved English with all my heart, no matter whether it was writing essays, reading books or learning poetry. Mathematics, on the other hand, was purgatory. I have never been able to understand Maths. Do not get me wrong, I can add up, subtract, I know my tables and I can divide but beyond that it was, and has remained a mystery I no longer wish to unravel. How long does it take to fill a bath with water, if Jack has several marbles and his sister a few more, or if a man on a cliff sees a boat out at sea—whatever is the relevance to me? I would turn the taps off when it was full, leave Jack and his sister to enjoy their game of marbles and if the boat out at sea was in trouble, call the coastguard. See, I think I understood more than I realised. I could never grasp the fundamentals of maths and angered more than one teacher with shrugs of my shoulders. It was not a shrug of defiance, as they always interpreted it, but a sign of despair.
I knew the penny would never drop and I could not wait to leave. Remembering my schooldays brings back all kinds of horrors.

I have to admit that I did love sports lessons. I enjoyed the energy and competitiveness of tennis, netball and hockey, although not quite so when an overzealous swing of one of my classmate's hockey stick took out my front tooth. These activities, excluding the tooth incident, were fun but spoiled by the fact that communal showers were to follow. I absolutely hated having to shower in front of everybody else. Nobody saw me without clothes—not even my Mum, so why did they expect me to strip off completely naked in front of my whole class plus a 'Nazi Type' gym mistress. She would stand at the entrance to the showers barking orders and never once did she fail to notice I had not joined the throng of naked bodies dutifully trotting through the showers like sheep to be slaughtered. I was always the one in the corner hoping not to be noticed, wrapped in an oversized towel but once spotted and told off I was the one that went round the shower at the end of the lesson at breakneck speed. I would go so fast that the water hardly touched me—what a waste of time! I am sure that that gym mistress got perverse pleasure from watching me squirm.

Sports days at the Grammar School, I always thought were on a par with 'Ascot.' Expensive cars would arrive in abundance—Rolls Royce's, Bentley's, and Mercedes. Those that alighted from the symbols of wealth were a sight to behold. Picture hats as I had never seen before, ladies dripping in gold and jewels and men dressed in the most expensive suits, complete with cravats.

My day was always tinged with the most excruciating embarrassment as I awaited the arrival of my lone Parent. Dad was always too busy working to attend, he could not afford to have the time off work as by now there were four of us children to feed. The honour of attending Sports Day was always left to my Mum. She, like me, was like a fish out of water but steadfastly determined, she did not want to let me down. Just before the proceedings were about to begin I could guarantee she would make her appearance, furiously pedalling up the long drive on her bike, dressed appropriately in her headscarf and 'mac.' She rarely left home without these accessories, just in case it rained.

I look back now and realise that she was probably the most genuine Mum there. So many of them came to flaunt what they had, having very little interest in the sporting activities of their daughters but Mums who just needed to be seen. At the time I could have won a medal for burying myself in a hole, as at that age it was so important to be 'one of the gang—to be accepted.' It was many years later that I was to learn the true value of true feelings and friendship.

Chapter 5

The Adventures of the 'Famous Three'

I was not a girl who made friends easily, I lacked, what most children have in abundance—confidence. I had two special friends, sisters who lived at the end of my road. One was slightly older than I was, the other slightly younger. Our adventures were straight out of Enid Blyton's 'Famous Five.' Even though there were only three of us it did not deplete the excitement we felt when embarking on our next adventure. The Hagbournes were the settings for most of our excursions. I am not sure that the villagers were aware that they lived in the most exciting place on earth. Haunted houses, abandoned behind thick overgrown hedges, Amazonian type jungles of uncut lawns and windows veiled in cobwebs so thick they could only

have been made by alien spiders. Derelict houses left
with doors hanging at various angles from damaged
hinges and creaking floorboards that had us conjuring up
visions of ghosts and ghouls of a bygone age, disturbed
and wreaking vengeance on us, poor mortals. We had no
concept at that time that we were trespassing on Private
Property—excitement and adventure were the name of
the game.

Another deserted property led us to believe we had
discovered a 'dead' body. Having crept through the
undergrowth of a very overgrown garden we tried to
peer through the extremely dirt laden windows. As this
was an impossibility we decided to explore inside and
climbed over the broken down front door. On our travels
throughout the rooms we suddenly were rooted to the
floor with fear. We had found a 'body'. We glanced at
each other and again at the hairy being sprawled on the
floor. Long matted hair, greying beard and odd shoes
exposing several toes peeping through a once colourful
sock. At last our searching had not been in vain. This
was what it was all about—murder, intrigue. Should we
look for clues? All around our 'victim' lay empty bottles
and cigarette stubs. Silently we scanned the crime scene,
maybe we could find a weapon? Suddenly, our 'victim,'
without any prior warning, let out a string of obscenities
as he tried to get into a more comfortable position. I am
not sure which 'detective' moved first but I think it was
'as one'. We leapt from that room, hurdled the broken
front door and cleared the Amazonian jungle in three
almighty bounds. In no time at all the Hagbournes were
behind us as we fled for home. I now realise that what
we had come across was probably an alcoholic tramp,

under the influence and sleeping it off, but at the time the 'body' was real and when we returned next day our fears had been confirmed. The 'Bodysnatchers' had been, no trace was left behind—only the empty bottles and cigarette stubs. What other explanation was there to three adventure hungry young girls? The girls of today with their make-up, designer gear and electronic entertainment have no idea what they are missing!

There was a farm just across the fields to where I lived that sold vegetables, potatoes and cheap windfall apples. On Saturdays it was my job to collect the weekly vegetable order. Due to the weight of the bags I always had to have help. The quicker this job was done the sooner my friends and I could go off on more adventures so they were always willing to be my 'pack horses.' Whilst awaiting my turn in the queue we noticed a barn next door which housed and old farm cart. All three of us came away with the same idea. What an adventure it would be to sleep one night in the farm cart. It would take some planning but nothing was impossible. We set to work. Blankets, pillows, torches, lists were made and arrangements were confirmed. That night would be ideal. It had been a lovely day with no rain, perfect for what we had in mind.

After tea, our watches synchronised, we went to our respective homes and bedrooms to await the witching hour. At midnight, when everybody else was asleep, we would make our move. It was arranged that hourly, torches would be flashed at bedroom windows to make sure we all stayed awake. The arrangement was fine for the two sisters who shared a room, they could take it in turns to sleep in between their hourly signal to me, but me, I had to stay awake until midnight. I struggled, but managed it, and at the appointed time after our last signal, I crept downstairs and out through the Dining Room window, remembering to leave it slightly ajar.

Away to the end of the road I crept, not unlike a tortoise, blanket and pillow attached to my back and torch firmly grasped in my sweaty hand. At the corner, we met and proceeded across the fields towards the farm. Oh how different it all was at night!. All that rustling in the grass, snuffling at your feet, shining eyes reflected in the torch beams and bats skimming overhead. This was not how it was supposed to be. At last we could make out the shape of the barn that housed the cart that was going to be our bed for the night. It was all so simple, toss up the blankets and pillows, climb up the wheels not forgetting to hang on to our torches. As we went to throw our legs over the side of the cart we disturbed several large menacing animals with long tails and beady eyes. They squealed, we screamed and grabbing everything that we had brought with us, fell off the cart and ran for our lives. The torchlight had gone out in our panic as we sped across the uneven ground in our hurry to put as much space as possible between us and those 'man-eating animals.' Maybe we were not the intrepid adventurers that we thought we were. Tired, beyond belief, we said our 'goodbyes' at the corner and returned to our beds via the part opened windows. Creeping through the darkened house I managed to get back into bed without being caught.
I tried to get to sleep but every time I closed my eyes I had visions of those awful animals running across my

hands and arms as they had done earlier that night. Little did I know at that time about RATS! Eventually I did drop off into a fitful sleep as exhaustion, mental and physical, finally took over.

As a Parent myself now—I look back with horror at the dangers that could have overcome us, as we, three very naïve teenage girls, pursued our life of make believe and adventure—or did we live in a different kind of time then?

Was it a time when children were allowed to be children, to use their imagination and the word 'bored' was never heard? What memories will the children of today have when they look back on a childhood filled with television, electronic games and hanging about aimlessly in gangs—their minds robbed of imagination and their only adventures watched on a television screen. It is such a shame that they do not know what they are missing!

At this time our local shopping centre consisted of one line of shops that went from one end of the 'village' to the other but only on one side of the road. One of these retail establishments was a shop called 'Locktons.' The shop was owned by a Family that lived in East Hagbourne. The Mother worked in the shop and was a slightly built, very haughty woman with her hair tied up immaculately in a bun at the back of her head. I remember there were two sons, one much older than I was and one, maybe just a couple of years older. He was our target!

They were very rich, living in a beautiful 'Tudor' house, skirted by our favourite stream where we spent many long hours fishing with a net and jam jar, our prizes being spectacular sticklebacks. The younger son was tall, bronzed and extremely attractive to the three adventurers. I am not sure what we would have done if he had even spoken to us but it was enough to just feast our eyes on him. This was the difficulty. He neither went to our local schools or hung around in our neighbourhood. We had no options other than to spy on him, but that was another problem.

We could not obviously go through their front gate, far too posh—so it was to the rear of the property we made our way. Behind the house the gardens were set out rather formally, a large striped lawn with occasional trees dotted about, surrounded by a wide shrubbery down either side. At the furthest point from the house a wide strip had been left to overgrow and the grass was waist high. Determined as ever, we followed the stream to the rear of the property where we did a 'death leap' over the stream and undergrowth, throwing ourselves headlong into the long grass. In the distance we could hear the 'putt, putt, putt' of a Suffolk Colt, a lawnmower only the rich could afford. As we raised our heads slightly, the smell of newly mown grass wafted across the distance between us and the gardener. We needed to get closer in order to spot our 'Adonis' through the window but there he was in his 'Ivory Tower' guarded by this 'conscientious manservant.'

Backwards and forwards, the gardener marched across the garden, we did not dare move for fear of being spotted. Elbows at the ready, our only mode of transport we slithered across the uneven ground to take up our vantage point hidden in the long grass. At the end of the rows as he changed direction, we leapt, one at a time, into the sprawling growth of a nearby shrub. We now had to progress shrub by shrub, nearer to the house.

No matter how long we lay there, on the more successful days, the days when the gardener did not catch us and chase us helter skelter through the undergrowth, over the stream and away up the lane—we actually never caught sight of our quarry. We spent many afternoons during the school holidays on this mission but to no avail. It was many years later that we found out why. During the summer holidays the 'Lockton Boys' visited relatives in sunnier climes across the Channel and during the winter holiday they could be found skiing in the Alps.

We realised then, on hearing this that maybe we were setting our sights too high—very rich and very poor do not generally mix! What would we have conversed about. I would have been enthralled to hear of his foreign escapades but could I have captured his imagination by tales of holidays spent in a caravan, our only excitement, apart from seeing the sea, was to sit in a local pub garden, sucking lemonade through a straw and trying to find the blue twist of salt in a packet of crisps. It would hardly have been captivating conversation in comparison.

The house is still there today but 'The Locktons' long gone. On walking through the Hagbournes as an adult I can cast my eyes over that black and white property and immediately be transported back to times when

Summers were hot and started at Easter and continued forever, a time of thunderstorms and when Winters had deep snow. It was a time of fun and freedom before the agonies of growing up started to take hold. Wonderful years, the memories of which will stay with me forever. I may not have been rich in money and possessions but my memories are a rich tapestry which can never be taken from me.

Chapter 6

In Fashion at Last!

I have mentioned before how difficult I found it to make friends and this included both those of my own sex as well as those of the opposite sex. I had very little confidence that was not helped by the fact that, unlike most of my peers, I could not keep up with the latest fashions. Mum's needlework was very basic—she had mastered the art of four panelled skirts but had to have a neighbour help her put in the zips. These skirts were always topped with her hand knitted jumpers, or if I was lucky, a twin set. My shoes were always a solid pair of 'Clarks.' There was not anything feminine or alluring there then! It was no wonder that I did not fit in. This was at a time when kitten heels, net petticoats in various bright colours and checked skirts were all the rage. It was a time for pretty blouses, pop records, dancing and generally getting to know boys. I never stood a chance. My Parents believed in keeping me a child until the day I got married, and they succeeded.

The one school friend I had that I had gone right through my schooldays with, had Parents who were completely different. She was allowed modern clothes, the freedom to go out with boys and allowed to stay out until what seemed unearthly hours. (I had to be in at 10pm until the day I got married). She even had a Saturday job and was allowed to baby sit for the owners children. How was that for being grown up?

I thought my route to being allowed to grow up was via a Saturday job. I thought if I had my own money I could afford to buy my own clothes and leap into the modern world. I should have known better. We did not have a television to feed me ideas and I was not allowed fashion magazines as they were deemed a waste of money so how this modernising leap was successfully to take place, I was not sure but I was not put off. I would earn my money and take it in easy stages.

I remember one craze which I thought I might be able to join in. Girls had started to wear long legged Broderie Anglaise knickers. The garment would be prettily decorated with a bow of coloured ribbon which hung just below the hem of the skirt or dress. My modern friend and I consulted on this and decided we could make them cheaper. We decided to play truant from school, visit our local haberdashery shop and buy all the necessary bits and bobs required.

It was obvious from the outset that we were not experienced enough to make the actual knickers, so we thought we would do the next best thing and buy them ready made. Here we hit out first obstacle as we could not buy Broderie Anglaise knickers with long legs. It seemed they were only made as the complete fashion item which was totally out of our price range. We looked round for a substitute. It seemed the only long leg knickers were 'old ladies drawers' in either apricot or powder blue. They would have to do. We bought a pair each, mine were apricot.

We purchased a length of Broderie Anglaise lace and a length of ribbon each. We could not return to school, so took an afternoon off to spend with my friend's Irish Grandmother. She was only too pleased to entertain us and kept us fed and watered with lemonade and Irish soda bread.

She helped us with our stitching and by school home time we were the proud owners of two pairs of long leg knickers complete with lace and ribbon.

On Saturdays, I now worked in a very old fashioned sweetshop and tobacconist that had been vetted by Mother. The owner, a rotund gentleman of very upright stature, thought it his life's work to make sure that men who smoked pipes had the correct one for their needs and was being supplied with the correct tobacco. As I was under age I was not allowed round to his side of the shop and I was kept busy on the sweets and chocolates side, weighing out various tasty morsels from large glass jars and wrapping boxes of chocolates. In order to reach all the glass jars it was sometimes necessary to climb a stepladder and on this particular Saturday, it was my downfall.

If anybody had noticed my little bow hanging slightly below my hem, they would have perceived that I was a 'modern miss,' for the first time ever. Not, I might add, after the incident that followed. I was up the ladder selecting the required sweets when a certain gentleman thought he would be clever and tweak the little bow in front of a shop full of customers. To my horror, the leg of the 'drawers' slithered down below my knee in full view of everyone. The impression of being a modern girl, now seen to be wearing 'old ladies drawers,' had been shattered. Needless to say that was the first and only time they were worn. I would have to save even harder in order to buy my modern attire, I could not afford any further 'bloomers.'

As you will have already learned I was hardly a modern miss. My Father never earned substantial wages which allowed for fineries and my Mother knitted for the Family. I never had modern clothes but I never went short of 'twin sets', which for those fortunate enough not to have had to wear them, were woollen short sleeved jumpers with matching long sleeved cardigans. I had them in various colours but they were all plain knitting. There was never a pretty pattern to make them look more attractive. Considering I was fifteen years old and my complete wardrobe consisted of two, four panelled skirts in grey and navy, (made by Mum, of course), several twin sets, a pair of 'Clarks' brogues and a school mackintosh—it was hardly any wonder that I didn't attract the boys.

This situation was to change one day when I met my very first boyfriend, He attended the local Senior School of which the playing field backed on to the cul de sac where I lived. I stood for hours chatting through the chain link fence until he became brave enough to pluck up enough courage to come round to the house to ask my Dad if he might take me out. He was slightly older than I was and remember how excited I was when he received a 'Blue Streak' racing bike for his 16th birthday. We felt like a couple of whiz kids on our racing bikes, his blue and grey and mine apple green and pink. My Parents had struggled to buy this bike for me as a reward for my doing so well in my exams. I loved it, it was my pride and joy and I joined a local cycling club. (I was the only girl with 14 lads) John joined the club with me and although he was not that keen on cycling, I think he did it just to look out for me, as what he really wanted was a motorbike.

Every Sunday we would turn up and cycle approximately 80-100 miles on a circular trip. I was not so bad on the straight flat roads but when it came to hills, I was very grateful for my friend.

He used to put his hand on my back and propel me along at breakneck speed. Derailler gears and leg muscles were not enough for me—I also needed help from human propulsion as well.

Sadly, when my friend was 17 his Parents bought him a motorbike and shortly afterwards, on his way to a speedway meeting in Oxford, he was killed as a result of a traffic accident. This was my first encounter with death. I was not allowed to attend his funeral service and sat crying in my Biology lesson at the appointed time. It took me a long time to get over his death and I still have the card with his funeral details in my Bible to this very day. As long as I live he will remain a very dear memory for me. My very first boyfriend who I remember as a perfect gentleman, who made me feel very special even at that very early age. It was at this time that I began to realise just how hard hearted my Mother was. I do not know if she meant to be or whether it was just her way but on my return from school, when she broke the news to me of his death, it was done in a very direct and blunt way. There were no words of comfort to soften the blow, and when I naturally burst into tears, there was no Motherly hug to accompany the earth shattering news. I had a finger and thumb placed over each shoulder, keeping me at arm's length and I was told "Pull yourself together girl. It is no good crying, no amount of tears will change what's happened." I suppose she was right, no amount of tears would change things, but a hug and a cuddle might have helped at that time. Sadly, I never did understand my Mother's way of thinking and it caused us to have a tempestuous relationship as I grew up.

A few months later, I was to have my second encounter with death. The young girl that lived opposite us in the cul de sac had 'disappeared' from the street. Adults spoke in hushed tones and us, mere children, were not allowed to know why. It seemed, I found out later, that the poor girl had found herself in 'the family way' and had been whisked away to a home for 'unmarried girls,' that was situated in Maidenhead. There were no details discussed in front of us until sadly, after the birth of her little girl, our friend died. We were devastated, she was our friend and we hadn't known anything about it—all we had been told was that she had gone away for a holiday and nobody seemed to know when she would return. Sadly, she did return briefly to the street, in a coffin on the day of her funeral. The whole street turned out and attended the funeral. This was to be my first funeral and I found it heartbreaking. What a waste of life, wiped out in her late teens.

We are talking about a time when it was thought to bring shame upon the Family. Pregnancy before marriage was a mortal sin and a girl was thought a 'slut' and a 'harlot' to behave in such a way. This was at a time when families shouldered the blame and girls were not patted on the back, given fistfuls of money and found rented accommodation to allow them the freedom to go off and have more children by a selection of unsavoury characters. Girls were frowned upon and few had the courage to bring home their offspring, pressure being put on them to have them adopted straight from the home.

After the death of their daughter, their only daughter, the sister of two brothers, everybody was astounded that they did not decide to bring the baby home. Of course, their daughter could not be replaced but just to have 'a little bit of her' in the form of the child, surely would have been a comfort. Her Family obviously did not see it like that, and had the baby adopted. They neither saw her nor showed any interest in having anything to do with her. The neighbours reeled with the shock! Nothing was ever heard of the child again for 40 years.

The Family, who attended church every Sunday, without fail, did not meet my criteria of being Christians after this. I was quite young, in my mid teens, but even at that time I could not understand the family's reactions. Was that how true Christians behaved, by turning their backs on one of their own? I did not think so! It made me realise that just by going to church every Sunday, it did not necessarily make you a Christian. To be a true Christian, it had to come from within, it was not what was shown to impress others but how you felt inside and how you behaved accordingly. The lesson I learned then has, I hope, remained with me and I do try to behave as I feel my Faith expects. I am far from perfect, and admit to making mistakes but then I am only HUMAN. I do have a conscience and if mistakes are made I do try my best to make amends.

Over the years that followed, bad luck seemed to follow that Family. Neither the Mother nor the elder son lived very long as both contracted terminal illnesses. After a respectful length of time the Father remarried and sadly was killed in a car crash outside his place of work shortly afterwards. I knew the younger son and he grew up, married and had a family of his own. Nearly 40 years after the birth of that little girl, her uncle tried to trace her. He was successful and met up with her just before her 40th Birthday.

Many years later I attended a Youth Club Reunion Party that many of my childhood neighbours had belonged to at one time or another. It was great to catch up and the details of 'the little girl' and the reunion with her uncle emerged. She was now obviously grown up, married with children of her own and strikingly like 'the Mother she had never known.' She had been trying to trace her 'proper Family,'supported in this quest by the very kind Family that had adopted her all those years ago.

Her uncle, formed a bond with her and her adoptive Family, but sadly that was not to last long. In 2008, he also contracted a terminal illness that took both his mobility and his mind and just before Christmas 2008, he succumbed to the inevitable, a young man in his 50's. At least he made the effort to make ' the little girl's' dream come true—She now knew who she was!!!

Chapter 7

From Rags to Riches

*W*hen I was fifteen something really exciting happened in our household. My Father had always promised my Mother that one day he would win the Football Pools. For those who do not know what Football Pools are—they were the equivalent of today's lottery. You had to guess a selection of games to draw when professional games were played on Saturday afternoons. The results were always broadcast on both the radio and the television on Saturday evenings and you made your claim very much like you do with the lottery today.

Over the years that my Father did them he only ever managed to win a few shillings, nothing substantial. One Saturday this all changed. My Mother desperate to replenish her yellow dusters went to a sale with neighbours at a local club where she knew she could pick them up for 1p each. One of our neighbours bought a late issue paper from a vendor outside the club and asked if my Mum knew the number of draws my Father had done. Great excitement ensued as the amount £800.00 winnings was mentioned. Dusters forgotten—Mum and neighbours returned home to break the news to Dad. My Parents were over the moon—£800.00 was a vast amount of money!! When they actually checked their coupon, astonishment and shock set in as the amount turned out to be considerably more. The amount was over £5000.00. We were rich!!!

In due course the cheque was sent through to Dad with a framed copy. We all looked at it, touched it and then sat down to discuss what we were going to do with it. We, as a Family, had never had enough money to warrant dealing with Banks. In fact, we had never been inside one, they were only for the very rich.

It was an exciting day for us all when we cycled off to our local Barclay's Branch. We must have looked like 'The Clampets', (a hill bill family from an early television programme) when we pushed ourselves through those large heavy doors. Unsure of what we ought to do we hovered at the back. Dad went up to the Counter and waited, and waited and waited. Several customers came in after us and were duly served and still Dad waited. He tried to catch someone's eye but was told everyone was busy when they so obviously were not. He tried once again to speak to a severe looking woman behind the Counter who looked extremely put out that 'this peasant' was trying to engage in conversation. Telling my Father he would have to wait yet again he pulled the cheque from his pocket and threw it onto the Counter explaining that he just needed to know what he had to do with it. She looked down her nose picked up the cheque and suddenly all hell broke loose.

Bells rang, chairs were brought out for us to sit on and within seconds we were being offered cups of tea and apologies for being kept waiting. What is that expression 'Money Talks!!!!' Suddenly we were being treated like celebrities—What hypocrisy!!! The Bank Manager appeared shook my Parents' hands and ushered us all into his office at the rear of the Counter. He congratulated them on their win and opened the account without any further fuss. We were now 'officially' rich.

This boost in our fortune happened just before my 16th Birthday and I was lucky enough to have the very first cheque from the brand new cheque book. We all stood and watched as Dad wrote out his very first cheque. How exciting—£20 cash! I had never had so much money and planned a shopping excursion to Oxford on the train.

Having cashed the cheque at the Bank off I went with that vast fortune burning a hole in my pocket. I bought a fluffy blue and green coat with a tie belt that on reflection made me look like a huge cuddly multi coloured bear, 2 pairs of pyjamas, pants, bra, socks, stockings and shoes, dresses, blouses and a couple of skirts. I had never owned so many clothes. I felt like a film star.

Mum and Dad were far more sensible. We had always lived in either a tied prefab when Dad worked at Harwell and we were now currently living in a 3 bedroom Council house in Didcot. All that was soon to change. We could now afford a house of our own. New private houses were in the process of being built behind Queensway on the fields that we had played on as children, now sold for housing projects to accommodate the growth of Didcot. Dad chose a plot and we watched with interest as the building grew. This was to be our new home. The day of the big move came and not for us a removal lorry like most people—no we had to move on the back of Fred Sutton's Coal Lorry. All our worldly possessions on display for all to see. I found it all terribly embarrassing. Eventually we all moved into our new home and very comfortable it was too. It was very basic and there was no central heating but Dad arranged to have storage heaters installed. These proved not to be very efficient but at least they took the chill off the air. Dad paid outright for the house stating that he had never had anything on Hire Purchase and he was not about to start now. This was where the bulk of the money went. Next came the furniture and carpets, real luxury and finally the car. We had, up to then, only owned bicycles but now we were the proud owners of a Morris 1100 car in Harvest Gold.

Dad could not drive and asked one of his colleagues from his local dart team to teach him. My Father, rather set in his ways, did not take to driving very easily. To Stan, his mate, it must have been like painting the Severn Bridge, a never ending task. Week after week after very long week Dad continued with his lessons. If Stan had been taking payment for these lessons he must have ended up as rich as my Dad. It seemed to go on forever, with Dad attempting his test on 3 occasions before finally being able to discard his 'L' plates. I am afraid that Dads' driving skills never really improved, neither did his attitude to other road users. He felt, because he had paid his road tax he was more entitled to be on the road than other drivers. He would cut people up as they tried to enter a motorway or dual carriageway from a slip road and would state that he had right of way and would never move over for them. He was a very selfish driver and I am sure he did not realise how many collisions he nearly caused with his 'dog in a manger' attitude on the road. Even my Mother did not like travelling with him and his Grandchildren were totally banned from the car for their own safety.

He continued to drive in that erratic way having many minor accidents along the way until at the age of 70 we, as a Family made the decision to write to the DVLA to ask them to revoke his licence. Our thoughts were for everyone concerned, Dad, Mum and anyone else he pointed the car at as all the mishaps along the way were never his fault, according to him. Funny That!!!!!

Our extraordinary wealth allowed us yet another luxury—a holiday at Butlins. According to my Father only rich people could go to Butlins and now here we were rich. We had only ever been away in caravans previously. Please don't feel sorry for us as my Parents always made sure we had a holiday every year. Dad would save all his shiny sixpences in an old 'cocoa' tin with the top welded on and the contents of that would allow us a week away in a caravan.

There was never any luxuries like eating out. We would do an early morning shop to include food for breakfast, food for sandwiches throughout the day and food for the main meal in the evening. Spending money was allocated to £1.00 per day for the Family which allowed us one ice cream each plus in the evening when we walked out to the local pub, Mum and Dad would have one drink each and the children (even at 16 I was still classed as a child) were allowed one glass of lemonade and a packet of crisps each. Trying to find that blue paper containing your salt before your siblings was a game in itself. We were very easily pleased in those bygone days. I often wonder how the children of today would cope with the simple way of life we had in my younger days. My childhood, yes even at 16, was filled with wonderment and excitement, every day being a new adventure. I feel very sorry for the children of today who at seven years old want to be dressing and behaving like grown ups. What childhood memories will they have to amuse them in their dotage? Will they have any memories at all as a good percentage cannot even face up to the lives they live and become involved in heavy drinking and drug taking to blot it all out in the name of 'having a good time!' I am convinced that children of today are no happier for having 'everything.'

Butlins was a whole new experience, swimming pools on site with huge fountains, indoor pools where you could sit underneath, drinking coffee and watching the legs of all the swimmers enjoying their daily dip. There were free fairground rides and amusement arcades to walk round, popping pennies into slots if the weather changed to rain. There were a whole range of competitions throughout the day and evening for all the members of the Family, Bonny Baby, Junior Princess, Sports for the boys, Donkey Derby's, Knobbly Knees and Glamorous Grannies—you name it and Butlins catered for everyone.

There were Redcoats on every corner, helpful and smiling, encouraging children and adults alike to make the most of the facilities. At night there were Glitzy Cabaret Shows with high kicking girls, Talent Contests and every conceivable dance catered for. We had a wonderful time. In those days it was almost unheard of for holidays to be taken abroad, so to us, we had reached the pinnacle of holidays and made the most of every moment. My first Butlins holiday was imprinted on my memory for ever. I also remember it as the place that introduced me to the famous 'Knickerbocker Glory.' Such Happy Days!!!.

Chapter 8

The Joys of Growing Up

Our house, a haven of safety whilst growing up, was never a social centre. Mum and Dad, even if they had any friends, were never social butterflies. Dad played darts for the local pub and Mum went to Bingo weekly. That was the extent of their social whirl and the friendship that they shared was enough. All the time I lived at home I never heard them exchange a single cross word.

As children, when someone knocked the door to see if one of us was available to play, the door was opened, an answer given and then the door was rapidly closed leaving the awaiting child on the doorstep. Never was a child allowed in to wait, play or sleep over and the only exception to them coming to tea was on Birthdays when Mum would relent and let only our next door neighbours children in for our Party. If ever I, or my siblings asked if someone could come in to play the answer was always the same, "No, don't you think I have enough to cope with having you lot, without entertaining all and sundry." It amazes me that I grew up to be as sociable as I am, it was not a skill that I learned from my Parents.

On the odd occasion that I was invited to stay at a friend's house, Mum always had to check it out first. She would contact the Mum in question to make sure she would be there during my visit, and to confirm what time I was to arrive and leave. I know she was trying to keep me safe but I was nearly 15 years old and all my school friends seemed to be able to come and go as they pleased. On one such occasion I was to stay over at my friend Angela's house. Angela's Mum was very laid back and Angela had all the freedom that I had only dreamt of. I was never allowed out once darkness fell (no decent girl roamed the street at night) so when Angela suggested we go to the local Fish and Chip Shop, where all the local girls and youths hung out, I was beside myself with excitement.

That night, did I but know it, my Future was mapped out with one chance meeting.

When I look back to how naïve and ignorant I was of all things worldly, it was no wonder that the 'Teddy Boy' with his winkle picker shoes, tight trousers and 'Teddy Boy' hairstyle, stole my heart.

He was aptly named 'Wiggy' by his peers and although
I was dressed in my school uniform (having been
allowed to go to Angela's straight from school) he
seemed genuinely interested in me. I did not realise
at the time that the interest in me was only to make
his current girlfriend jealous, but I was flattered. He
chatted and I listened and we agreed to meet up the
following afternoon at his house where, it seemed, all the
youngsters used to meet up to listen to records and to
play cards.

I stayed that night at Angela's and talked and dreamt of
my new found 'hero.' Next day on my return home I
did not dare mention my afternoon assignation. I hunted
through my clothes to find something suitable to wear
but as my 'hip-chick' social life was non-existent, knitted
twin set, four panelled skirt and 'Clark's' brogues were
the order of the day and off I set to meet my 'Knight in
Shining Armour.' As it was afternoon, Mum and Dad did
not worry about where I was going. I could not go far, I
did not have any money.

On arrival at the house, opposite the Fish and Chip
Shop, which had been pointed out to me on the previous
evening, I knocked and waited. I could hear the music
from within as my knees began to knock and I wondered
what I was doing there. Suddenly the door flew open
and I was amazed at the number of faces there seemed
to be. I was taken into a back room where the latest
records were playing at full volume and a card game was
in progress. I did not have a record player at home and
my only chance to hear the latest music was for an hour

on a Wednesday evening when I was allowed to listen to Radio

Luxembourg (the volume turned right down) while my Parents played cards with my Gran. She was our only visitor and every Wednesday she made the pilgrimage on the bus from Harwell village to Didcot, in order to join us for tea and a game of 'Pontoon.'

Sitting in the back room of that house, I felt as if I had arrived. I had at last caught up with my teenage years. Everybody seemed to be smoking and singing (they knew the words to all the songs) and generally having a good time. I sat next to 'Wiggy' who seemed to be the leader and I have to admit that I felt very special. During the afternoon, his Mother brought through cakes and non-alcoholic drinks and people came and went. I found it very exciting and was asked if I would like to stay to tea. Oh my!! I could not believe my luck but there, as time wore on and dusk fell—the nagging doubts started to creep to the forefront of my mind. I felt so grown up—I was—I was now nearly 15 years old.
In the course of the evening 'Wiggy' asked me if I had to be in at any particular time? What could I say? Yes, I have to be in before it gets dark or be like everybody else and go home when they pleased. Fingers crossed behind my back—I declared that I had no curfew hour. As time passed and 8pm loomed and went my nerve gave out and I said I would have to go. He asked if he could walk me home, so we set off hand in hand. It was so romantic, the night was black, only broken by the occasional street light where we stopped for a kiss and a cuddle. 'I was in love.' I floated homewards on a fluffy cloud of dreams.

This was what I had read about—this was all part of growing up, what a wonderful feeling, but no, my dream was about to be shattered!. In the distance I could see her coming towards me like 'Colossus on Speed.' She loomed up in the darkness shouting, "Irene, is that you? Stop sucking each other's noses and get your arse indoors now!!!" I froze on the spot as my beau disentangled himself from me and disappeared in a cloud of dust. I felt the cuff of my ear as I ran past her at breakneck speed, not waiting to hear the list of expletives that followed me up the road with 'her' in hot pursuit. I ran like the wind in order to reach the safety of the bathroom (the only room in the house with a lock) before she caught up with me. How could my perfect day end up like this? I raced in, up the stairs, threw myself through the door and slid the bolt into place. I was safe, at least for the moment. I sat on the edge of the bath and waited for the continual torrent of abuse that had followed me up the stairs. From behind the door I heard it all. "How disrespectful I had been to cause them to worry! Who did I think I was staying out until this unearthly hour? (Remembering it was still only 8.30pm) Was I becoming a 'tramp' and an 'whore?' Where had I been all this time—I had been out since 3pm that afternoon?"

When Mother's temper had subsided enough for her to listen I tried to explain where I had been and what I had been doing—listening to records and playing cards. Whatever it was I had been doing seemed to trigger off her anger again and I was accused of being at an ORGY (pronounced with a hard 'g'.) Mum never did get the pronunciation right, bless her, but the reality of the situation is that even now being in my 60's—I have never been to an orgy in my life!!! What a sheltered life I have led!.

My romance, despite my Mum's attempt to sabotage it, blossomed and although my Dad did relent a little with my curfew hour, I was allowed to remain out, if I was going somewhere special (the cinema for instance) until 10pm. This rule remained in place until I married 'Wiggy' just before my 19th Birthday.

If I did have an outing to the cinema I had to go extra early to see the end of the film first, because the normal showing did not end until 10.30pm and I had to be in long before then. My Parents were sticklers for rule keeping and 10pm was 10pm—not a minute later! You can tell by this that we could never be called 'little ravers!' During our courtship I was very rarely allowed to go dancing—dances finished far too late for 'decent' girls to attend and as for holidaying together that was almost out of the question except on one occasion. We were allowed to visit my Mother's sister who was told never to leave us alone together. We were always to be chaperoned. With hindsight, I wonder why he ever stayed with me?

Unbeknown to my Mum and Dad, they need not have worried about my straying off the straight and narrow. My greater fear was that if I had become pregnant, I would not have the courage to tell them. It would have been too great an ordeal—that was protection enough. Apart from that I had not forgotten my friend who had died having her baby, had that been a complication or could that happen to me?

At school we had learned about the birds and bees but absolutely nothing about human reproduction. I knew I should stay out of the way of a besotted bee or a rampant robin, but a man—well, that was a different story!

My Mother was never one for speaking about issues below the waistband so even the normality of just 'becoming a young lady' remained a mystery to me. Out of the blue one day, Mother grabbed me by the arm, threw me headlong into the toilet—quickly followed by a sanitary towel and a belt with loops on it. I had no idea what it was or what I was supposed to do with it? Ignorant, even at 16 years old, I thought I was being punished. A hushed discussion through the closed door vaguely revealed all and I was sorted. During this discussion I was told for the next week I would not be able to wash my hair, have a bath or go swimming.

The penny then dropped about my friends. There had been days when they said they had been unable to wash their hair or they had not been able to go swimming on days we had arranged to go. They would say "Sorry, I can't go, I've got you know what." At the time, I had no idea what they had been talking about but as everybody else seemed to understand I did not want to show my ignorance. At last, all was revealed.

Life got no better as marriage approached. I still had no idea what to expect or where babies came from or how they came into the world. Those 'treats' were yet to come. When I think how knowledgeable young girls are today, I cannot believe how ignorant and 'green' I was in those far off days of my youth. My interests were not in sex or drugs but in the romance of stories such as 'Little Women' and 'Good Wives' or the mysteries of 'The

Nancy Drew Stories.' I look back on a childhood that lasted forever and although it did not equip me for what was to come, it has helped me to retain an element of fun when it comes to special times like Christmas, Easter and Halloween that I can now share with my Grandchildren. I do hope I never become a 'grumpy old lady.'

Chapter 9

A Marriage made in Heaven?

My courtship was a non-eventful time. It was expected of us to marry and we drifted into a pattern like so many couples do. We would see each other most nights and either spend it at his house or our house, with a trip to the Pub at weekends to break the monotony.

Our relationship was an on/off affair at the beginning and during that time I worked as a telephone operator at Oxford General Post Office. A rather dashing young lad, who was training to be an engineer, caught my eye. He was slightly older than I was but I knew he had his eye on me, and he had his own car. Very impressive! For several days he followed me to the train station when my shift had finished. After a few nervous attempts at work to open a conversation with me, he did eventually pluck up courage to ask me if he could give me a lift to the station. We chatted on the way and he seemed quite nice. Unfortunately, the relationship never actually got off the ground due to unforeseen circumstances. As my train pulled into the station, he leant over to give me a quick kiss. Unexpected as it was, I moved, and our faces bumped. In the collision he had dislodged my front tooth crown—a result of an overzealous swing of a hockey stick. I felt it 'ping' off and knew I would be left with the metal rod that had replaced the root, sticking out of my gum, as I watched in horror as it landed in the foot well. At that very minute I felt like 'Cinderella' at midnight. Without a word, keeping my mouth well and truly shut, I grabbed the offending article (hopefully before he had seen it) and fled into the station. On the train, I looked in my compact mirror, and felt I resembled an extra from a horror film, instead of a front tooth I had a 'metal fang.' Very attractive! I never spoke to the lad again I was too embarrassed—I'm not sure what he thought, or if he had actually seen anything, but if he thought his fumbled kiss had offended to that degree I expect he spent the next few weeks practising kissing his hand or a mirror to improve his technique. It took a couple of days before I was able to see a dentist so I couldn't even explain why I had behaved the way I had. I expect he just thought I was a 'weirdo' and thought he had had a lucky escape. The romance was over before it had begun. At that time I must have been destined for 'Wiggy.'

My relationship with 'Wiggy' was what might be described as a stormy affair. We eventually got back together and decided to get engaged. I had seen the engagement ring I wanted in a jewellers in Oxford. In my meanderings at lunchtime whilst working as a telephone operator I had spotted this little ring. I am not really sure that it was an engagement ring, more a little dress ring, but it had caught my eye and I had fallen in love with it. I spent many months checking to see if it was still in the window—long before I had anyone interested in marrying me. That little ring must have been earmarked for me as when it was bought—it saw me through two marriages. (I will explain in a later chapter)

'Wiggy' did everything right. He firstly asked me, and then he asked my Dad 'for my hand' although I guess, by this time, it was more than my hand he was after. Dad agreed and wedding plans were put in place. When I consider the girls planning their wedding today, including both my daughter and daughter-in-laws, life was so different back then. I had no original ideas of my own about what dress, venue or carriage I preferred, but I did know what I wanted my bridesmaids to wear. Everything was arranged for me. My wedding dress was to be made by my Auntie Mary (she had previously been employed by Norman Hartnell, the Queen's dressmaker). My wedding cake was to be made by a neighbour who made cakes for all and sundry (it was to be 3 tiers, I was told) and the reception was to be held at the local 'Labour Club' at reduced rates, due to my Parents being full members. Taxis, to finish off the package were to be hired from the local cab firm. Entertainment was covered by the local pub pianist, a middle aged lady who liked a drink, but knew all the old pub songs. Well, you could not have a wedding for 'Londoners' without an old

'Joanna' and a sing song! That seemed to cover all aspects of my wedding except for the bridesmaids. 'Wiggy' and I agreed on who should be our bridesmaids and thinking about it now, I think that was the only decision we ever did agree about! We were to have my younger sister, his toddler sister and his niece. They were perfect for what I had in mind. I wanted them dressed in crimson velvet dresses trimmed with white fur, carrying white fur muffs. Perfect I thought for a January wedding. I had seen the combination whilst watching 'White Christmas', a couple of years before and my mind had been made up. This, I did not know at the time, was an ominous sign for the marriage. Everybody smiled to my face, but behind my back they were talking about 'blood and bandages.' In Folk Lore it seems the combination of red and white at a wedding is a sure sign that it will fail. How right they all were! Those 'Folk' whoever they were, knew their stuff!

My hen night was a very tame affair by today's standards. A small party, and I mean small, consisting of my Mum, his Mum, his two grown up sisters, my Auntie Vera and of course, not forgetting the Bride to be. We all met at a local pub, in the saloon bar as we did not want any rowdiness, to have a cordial drink. We met at 8pm and were back indoors by 10.30pm. You can see from that what a riotous affair it was!! There were certainly no male strippers, saucy tasks to perform or blown up condoms in sight. In fact, nothing of any consequence was ever mentioned, not even a dirty joke or innuendo. 'Nice' women did not discuss anything ' a bit sordid', and we were if nothing else, 'nice' women.

The day of the wedding came—a cold wet day in January. Dad was so proud as I made my appearance. I like to think of myself as a 'vision in white' but as I was neither glamorous, nor very confident, the saying 'All brides look beautiful' was my only hope. I can remember getting out of the taxi at the church and thinking, I missed my friend (my first boyfriend) whose ashes were buried alongside the church wall. Was it right to be thinking of a lost relationship on your wedding day? The signs were all there, but as the saying goes, 'love is blind,' and all I was short of was a white stick.

At this time, I had a cousin who was an actor, and believe it or not, his fan club (small as it was) was gathered outside the church in order to catch a glimpse of him. My Dad, as proud as a man could be, walked me, like the innocent victim that I was, up that aisle like a lamb to slaughter.

The day went without a hitch. Everybody had 'a good old knees up' and at 6pm, my new husband and I ran up the road, in pouring rain, to catch a train to our honeymoon destination. There was no flight to the Maldives, Bahamas, or Jamaica for us. We were heading for a 'Butlins' hotel in Margate, Kent.

We waved from the train window as our fellow revellers slowly disappeared from view and took our seats on our way to Paddington Station where we had to change trains. I looked at my new husband and down at my shiny new gold band and a slight doubt entered my mind. Had I really done the right thing? Did I really want to spend the rest of my life with this man or would I rather be back in Didcot within the safety of the Family Circle, back home with Mum and Dad? I put it down to nerves and concentrated on holding my left hand at various angles to see who would notice we were newly weds—oblivious to the confetti that adorned our attire and had gathered round our feet like 'slipped halo's'. Arriving at Paddington, we had to wait an hour for our connection so we made our way to the Buffet for a cup of coffee. I think it was while we were having this drink that I had the revelation that all was not as it should be.

I suddenly missed my Mum and Family so much that I found it difficult to hold back the tears.
Instead of a comforting word and a cuddle, I got an unkind comment about 'cutting Mummy's apron strings.' This confirmed my worst fears. Who was this 'monster' I had married? There was no going back, I had made my bed, and that was another thing, I had no idea what to expect later. Today, you will read this, and not believe that someone of 18 nearly 19 years old could be so naïve, but, believe me, I was.

We caught our train in silence and whilst he slept most of the way to Kent, I sat and seethed about his lack of understanding. We managed to get a taxi at the end of our journey, which took us to our honeymoon hotel, amidst good wishes from our driver. We booked in and were shown to our room. Oh my goodness, too late to turn back!!

He apologised for the earlier incident and put it down to tiredness and the pressure of the day. We looked round the room with it's en suite bathroom (a real luxury in those bygone days) and he positioned himself on the bed, and beckoned that I do the same.

Panic set in, and I swung my case up beside him to put a barrier between us. "Let's get ourselves organised, and hang our clothes up," I found myself saying, hoping to put off the inevitable. Disappointment showing in his eyes, he started to unpack his case and surprised me with a parcel, all beautifully wrapped and ribboned. How thoughtful, he had bought me a present. Another diversion, I thought, as I slowly unfolded the shiny silver wrapping.

A silver box—I carefully lifted the lid to find the most gorgeous negligee. I held it up as I thanked him and then my heart sank. It was sheer, you could see through it!! Where was my Mum and Dad when I needed them?

I made my excuses and went to the bathroom, where I bathed, cleaned my teeth and did my hair. Never had it taken so long to do my ablutions. I thought that if I stayed in there long enough my new husband would go to sleep. It was not to be. It shows you just how 'cabbage like' I was, even on my wedding night—my Mother's lack of information had a lot to answer for. I was completely out of my comfort zone. My normal attire when going to bed were fleecy pyjamas, warm woollen bed socks with a warm fleecy dressing gown for extra warmth. I am talking of days when central heating did not exist for the working class and lino, not wall to wall carpets, were the norm.

I crept from the bathroom without a sound, slithered onto the edge of the bed and tried to get in without disturbing what I thought was a sleeping husband. No such luck. Well, the rest is history. My first night was not to be remembered for earthmoving passion but for a night of tears, of homesickness and an almighty row, with me wishing I had never met him and him wishing he had married his former girlfriend. Right at that minute, I have to admit, I also wish he had.

The rest of the honeymoon was almost as successful as our first night. I spent most of it alone, walking the length of the beach wishing I was back with my Mum and Dad. He spent it. playing bar billiards in the hotel bar with some new found friends. It was the start of a very stormy marriage which was to last for three and a half years.

Chapter 10

Facing the Families

Our arrival home from Margate was a farce. Our Families were eager to hear about our holiday and so not to disappoint or worry them we pretended we had had a wonderful time. It was only in the privacy of our home, a caravan we had bought prior to the wedding, that an uneasy truce was reached.

He did what most men do when there is a problem 'at home'—he either went to the pub or to the club on the premises where he worked. I immersed myself in 'playing house.' I didn't mind staying in listening to the radio (we did not have a television in those days), or either knitting or reading. I kept myself busy cooking, cleaning, washing and ironing and very occasionally, if he invited me, going for a drink with my husband. This was not altogether a good idea as when he had been drinking—I saw a side to him that I had never seen before. I knew his Father had been violent towards his Mother at times, but now I was facing 'domestic violence' for the first time. It started with an odd slap here or a shove there but it escalated to such a pitch that I no longer wanted to go out at all and always tried to be asleep when he returned home. I had never encountered this before and I was convinced that it was my fault. It seemed to me that I would antagonise him without even meaning to. Who would in a situation like that? He was very crafty as my bruises were always where they would not show and in front of others he was the perfect partner. I felt I could not speak to my Mum and Dad as they had never had a cross word, let alone exchanged punches, and they would not understand. In desperation I tried to have a tactful word with my Mother-in-Law hoping she would discreetly speak to him about his behaviour. If she ever did, it did not make any difference, his behaviour never changed!

I am speaking about a time when 'domestic violence' was allowed to happen. Police would not interfere between husband and wife as long as murder was not committed, everything else, although frowned upon, seemed acceptable. The general feeling was that a woman should not upset her man and I obviously did this on a regular basis—it was obviously my own fault. Of course, today things are very different, nobody has to suffer abuse, but back in those days what happened behind closed doors was nothing to do with anybody else,—you just got on with it!

During the day, I worked full time so I could forget my misery. Most nights he went out so my evenings were relatively peaceful. If I was still up on his return, his conversation would be littered with girl's names from the dairy where he worked. Once again I showed my gullibility, I could not see what was being unveiled right before my eyes but if it kept him happy, I was relieved.

We continued to live in this uneasy state for a couple of years. Divorce was unheard of, only existing in the lives of the rich and famous. I had made my bed—I now had to make the most of it. How easy it all is for the youngsters of today. If it does not work out, walk away—there is plenty of help at hand. In those day's life was not so simple. Do not get me wrong, I do not regret one single day of my life. The hardships I suffered during those bleak days, made me the person I am today, strong, compassionate for those less fortunate but experienced by life's hard knocks to help others through emotional times.

One day, I woke not feeling too good, but made my way to work as normal. I reached the railings of the church where we had been married, only to find myself retching uncontrollably. I hung on the metal railings thinking I was going to die. If I had eaten something that had disagreed with me—this was a very violent reaction. After a short while normality resumed and I continued on to work. Everything seemed to have settled until next morning. As I caught sight of those railings I was off again—retching uncontrollably. I could not understand it, had I suddenly become allergic to the sight of those railings—if so I would find an alternative route to work?

This continued for the rest of the week and I began to worry there was something wrong. I usually was very fit and never needed to visit my doctor but this was an exception—it was not only dragging me down but making me late for work. I could not have been less prepared for the shattering news he was to give me a few days later. I am sure you guessed it long before I did—I was pregnant!!!

Chapter 11

Strength born of Adversity

Oh no!—I couldn't be—Pregnant! I had never considered having children, they were what other people had, but not me!. We were supposed to be going out for a drink with my Parents on the day I got the news. I felt suicidal. I went home and told my husband who, I might add, surprisingly was over the moon with the news. He could not wait to tell everyone and my Dad seemed pleased but my Mother's remark was "You silly cow." I do not think my Mother had a maternal bone in her body and was never pleased to hear when anyone was pregnant, even though this was to be her first grandchild. I tried not to think about it as I grew steadily, bigger and bigger until in no time at all I had turned into a 12 stone lump.

Our relationship at this time did not improve although
occasionally he would take me to the local Marlborough
Club to have a drink with his Parents. It was on one of
these occasions, that I said something he did not like, as
we were leaving the Club. His violent streak came to the
fore, he was never one to discuss things rationally, and
punched me clean over a low garden wall. I ended up
flat on my back in someone's front garden not unlike a
tortoise upturned on its' shell. I was 8 months pregnant
at the time and I looked like a galleon in full sail—I
was huge! I was laid on my back with my legs in the air,
hardly looking a glamorous sight, struggling to regain my
feet. He had walked off in a temper leaving me to my
own devices.

I know, with hindsight, I should have left him then but
as I have said so often before, I was not worldly wise and
my bed had been made. Nobody had forced me to marry
him, although he did not show his violent side prior
to our marriage. I would try to make the best of it and
maybe, just maybe, he would change after the baby was
born?

I worked for as long as I could keeping good health
throughout the pregnancy. During this time I attended
the antenatal classes which proverbially 'Put the fear of
God in me.' My naivety and ignorance in these matters
became more apparent as I progressed through my 'term.'
It was during one such class, a midwife showed us all a
model of a female body which came apart in sections.
She was in the throes of explaining how the baby comes
down the birth canal when one young girl jumped up
and ran out screaming that she no longer wanted to have

her baby—she had changed her mind. I have to admit
that my feelings were exactly the same and I would have
followed her out of the door if I had not been rooted to
the spot with shock! Oh my, what had I done and there
was no going back! I later attended a film, shown by the
clinic in the local Baptist Church Hall called, 'To Janet
a Son.' This confirmed the nightmare—Yes, that was
how a baby came into the world and why had nobody
explained this detail when I got married. Fear gripped
me and never left me for those last few weeks until that
inevitable day I went into labour.

I had listened to a Boxing Match on the radio in the
early hours of the morning and it seemed that I had
only just gone to sleep when I was gripped with the
most agonising pain. Already alerted by my writhing and
screams, 'Wiggy' was already leaping into action to find
a phone box in order to ring an ambulance. The night
had been a particularly wintry one and on opening the
door he was confronted with a deep fall of snow. Shoes
discarded and wellies donned, off he set to get help.

The ambulance could not reach me where we were on
site so between two burly ambulance men I was half
carried and half dragged to the awaiting vehicle, Labour
lasted from 7am until 5pm when my son finally put in an
appearance. The intervening hours were soon forgotten
as I looked with such pride at the little wrinkled person
I had produced. The surge of 'motherly love' that I felt at
that moment has been sorely tested over the years of his
upbringing. He grew into a defiant toddler, an arbitrary
youngster and an extremely rebellious teenager, but as a
grown man he has proved to me many, many times over

that I was right in my first assessment of him—a son who fills my heart with pride. He has shown me that he has great commitment to his Family, friends, Company and workforce. He has at last, proved to me that maybe I did do things right along the way, even though, at times, he took me to the depths of despair. I look back now and think, all that we went through has made him the man he is today, a pillar of society and a son I am so proud of!

As a new Mum I was so proud and protective. I realised, beyond the original excitement at the thought of becoming a Father, Wiggy really did not have much Paternal Spirit about him. I took Karl with me whenever possible trying not to leave him with his Father unless it was absolutely necessary.

One Saturday, a week after I was discharged from hospital with my new charge, I decided to do my weekly shop. I wrapped Karl up warmly, placed him in his pram and set off for the shops. Wiggy had gone to the local Works Social Club as he normally did if not working and I knew he would not be home before teatime. I was not bothered as I had my shopping to do. On arriving at my local grocery store, there were no huge Supermarkets in those days, I ordered my shopping and chatted to the assistant as I did so. Carrying as many bags as I could I endeavoured to struggle home. My hands were red raw but a nice cup of coffee with my feet up would soon remedy that. I put the kettle on and started to unload the bags, filling the depleted stocks in the cupboards. Nearly done—Oh how I was going to enjoy that cup of coffee—after all I had certainly earned it!!!!!

Something began to nag at the back of my mind. Had I forgotten something? No, I mentally went through my shopping list—I had remembered everything, so what was it nagging at me? Oh No, I felt sick to my stomach—I had forgotten something—my new baby!!!. I had walked right past his pram outside the shop (it was safe to do that in those days) and struggled to carry all those bags when they could have been carried under the pram. How could I? What sort of Mother forgets her child? (It was a dilemma I found myself in on numerous occasions with a later son)

At breakneck speed I dashed back to the shop where the pram and sleeping baby remained as I had left it. I looked round feeling thoroughly ashamed to see if anyone had spotted my mistake but everyone seemed to be going about their own business so off with the brake and away I went.

This having a new baby is going to take some getting used to,—I must remember I have him when making future excursions. I soon got the hang of it though, as they say Practise makes Perfect.

My marriage to 'Wiggy' did not improve after our son was born. His parenting skills were very limited as he had very little patience and I was left to cope whilst he increased his 'socialising activities' outside our home. The caravan we had bought proved to be a millstone round our necks as the roof began to leak and we found it increasingly difficult to keep healthy with everything damp and musty. We made one last ditch attempt to get more points to enable us to get council accommodation by selling the caravan and going back to live with our respective Parents. 'Wiggy' returned to his Parent's house and I, with our baby son, took up residence in the smallest bedroom in my Parent's house. A bed, a cot, and not much room for anything else, did eventually do the trick and after several months of living apart we were allocated a 2 bedroom flat. A 'proper' home of our own—things had to get better! We were both excited about the news and moved in as soon as we could, with the help of both Families. It was not until after everybody had gone that we realised how little we had. The caravan had been fully furnished so we had not had reason to buy large pieces of furniture. We were now left with an almost empty flat. We had managed to buy a double bed for our bedroom, a cot, a present from Grandparents, was all that was in our son's bedroom and the sitting room was bare except for a standard lamp that had been a wedding present, and a tiny drop leaf table that had been taken from the caravan. The kitchen was no better, we had brought the cooker with us from the caravan but save a 'Burco' boiler there was nothing else although we did have a small balcony on which to dry our washing. We had no wardrobes, dressing table, three piece suite or anything that might make it feel more like home. Never mind, it was ours and we had a lifetime to make it comfortable.

Over the next few weeks we managed to buy a wardrobe and a very small, uncomfortable cottage suite. There, it was beginning to take shape already. I did not work at that time and relied upon my husband's money to keep us. In the first few months 'Wiggy' worked hard and wallpapered each room to our liking. I thought he had changed. He did not go out as much, he could not afford to, and although we were not ecstatically happy—we rubbed along together. Even though he had become less violent towards me, he still had a cruel streak. At night, I would put spikey rollers in my hair, as was the fashion of the day. He would take great delight in pushing them into my head so they hurt me. He said he only did it for a laugh—some laugh—it certainly wasn't me who was doing the laughing. We never had a lot of money and we were finding it difficult to keep the place comfortably warm. We took to wearing thick woollen jumpers, our sons' provided by a 'knitting Nanny.' Although bodily our son was warm, his little hands were always cold and puffy. His Father would take great pleasure in tapping his hands with the handle of a child's broom—taking perverse pleasure in seeing his son cry. Although he was never violent towards our son, neither was he kind. I began to feel more and more defensive of my offspring trying to keep him out of his Father's way if only to keep the peace.

Once the decorating was complete, it seemed that my husband's commitment to us became too much for him to bear. It was during a rather volatile row that he snatched up our son and suspended him over our 2nd storey balcony, dangling him by the woollen straps of his romper suit., threatening to drop him. That, for me, was the final straw—enough was enough. I tried to calm the situation and we agreed he should go. I found out afterwards that he was already 'involved' with a girl he worked with and had only been looking for an excuse to leave. He certainly did not need to go to those extremes, he could have just walked out, I would not have tried to stop him!

The day he left, he packed his car with half our worldly goods and drove off into his new future, footloose and fancy free. I watched him go from my son's bedroom window and then sat on my uncomfortable cottage suite and broke my heart. I am not sure if the tears were with relief, sadness for all the misery I had suffered at his hands, disappointment at being a failed wife or simply fear of what the future now held for us. I can remember crying until I had no more tears to cry, but from that desolation came an inner strength that I never knew I had. I looked at my son and realised that he did not have anybody else to rely on, only me. Our future was sealed, I would not let him down.

Chapter 12

Dancing on Ice

uring this time my self esteem was pretty low as over the years 'Wiggy' had worn me down and I had very little confidence. It was around this time, that I met a male friend of one of his cousins. He happened to be a driver at the Dairy where 'Wiggy' worked. He knew we had parted company and asked if I would like to go ice skating at Richmond. It seemed a trip had been arranged through work and here was my chance to join them. Mum agreed to baby sit and then I was faced with what could I wear?

My Mum used to send away for parcels of remnants (oddments of material), and it was in this that I found my 'ball gown.' Well, maybe not a ball gown exactly, but a length of olive green material, enough to make a skirt.

Well, even that is an exaggeration, it was more like a pelmet as it measured only 18" from top of waistband to bottom of hem.—no matter—it was new. It consisted of four panels (the only pattern Mum had, a throwback from my schooldays) and I topped it off with a pastel peach fine knit jumper, a new jumper I had had for my birthday. My black well polished knee length boots finished off the outfit. My secret was, that although they were highly polished on the uppers, they had no soles. Every day I used to call round to the local shop to pick up a thick cardboard box in order to cut out several pairs of inner soles for my boots. To replace the boots would have cost a lot of money, money I could ill afford. There were far more important things to buy, shoes and clothes for my son came top of the list, after the essentials of food, heat and light. I had no extra money for fineries. The date went well, his friends actually spoke to me even though 'Wiggy' had convinced me that 'nobody liked me.' I really enjoyed the outing although I did not go on the ice for fear of falling over and showing my 'credentials'—my skirt had proved to be shorter than I thought. That did not matter I enjoyed watching everyone else, including my date, as they all seemed to be at home on the ice. They had obviously all been before. We all stopped off for a drink on the way home and for a few short hours my financial struggles were forgotten. On our return to the flat, where my Mother was waiting, he said a gentlemanly goodnight at the entrance hall and asked to see me again. I explained that I had a son and it was not always easy for me to get out. He seemed to understand and said he would call round. We became firm friends (friends being the operative word) and he took my son and I to meet his sister and her husband. We got on very well and after several weeks he invited me to meet his Mother and Father who lived in Maidenhead.

I thought it would be too much of a shock for his Parents to meet my son on our first visit so I left him with my Mum. The meeting went well to start with. His Father welcomed us and made us a drink while his Mother, a hard faced lady, sat in her armchair like a judge presiding over a court room. To say I had the 'third degree' was an understatement. She wanted to know all about me. When it came to 'What did I do for a living? I tried to explain that I could only work part time as I had a child. That was all it took! She, in no uncertain terms, told her son to take his 'harlot' out of her house and not to return In his defence, he tried to explain the position I had found myself in but to no avail. She heard the word 'married' and I do not know to this day if she thought I was having an affair with her son behind my husband's back, but they had a row and before I had a chance to empty my cup I was being shown out by a very apologetic Father. I am not sure if her son ever returned but I certainly did not!

I am not sure if it was a reaction to his Mother's anger or whether it had been on his mind anyway but on the way home he proposed to me. I was taken aback as nothing of such a serious nature had ever been discussed. I quite liked him <u>and</u> he always treated me with the greatest respect and it was comforting to have somebody in my life again, but marriage?
Well, it was a good job I was still married as no pressure could be put upon me to make a decision.

I have to explain that he had a car that was his pride and joy. He cleaned and polished it continually both inside and out. I noticed over the time with him that it was ok for me to travel in it I did not touch anything but when we took my son out he was forever telling me not to let his 'sticky fingers' touch anything. As I never took my son out with 'sticky fingers' I took umbrage at this and knew our relationship was doomed. He had never been married, had no experience of children and was, I realised just too selfish and set in his ways. My son came first and we parted company but remained friends until he left England to live in the sunnier climes of South Africa, never to be heard of again.

Back on my own again I found life a bit lonely and immersed myself in my books. I collected paperbacks from everybody and anybody. I read constantly when my son retired to bed each evening. I had boxes of books that I had read and I was not sure what to do with them. One day whilst in our local market square, the problem of what to do with the books was solved. A new shoe stall, in the shape of an open sided lorry appeared. I recognised the owner as a Scottish lad from the Power Station who, when I was pregnant, kindly gave me a lift home from work on several occasions. He wheeled and dealt in all sorts, clothes, shoes and books, anything he could make money out of. He recognised me and in conversation, the situation I was in, was mentioned. I explained about my boxes of books and asked if he could use them. We struck up a deal. I would supply him with all my books and he would supply me with a pair of shoes when I needed them. It proved to be an excellent arrangement and we remained friends for many years.

He went on to do very well for himself and currently has a shop in Oxford's Covered Market. Although he was a ruthless business man, he had a 'heart of gold' and I will never forget his kindness.

The flat was now becoming more homely. I had managed to buy a single bed for my growing son, we now had a square of carpet in the sitting room, lino with rugs in both our bedrooms and a 'formica' table and four chairs in the kitchen. I have to admit that it was taking longer than I thought but at least I felt that I was achieving something. The only room I had not done anything to, was the long hallway from the front door to the kitchen door. The floor was concrete and quite cold looking. One day, I had a brainwave! I would paint the floor with 'Red Cardinal' Floor Paint. What a success! It looked warmer and I polished it until it shone like glass. The reality was that it became a death trap. Unsuspectingly I would come out of the bedroom door in my socks, slide the whole length of the hallway and end up in a heap in the kitchen. My overzealous polishing had turned it into an 'ice rink.'
Who needed to go to Richmond? All I needed were two dusters on my feet and I was away.
Later, when I could afford it, I bought a 'runner' (a length of carpet that was not fitted) for the hallway. I am not sure this improved the safety aspect as I would then take one step through the front door and 'surf' to the kitchen.

When lack of funds did not allow for any other activity, my son and I would take up the 'runner' and spend many a happy hour, practising our skating up and down that hallway. Who needed to go out for entertainment when we had it there for the taking? No expensive skates for us, just four fluffy yellow dusters and four elastic bands to hold them to our ankles. We were 'Dancing on Ice' long before producers thought of the idea for television!!

Chapter 13

Every Cloud has a Silver Lining

During this time my social life was almost non-existent, my finances did not allow for anything other than necessities. My life was pretty much in a rut of visiting friends and Family during the day and sitting reading or listening to the radio (if I was lucky enough to be able to afford the batteries) during the evenings. I cannot say with hand on heart that I did not long for something more. My life seemed very dull in comparison to others and at times I felt quite depressed that I could not see it improving for the foreseeable future. How could my life change? I saw the same people, day in day out, week in week out, never having the opportunity to meet anyone new. Should I just be grateful that I had a healthy son and make the most of my miserable existence?

For six weeks nothing happened to change my mind
until one evening my Mother came to my rescue. She
played darts for a Ladies Team and they were playing a
home match in the local pub. Without warning she came
round to collect me, complete with sibling to babysit
and pocket money to spend. What an opportunity! She
insisted that I needed a night out but little did she know
what Fate had in store for me!

I only vaguely knew the other dart team members so I
just sat quietly in the window seat grateful to just listen
to some different conversation. I was not, at that time,
interested in Ladies Darts so passed the time people
watching.

Suddenly the bar door burst open and in poured a group
of rough looking characters, loud and obviously some,
the worse for wear, from visiting other hostelries en
route.
I was not impressed by their rowdiness and turned
away when they began to speak to certain members of
the Dart Team. Just at that moment the half time food
appeared and Mum came and joined me at the table.
Sandwiches, hot sausages and jacket potatoes were being
offered round. Mum insisted that I ate something so I
settled for a jacket potato. As I was eating it I felt eyes
boring into me and looked up in time to see one of
the rowdy gang staring at me across the bar. I quickly
looked away as I did not want him to think I was at all
interested, but not before I noticed what lovely blue
eyes he had. I turned towards my Mum, even though I
could see him out of the corner of my eye, still staring.
I remember asking her how to eat a jacket potato in a

ladylike way as I was under scrutiny. Mum, in her usual
tactless way, looked directly at him and said he had been
looking at me ever since he walked in. He had, in fact,
asked one of the members of the Team, who I was. What
a cheek—How dare he?

During the course of the evening I discreetly checked
him out. I quite liked what I saw, those lovely blue eyes
and a grin that went from ear to ear. On the down
side he was acting the fool, kicking his legs in the air
whilst strumming an air guitar and singing very loudly
completely out of tune. On reflection, he was not my
type at all—What was I thinking about?

He fascinated me as I watched him chatting easily to
everyone, grinning at me when he thought he had
caught my eye. Towards the end of the evening, he
approached the table and asked if I would like a drink.
No thank you, I most certainly did not, I didn't know
him from Adam! He was obviously one of the 'Power
Station' lads and we all knew how rough they were. He
turned his attention to my Mum and offered to buy her
a drink if she put in a good word with her daughter.
He was charm itself and Mother succumbed. Whilst he
was at the bar she pointed out I was always grumbling
about not getting the opportunity to meet new people
and here I was turning the chance down. Mother had
completely fallen under his spell.

When he returned to the table with a drink for us both,
he asked my Mum if he could walk me home. Did he
not realise I could speak for myself? He sat chatting at
our table and I have to admit that I warmed to his charm

as he introduced himself as Bryan, employed at the Power Station as a pipe layer for Film Cooling and living on the caravan site in the Power Station Compound. He went on to explain that he had moved there from Shropshire and was looking to make new friends. Those eyes, that grin, I was hooked!

I was very conscious that he probably thought I was single so I took the first opportunity on our way home (yes, he did persuade me in the end) to explain my marital situation and the fact that I did have a son. He did not seem perturbed by this news and in turn he told me about his Family. I was shocked as he seemed to be one of at least 30. I was one of four—did families really have that many children? Fortunately for his Mother this was not the case as I was to find out later. He had been one of 12 but each brother and sister not only had the names they were given at baptism, but several other nicknames throughout the Family. It was extremely confusing for newcomers to the Family but eventually I got the hang of it and understood which one he was actually speaking about.

I felt sure on that first journey home that he thought I was an easy pick up but he proved to be a real gentleman even when I refused to let him in for coffee. He thanked me for allowing him to walk me home and disappointed me by not asking to see me again. Oh well, such is life He was such good company, and I had hoped to see him again. Life can be so cruel sometimes. I said goodnight at the entrance to the flats and he kissed me chastely on the cheek and disappeared into the night. I opened my front door and picked up where I had left off—being a dutiful

Mum. It did not stop me dreaming though—those sparkling blue eyes, his sense of fun. What a shame I was not for him—he seemed so perfect.

Back to reality as the weekend passed and Monday returned with the normality of the usual circuit of family and friends. Somehow I could not get the vision of the young roughneck out of my mind. Was it because I had been on my own for a while? Did I really like him or was my judgement now impaired? Who could tell?

On Wednesday evening I was sitting reading at about 9.30pm when I thought I heard a tap at the front door. I was not expecting anyone and thought I must be imagining it. No, it was definitely a soft tap.
I was very conscious of how vulnerable I was living on my own and approached the front door with trepidation. As I did the letterbox opened and lo and behold a pair of sparkling eyes confronted me. My heart leapt. He apologised for calling so late but he explained he could not remember where I lived and had spent most of the evening knocking at doors in the 6 blocks of flats trying to find me. He obviously had eventually, been pointed in the right direction. Little did I realise that by opening that door I opened up a whole new episode in my life which was to completely change my future for ever.

He came in, had a coffee and we spent the next few hours chatting. I found him very easy to talk to and he seemed genuinely interested in my plight although I was never one to bemoan my fate—if anything I always made light of it to others no matter how I felt. That very afternoon I had been invited to a lingerie party and the invitation was on the mantelpiece. Bryan noticed it and asked if I was going. I told him I would not be going as my finances did not stretch to such luxuries and he immediately pulled a £10 note from his wallet and put it with the invitation. He stated that now there was no reason not to go so I should go and enjoy myself. I did not want his money and felt that if I accepted this payment he might expect something in return. I obviously did not know at that time what a generous, good natured character he was. He insisted that I keep it and made his excuses and left. The money worried me and I left it where he had put it. I never bought anything at the lingerie party, meaning to repay his money if he returned.

I did not have to wait long as on the following Saturday evening he returned and asked if I could arrange a babysitter. Luckily I was able to and we had our first proper date. He did not have a car and travelled everywhere in a taxi. We went out to a village pub where he bought me the biggest box of chocolates that I had ever seen and then we returned by taxi at the end of the evening. It was a memorable date and he made me feel very special. I almost began to believe in myself again.

There was a slight downturn to the evening when he asked if he could stay the night. I was horrified and refused. He explained that as he had sent the taxi away and I didn't have a phone in the flat he would have a long walk to the nearest phone box to summon another. He apologised for giving me the wrong idea but explained he was happy to sleep on the sofa or even the floor, and that is exactly what he did. With my coat as his only blanket, he started off on the two seated settee (which was uncomfortable enough to sit on let alone sleep on) and finished the night on the floor whilst I slept soundly behind a locked bedroom door.

This was the beginning of a romance which was to last for over thirty years.

Chapter 14

A Leap into the Unknown

During the following two weeks, I continued to see Bryan, not every night but maybe once in the week and one evening over the weekend. We got on very well but something was not quite right. Call it woman's intuition but I was sure that all was not how it seemed. I suspected that he was married., but when asked, of course, he denied it. I thought I would put him to the test and invite him for Sunday lunch.

At that time Families sat down to a Sunday Roast and meals were planned round a man popping to the pub for a 'swift half' before his dinner. It was a Family time and a man had to have a good excuse for missing his Sunday Lunch.

With a view to finding out once and for all, I invited him to lunch the following Sunday. He readily agreed and said he would arrive about 11am. Maybe I had been wrong after all?

On the dot of 11am he arrived and spent, until dinner was served, pacing around the flat looking out of windows. Although my flat did look out over a local park I was not aware that the aspect was so great as to warrant such interest. Dinner served, we sat down to eat and the conversation flowed easily although I did suspect he was a little tense. Did my cooking not come up to par? Maybe he thought I was pushing the relationship too fast by inviting him for a meal? I was not sure but he had plenty to say and he made me laugh and for the first time in ages I felt totally relaxed and at ease.

Dessert served, eaten and cleared away, I settled my son for his afternoon nap. Suddenly there was a rapping at my front door. Not expecting anyone to call I cautiously opened it to find a young man standing there asking to speak to Bryan.
Bryan explained that he was supposed to be working that afternoon but had left a message to say he wasn't going in but could be contacted at my address. They went down the stairs together and I could hear raised voices, presumably because he had not turned up for work. My naivety knows no bounds as I was to find out a little later.

Bryan returned, apologised and our afternoon continued with him telling me all about his childhood, growing up within such a large family. The only interference was from my son who seemed particularly grizzly and would not settle. On one of my many trips to his bedside to try to settle him I was startled by my letterbox lifting. As I had not heard anyone knock I was a little shocked, to say the least, especially as I did not recognise the eyes that looked back at me, nor the voice that followed the look. Suddenly the door was being hammered and kicked by a woman who obviously was not there for a friendly visit. Son ignored momentarily, I confronted Bryan who told me not to worry it was only his wife!!!!!!

As he opened the door to her, she flew in, pushed him the length of the hallway whilst screaming abuse, back into the kitchen where she instantly grabbed the carving knife I had been using and lunged towards him.

That was enough for me. No man was worth being party to a murder, so I grabbed my son from his bed, wrapped him in a blanket and ran to a neighbouring block of flats to some friends. As I picked Karl up from his bed I realised why he had not been able to settle, his face and glands in his neck were all swollen—he had contracted mumps.

What a day!—An irate wife and a son with mumps, this was certainly not a day I could call boring! I had a coffee with my friends and spent the next couple of hours chatting with them hoping that by the time I returned home, my visitors would be long gone. Having given them enough time and space to either slaughter each other or to have made up and disappeared from my life. I returned home with the thought in mind of dosing my son up and getting him back to bed.

As I lay him in his bed, fitfully sleeping, I heard voices coming from my sitting room. Surely they could not still be here as I had been gone for over 2 hours?

I poked my head around the door, after all, this was my home, and mentally noted how attractive his wife was. She was very slight of figure, black thick hair worn shoulder length, very pretty and dressed in a red and white soft leather fringed dress complete with white leather fringed boots. Oh my, how could I compete with her? I later found out she had previously been crowned 'Miss Shropshire.' It did cross my mind at that time, that when he looked at me—did he see what I saw when I looked in a mirror?

I have never been an outstanding beauty, always carried a little more weight than I would have liked and due to lack of finances, never at that time, was I glamorously dressed, more serviceably clad. I was not sure what I was supposed to do in this situation. Casting my eyes over both of them who were, by now, chatting amiably, I could not see any obvious signs of violence, no stab wounds oozing blood, no black eyes, lumps, bumps or bruising and my frugal pieces of furniture seemed intact. Was this not a strange situation to be in?

Bryan asked me to sit down as they had something to discuss with me. Oh no, I had heard about people like them. Please don't put me on the spot, I will look so disgusted—I am just so not into anything like that. Aren't there magazines for that sort of thing?

Why me—is this day going from bad to worse?

Imagination ran away with me, it was nothing like that but something equally bizarre. He explained the situation and introduced me to his wife. He went on to tell me that although they did live together in a caravan on the Power Station site they did lead separate lives. He further explained that he did not love her, in fact never did, but had married her simply because he had made her pregnant. She understood the situation at the time of the marriage but had hoped he would grow to love her. He never had and she always knew that one day he would find someone he really wanted to be with.
I found all this honesty quite embarrassing but nothing could have prepared me for what came next.

Bryan told me that no matter what the outcome of the afternoon he would not be returning to the caravan and his wife. His wife, realising that it was all over decided that that evening she would return to Shropshire to be with her Family.

Bryan then turned to me, in front of his wife, and declared his love for me and asked if we could become an item. I was both shocked and embarrassed. Encouraged by his wife who pointed out that from what he had told her, I had nothing to lose and as she was going to be out of his life once and for all, I agreed. It was hardly a fairytale start but, in truth, what did I have to lose? My life at that time was a constant juggle to make ends meet, no luxuries, no fineries and little to look forward to but most of all the desperate loneliness I felt when I shut my front door. I was very lucky to have my healthy son, I never once lost sight of that, but conversation with a 18 month old can be very limited, no matter how much input you give them.

It just felt so right—but how to tell Family and friends that after only knowing him for 3 weeks Bryan was moving in. This was not like me at all, everyone would be horrified. What happened to my standards, where were my morals? Would everyone look down on me as a slut and a harlot? I was not sure about anything except the fact that I wanted to be with him and he seemed to want to be with me. I would bite the bullet and face the consequences and time would tell. That almost instantaneous decision was the best decision I could have made. The next 30 plus years proved to be a tempestuous affair—more ups and downs, troughs and peaks, mountainous moments and depths of despair than most people experience in a whole lifetime but every moment was worthwhile. I can honestly say from that moment onwards I lived life to the full.

Chapter 15

On The 'Up'

I have in previous chapters already explained how austere my life was, living on my own with a small child. I have to admit that my Family did offer financial help at times but I was fiercely independent and refused their assistance.

Bryan moving in opened up a completely new element to my life. Going shopping was a whole new experience—I could now afford to fill my trolley with all kinds of goodies. It was a veritable joy—something I had not been able to do for a very long time. I now had a full store cupboard, my cupboards were so full they were bursting at the seams and life in general began to take on a rosy glow.

I had never owned a television but that was soon to
change. I came home from visiting my Mum one
morning to find a strange television situated in my
hallway. I say strange because I had not seen one like this
before. It had a coin slot attached to the top of it—very
peculiar. When I lived at home, our television plugged
into the wall and you just switched it on—this one was
slightly different.

Anyone who knows me well would understand why I
did not touch it. I am absolutely useless with anything
electrical or mechanical and although I am academically
quite bright—I have no logic at all. I therefore thought it
best to leave it where it was until I could find out more
about it.

On returning from work, Bryan explained that it had
been his when he lived in the caravan. He explained that
you paid for your viewing by putting money into the
coin slot. Periodically a service engineer would come out
and empty the coin box—this would be your rental for
viewing.

I noticed that the money box was hanging off and
empty so wondered if the engineer had just retrieved
the rental and forgotten to re-attach the box (naïve once
again). At this point I have to explain that I had had a
very sheltered upbringing. I was neither worldly wise or
dishonest in any shape or form but living with Bryan was
going to open my eyes to various aspects of living life 'on
the edge.'

Bryan explained that he didn't really feel it was worth the rental money as the picture on the television was not very clear. Due to this he had decided to open up the money box, pocket the contents and just use one coin over and over again. The television worked like this for months until eventually the picture disappeared altogether and it was time for a replacement. Today I am more worldly wise and would just dispose of it but in those days I worried about doing the right thing and felt I had to contact the engineer so he could come and collect it. How was I going to explain about the lack of rental money and the money box hanging off at an obscure angle? Not a problem!!

Bryan always came up with a feasible answer. I was to tell the engineer that I had just moved into the premises, the television was in situ on my arrival and as far as I was aware the previous tenants had emigrated to Australia. Sorted!! I have to admit that I had all my fingers and toes crossed during his visit but unpractised as I was at lying, I must have done a good job as he went away apologising for the inconvenience. I was now on a slippery slope!

A week later I was the proud owner of a brand new television—this time a legitimate one.

On another occasion I came home from the shops to see muddy footprints on the outside wall underneath my son's bedroom window. As I have previously explained, I lived in a second floor flat so thought this quite odd. It was just a fleeting thought as I struggled to get shopping, pushchair and toddler son up two flights of stairs. I entered the flat and carried my son into the sitting room.

Oh no—I must be in the wrong flat, that stereogram was not there when I left. I picked Karl up and made my way back out, but wait—this is my flat, I entered it with my key. This is my carpet, but how did that stereogram get there when I have the only key?

Suddenly I recalled the footprints on the outside wall and opened the door to my son's bedroom. The window was shut but there were muddy footprints on the window sill and on the lino. I did not understand! How had anyone got through a closed window? I thought burglars were supposed to take your belongings not furnish your house once they broke in. No, it was ridiculous. I could not think of a sensible explanation, all I knew was that I did not own, neither had I ordered a stereogram, what would have been the point, I had never owned a record in my life.

All was revealed on Bryan's return. A chap he worked with had bought in on Hire Purchase but could no longer afford it. He explained that he did not owe much on it and would be willing to sell it on for the amount he owed the Hire Purchase company so he could clear his debt, hence I became the proud owner of my very first record player. It seemed that on going shopping I had left the small window open in Karl's bedroom. Bryan had entered the premises by reaching in through this small window and opening the larger one before climbing in, hence the muddy footprints everywhere. Once in it had been easy to open the front door, trundle the piece of furniture up the stairs with the help of his workmate and place it in the sitting room to await my return. Window and door shut behind them—mission accomplished.

I was not sure if the money Bryan paid over ever found it's way to the Hire Purchase Company or whether it ended up in a local hostelry but somehow it did not matter. I was now the proud owner of my first record—Freda Paynes 'Band of Gold' which was played over and over and over again.

Can you see how my life was changing from staunch upright citizen to accessory to theft and now accomplice to fraud. I felt a bit like Clyde's Bonnie!

Chapter 16

A Time of Uncertainty

I had not mentioned before that Bryan had a 4 year old daughter who returned to Shropshire with her Mother as I did not feel it was relevant at the time. Weeks into co-habiting with me, with unrest at the Power Station, Bryan began to feel guilty about not seeing his daughter. He talked of changing his job and wanted to visit her before he took up new employment. Although I was unsure about him visiting his estranged wife I realised I had no hold over him and had no choice but to agree to his returning to Shropshire. His Family all lived in that County and he told me he would be staying with his Parents during his visit.

I hated the thought of him not being around, he was such a large character but after promising to write to each other daily, I waved him off at the local railway station. He had made sure there was enough money in the bank to see me through for the next few weeks so I felt sure I was worrying unduly and he would be back. Little did I know how long it would be before I heard from him again.

I kept my promise to write daily, filling my letters with local gossip, idle chit chat and a daily diary of my growing son's antics. I wrote day after day after day but got nothing in return. Could he have forgotten us already? Had he made up with his wife? Was he ever coming back? The doubts crept in and despair took hold. I could not understand it—we had been so happy. What had gone wrong? Six weeks passed and I had heard nothing at all. I began to fear that my lonely existence was just about to return, made worse this time, because I had known such happiness since Bryan moved in. I could not bear to think about it. What had gone wrong? Was it something I had said? Shropshire was so far away it may just as well have been on another planet—we were worlds apart. Then out of the blue I received a letter. It was blunt and to the point. 'Be at the phone box at 8pm Friday night.' Bryan. (I have to explain that Bryan had made a note of a number of a local phone box before he went away, just in case he needed to speak to me, this was obviously of some urgency.)

My mind went into overdrive, swaying one way then the other. Had something happened to him, that being the reason he had not been in contact? On the other hand had he decided to go back to his wife? Was this phone call just to finish with me?

I would just have to face up to it whatever it was and Friday evening could not come quickly enough.

With my brother babysitting my sleeping son, I sped off down the road to await my Fate. I made sure I was early. I did not want to miss the opportunity to speak to him and find out what had upset our relationship.

Brrr, Brrr—I snatched the receiver up and pressed it to my ear. Why was he grumbling at me, the reception was not very good? I could not hear him clearly but through the crackling he seemed to be cross about not receiving any letters. I tried to get a word in to tell him I had written every day but had received nothing in return and then he calmed down. Oh My, What was he saying, he was coming home?

My spirits soared. I asked him why he had not contacted before and like me, when he did not receive anything, he also felt the relationship had broken down and maybe I had changed my mind. Pride had prevented him from contacting me sooner but after a conversation with one of his sisters he had been persuaded to make the first move. We found out later that his Mother, intent on getting a reconciliation with his estranged wife, had intercepted the mail and burnt each and every one of my letters. Her plan failed miserably and Bryan returned to our two bedroom flat, be it only for the weekend.

It was harvest season in Shropshire and Bryan had gained employment on a local farm, hoeing beet for the sugar industry. He remained in Shropshire for another month coming home only once during that time. On his return to Shropshire after the phone call episode I received a letter from him on every second day. I wrote daily. I was impressed with his handwriting. It was so clear and neat and the letters were put together so eloquently for a man. I treasured every one of them, reading and re-reading them until his return. During his time of absence, I received a weekly registered envelope with a wad of cash to keep me going. How had I ever doubted him? He was my Saviour, I idolised him. I could hardly contain my excitement when he said he was returning home for good. All uncertainty vanished, our Future was sealed, my life was just perfect.

Chapter 17

My Introduction to the Family

*A*s money had been sparse during my childhood—I had never known the pleasure of 'eating out'. Bryan was the one who introduced me to the experience of eating out in a Chinese Restaurant. I thought it so romantic, an experience I had only read about in the novels I always had at hand.

Alighting from my carriage, a local taxi, I felt a little nervous as we entered the restaurant. Bryan had obviously eaten there before as they seemed to know him personally. I felt so important, out with such a well known character. The Manager, greeting us at the door, at first seemed a little uncertain about letting us in muttering something about someone running out without paying. It surely must be a case of mistaken identity—not my hero!

I was right of course, as Bryan explained to him about his twin brother, who only ever wore a sports jacket and casual trousers unlike himself who always wore a suit. Dubious as to the credibility of this, the Manager agreed to us dining there only if we sat right at the rear of the restaurant, next to the kitchen door. I did not care where we sat I was enthralled by this new way of living. Could my life get any better?

I thoroughly enjoyed myself, the Chinese food, the soft lighting, the ambience of the place, to me it was complete perfection. During the meal I brought up the topic of his twin brother who I could not recollect hearing him mention. He grinned that grin that melted my heart and confessed that it was actually himself that had run out without paying, there really was no twin brother. I was horrified and said I hoped he was not planning to do that on this occasion as I had never done anything like that. He laughed, told me not to worry and then confessed he had not enough on him to pay for the meal we had just consumed. I had not taken out my purse and we are talking about a time when credit cards were unheard of and everyone paid in cash. I was panic stricken. He told me it would be fine, when he said the word I was to get up quickly and make my way to the door. He would remain seated (as if we had had words and I had just walked out on him) then when no one was looking he would make a quick dash for the door. I was to be ready to run like the wind when he joined me outside. Oh, it was never like this in the books!

I could not look at anyone I just sat there petrified. On the word 'Now' I jumped up from my seat, got my head firmly lodged in a long tubular lampshade that hung down over the table and remained, static with fear and embarrassment. At this point he roared with laughter and said he had been joking. He then called for the bill which he settled in full. I could not get out of that restaurant quickly enough. How could I have been so stupid? It was a long time before he persuaded me to 'eat out' again but this was only the beginning of the journey that paved the way to my seeing how the other half lived, and I don't mean the rich and famous. I still had the encounter with the Family to look forward to.

We had only been together about 3 months when Bryan received and invitation to his brother's wedding. The invitation was to include a guest and I hoped I would be the chosen one. Prior to the event, we went shopping for an outfit. Considering this was to be the first time I would be meeting the Family I really wanted to make a good impression. Shopping with Bryan was a real experience as I was told never to look at the price of anything, whether it was suit, hat or shoes. If I liked it and I looked good in it then I was to have it. I felt a million dollars on the day. I had chosen an emerald green military style trouser suit complete with gold buttons topped with a cheeky cockney style emerald green peaked cap. I looked as if I had stepped straight out of a boutique on Carnaby Street.

We arrived early at the church in Shropshire and took our seats towards the front. That was a big mistake, as I was in full view of all the Family. I felt like a prize exhibit. I could feel their eyes boring into my back and almost hear their muttered comments, but not enough to be able to decipher whether it was of approval or not. The wedding service passed without a hitch and afterwards we made our way to the reception where I subsequently was introduced to 'The Clan.' There seemed to be so many to remember as all but two were married so there were in-laws to remember as well. Then came all the children, the Family had a population explosion all of their own. Had anyone in Shropshire heard of birth control?

After the speeches, which were very short and to the point—a buffet was served. All quite normal you may think, for a country wedding, I certainly did. I tried, failing miserably most of the time, to make small talk with those Family members who deigned to speak to me. That was not very successful so I tried to make myself as inconspicuous as I could by sitting quietly in a corner hoping no-one would notice me. Bryan, meantime, socially mingled, coming back every now and then to refill my glass.

Suddenly all hell broke loose. Most of the brothers had been playing cards in a corner, fortunately not the one I had chosen, when one accused another (very loudly, I might add) of cheating. That is all it took. Tables went flying, chairs were hurled like missiles and grown men threw themselves into what could only be called a free for all. Goodness—Was this a wedding? Women were screaming, children were crying and by this time most of the men were locked in battle. I had never seen anything quite like it in my life. I felt like an extra in a Western Movie. One lady, who later became my sister-in-law shouted at me to get out of the Family while I could explaining that they were all mad and if I had any sense I would not have anything to do with any of them. (Words that would come back to haunt me many times over the next 30 years) It made no difference to me at that time—I was in love, my Bryan was not like them. Actually, where exactly was he as I could not find him in the room? Suddenly a door opened and in he raced, threw his jacket at me as he sped past and threw himself into the melee. I wanted to go home, this was not for me, I felt completely out of my depth.

My introduction to the Family had not gone as well as I had hoped but maybe there would be time over the rest of the weekend to make amends. Begrudgingly, Bryan's Mother, had agreed to us staying at his Parents' house. At first she had refused outright, but after Bryan had threatened never to darken her doorstep again if I was not made welcome, she backed down and through gritted teeth, welcomed me into her home. I tried to be as helpful as I could, laying the table, making tea, buttering bread and whilst going about these tasks, trying to make polite conversation. It was very difficult, she never made it easy and I could feel her resentment.

On returning from the wedding I made my excuses about being tired after the journey and escaped to the bedroom we had been allocated, where I lay on the bed and fell asleep. In the morning I was awakened to the smell of breakfast cooking. I rose, washed quickly and went down to be met by a sea of faces. Bryan was already up and tucking into a hearty breakfast and said that as my breakfast was already cooked, I should join him.

During the course of the morning Family members arrived in droves. The house, ill equipped for a huge Family consisted of a small kitchen, an even smaller scullery and a sitting room. In the middle of the sitting room was a table with four chairs and to one side of the fire was Fathers armchair. Around the perimeter of the room were various upright wooden chairs and a sofa. There was never enough room for all the Family to sit down at one time and the sitting room was very much like a doctor's waiting room. When someone vacated a seat to either go to the toilet or to make a drink, another standing member would take their place. It seemed to be a permanent sea of movement. The children were always banished to play in the garden, no matter how inclement the weather and on reflection they were probably safer out there.

The conversation topics when Family members got together were either, football, politics, racing or farming. Nobody seemed to be listening, everybody had an opinion and the more they talked the louder they got and the louder they got, the more heated became the conversations until invariably an argument erupted. It brought a whole new meaning to close knit Family—their close knit meant arms and legs locked in battle! Whilst all this was in progress, the seated members disappeared in a smoky mist as everyone seemed to be chain smoking.

If discussions were not underway then domino games were in progress. To most people, a game of dominos is a relatively quiet game, but sadly not in this household. All would be well until a game was coming to a close, when a domino would be laid that someone else did not agree with and before you knew it, tempers had flared, punches had been thrown and the dominos would end up as firewood burning brightly on the back of the open fire, Happy Families!!!!

Bryan's Father was a character in himself. He was extremely proud of his large Family and when we all went out for a drink together he was only too pleased to say, 'these are all mine.' It was a strange household, Father, Mother, 2 surviving daughters (one had died when aged 21yrs) and 9 sons. It was expected of the Mother and two daughters to wait hand, foot and finger, on the males in the Family. This was not something I had been used to as my own Father would help my Mother do her chores and my brothers were expected to help out as much as I was. This arrangement within their Family did not sit comfortably on my shoulders and I hoped Bryan did not expect the same from me.

On the Sunday after the wedding it was decided that all the men would meet up at lunchtime for a drink, while their women were at home preparing and cooking the dinner. I saw Bryan's Father disappear in a scullery full of steam rather than lean over and switch off the boiling kettle. I was astounded when he called his wife, to leave whatever she was doing upstairs, and come down to switch off the kettle. How lazy was that? Down she trotted, obediently switched off the kettle and then returned to her duties upstairs.

During this time, having enjoyed my breakfast, I sat on the sofa sipping my coffee and attempting to do the crossword in the 'Shropshire Star.' Having finished his ablutions in the scullery, Father, as everyone called him, came and sat in his armchair by the fire. Suddenly, he barked 'Get my shoes.' Not realising that they had a well—trained dog, I looked round to see if I could see it. I thought it strange that I had not spotted it during my stay. Once again the order was barked 'Get my shoes.' I looked up from my crossword to find Father glaring at me. I felt sure that he could not be speaking to me in that tone of voice and said as much. He told me, in no uncertain terms, to do as I was told. I looked down at my feet expecting his shoes to be within my reach but lo and behold, he told me that they were upstairs under his bed. Even in those far off days, I did no man's bidding and told him to get them himself. He was not at all amused and on Bryan's return to the room, he declared ' Southern women were no good as they would not do as they were told.' Bryan was advised to get rid of me. I felt really uncomfortable but stuck to my guns and refused to obey orders. Bryan tried many, many times during our earlier years together to mould me into a domesticated slave and I have to say with a certain amount of stubborn pride that he never did succeed. It was a constant battle that often resorted in him saying 'I would never beat him,' meaning I would never get the better of him. My reply was always the same, 'I am not playing your games, I may do things if I am asked properly but never if I am told.' It caused many arguments but we were both extremely stubborn characters.

In general, I was not accepted by the majority of the Family. They thought I was stuck up (this was because I had been educated in a Grammar School where we had been severely reprimanded for not speaking properly, so I had a slightly 'posh' accent) I did not drink or swear and I was certainly not classed as a loud person, therefore I had very little in common with them all and did not fit in. At the close of the weekend I was very happy to be leaving Shropshire and 'The Clan' behind, to return to my kind of normality—if life with Bryan could ever be called normal.

Looking back over the whole episode it was to epitomise my relationship with the Gough's, with the exception of one sister, who did befriend me, and we have remained distant friends for a lifetime.

Chapter 18

A Nomad at Heart

Home, Sweet Home! Over the next few months, Bryan managed to get a job as a scaffolder, at Didcot Power Station and we began to improve the look of our meagre flat. We decorated it throughout and we bought new furniture and furnishings to make it a cosier home. It was wonderful, I could not wish for more. We were extremely happy. I should have known better than to rest on my laurels, as the saying goes. One Saturday morning Bryan went into town for a haircut and once again—life was 'up in the air.'

I was watching for his return when all of a sudden I saw him staggering across the green as he made his way homeward. Was he alright as he seemed to be struggling to walk? Drunk!—he couldn't be drunk—it was only

107

1.30pm. Surely not! Unfortunately, drunk he was, not
only drunk but about to drop a bombshell. As he fell
through the door way he told me to pack his case as he
was off. What had happened, we had been fine when he
left for town. What could have made him want to leave?
I had got it wrong again!

He had been drinking with some lads who had been
working at Port Talbot. They had been earning far more
than he was getting at Didcot so he was off to chase
'bigger bucks.' He said he had a taxi arriving in five
minutes and needed his case ready to go. Pants, socks,
clean working clothes, shirts and trousers for going out
and toiletries. E verything was thrown rapidly into a
suitcase and there was just enough time to make a hasty
arrangement to ring our designated phone box the
following evening. The taxi arrived, Bryan lurched down
the stairs, missed his footing and fell down one flight
with clothes spilling out the full length of the staircase.
There is nothing like making an exit. Hastily cramming
clothes back into the case, I managed to get both case
and Bryan into the awaiting taxi with instructions to
take him to the local Railway Station. In a blink of an
eye, he was gone. I would just have to await the outcome
of the phone call the following evening, that is, if he
remembered to call.

The following evening, I waited in the phone box unsure
whether Bryan would remember to contact me. Ten
minutes after our allotted time and still silence. Should
I wait or should I go? I was just about to go when the
familiar ring broke the silence. Excited to speak to him
I asked how was it in Port Talbot? He answered 'Port

Talbot, I am not in Port Talbot, I am in Kincardine, in Scotland.'

On the train travelling down to Port Talbot he had met some other lads travelling back from Kincardine. The prospect seemed better in that neck of the woods, even 'bigger bucks,' so the lure of even more money had sent him North. That is what it was like living with Bryan.—life was never dull, if a little uncertain at times but always challenging. He was away for 4 weeks before I saw him again although we spoke twice weekly in our own special phone box. I had hoped he would write to me but once a week a registered envelope would be delivered with my name:—Iren followed by the bare bones of my address. On the inside would be a piece of notepaper torn from a spiral notebook with the words, 'her is £ s d.' Remembering this was a time of pre-decimalisation these were the symbols of money and true enough the envelope always contained a fistful of notes, my housekeeping from Bryan. What had happened to those eloquent, flowery love letters I had once received? It was mystifying! Bryan had obviously entrusted my money to a friend to post as the note, I guess, was written by a well trained, if not enebriated spider. The Power Station 's address, in Kincardine, was eligibly stamped on the envelope so I started to write daily to him. I got nothing in return so decided to speak to Bryan when he next rang. He explained that the shifts were long and he didn't have much time for writing but would explain better on his return. I accepted this as I had no choice and looked forward to his long weekend leave.

I now no longer had to work. The bank balance was healthy and my son was growing fast. We enjoyed playing together in the local park, going on Nature walks or even fishing for sticklebacks in a local village stream. Life was wonderful, except for the loneliness of the nights without Bryan. I could now relax when I went visiting, no longer under the constant stress of how to make ends meet. The weeks flew past and the weekends when Bryan was home were idyllic. It was a lovely feeling of cosiness to be so secure in a relationship.

On one weekend home Bryan seemed hell bent on collecting raffle prizes for a raffle he was organising on his return to Kincardine. He went to a local social club where there was a sale of repossessed goods and bankrupt stock. He thought he might pick up a few bargains to take back. I asked him details of this raffle—I had not realised what a charitable fellow he was. He explained that he had put word about that he was going to raise some money for an old destitute lady he knew. His work colleagues were all earning extremely good money at that time and told him if he organised something, they would all give generously. I could not think to whom he was referring so thought it must have been someone he had met in Shropshire, maybe a friend of the Family. What a lovely man I had become involved with!

After the weekend was over, with a couple of suitcases full of prizes, he returned to Scotland. The raffle finally took place, and true to their word, the men generously supported it. It was a commendable cause and Bryan sent me the £1,000.00 raised.

I was so proud of my man. It was quite worrying having that amount of cash in the flat but I hid it away to await Bryan's return. What a shock I did get when he did return—that 'little old destitute lady' turned out to be me!!!

I did not understand as I was only in my 20's and certainly not destitute! Bryan laughed and said, 'Yes, but you are a lady.' What could I do with him? He said that we were now £1,000.00 better off and all his work colleagues in Kincardine were content with their prizes in the knowledge that they had helped a good cause. Everybody happy!!!

During his first visit home from Kincardine I did manage to unravel the mystery of the letter writing. When I asked him why he had not written to me properly as he had in the early days, when he had sent me lovely letters beautifully handwritten, I must admit I was not prepared for his answer. He seemed a little uncomfortable with the question and made me promise not to laugh. He then confessed to me that he could neither read nor write. I thought he was joking and burst into laughter but I could tell by his face that he was serious. I apologised for my lack of sympathy and ignorance, but I had not considered that there were people around with this problem. I had been well educated and thought everybody had reading and writing skills. He then went on to explain that as a child he could not hear properly (this, in fact, was an understatement) and because his family farmed, practical skills were more important than academic ones. As long as he could physically work—education had been unimportant. On the odd

occasion when he did go to school he was made to stand
in the corner wearing a 'dunce's' hat. This would not be
allowed today but in those far off days it was a popular
punishment for children who did not listen or abide by
the rules. It was during one of these punishment sessions
in the corner that Bryan made a concerted decision
not to try any more. Now it would be his choice not to
learn. The sad part about this was that Bryan had been
born partially deaf and by later life became profoundly
deaf, unable to be helped even by the most up to date
technical aids.

Due to the number of children in the Family, he had
been overlooked and his deafness never picked up
throughout the whole of his childhood. He grew
up unconsciously finding strategies to overcome his
disability. He always shouted, thinking if he could not
hear himself, possibly others couldn't hear him either.
He learned to lip read, to a certain extent, without even
realising it and spoke, what we called 'gobble de gook.'
He would be able to lip read the beginnings of words
but failed miserably with the endings, so would make up
his own. This caused for some strange conversation over
our life together. eg our workforce in later life would be
sent to Ashby Dooble Ash instead of Ashby de la Zouch.
Within the Family it could be comical but when outside
with people we had not met before it could be highly
embarrassing for us but to Bryan, he never cared a jot. I
think, sometimes, that is what endeared him to people,
they thought he was a bumbling idiot until they got to
know him and then would realise what a clever man he
was—it was a very clever ploy really, if unintentional.

When he told me about his inability to read and write I found it difficult to believe him as I thought he read a newspaper daily. On reflection I noticed he always turned to the racing pages before looking at anything else. He told me he was scanning the pages trying to recognise the names of three good horses he had memorised. Very Clever!

He would read a joke in a pub and laugh like everyone else. The reality was that he had no idea what the joke was about but had noted how long it had taken the others in the group to laugh and did the same. What a clever way to cover himself? When filling in forms he always made out that he had forgotten his glasses, this was another ruse to cover his embarrassment at not being able to read the form.

We discussed this situation and decided something must be done about it. He would have to learn and I would set about teaching him. It proved to be a far harder task than I had imagined but I would not give up, he had changed my life dramatically and I would do my best to make life easier for him. Let battle commence!!!!

Chapter 19

A Learning Curve

$\mathcal{I}$ have always liked reading and writing since a small child and found it very difficult to understand how someone could survive without these skills. It made me more determined than ever to remedy the problem with Bryan. I thought I would start at the very beginning with a 'Janet and John' reading book to see where that lead us. Bryan was very keen at first and sat down eagerly thinking the process would only take a couple of weeks. We went through all the basic sounds and combinations of the letters, before we actually started to read. I thought by doing this he would have an understanding of the sounds. How wrong could I be? I have to explain that during his childhood upbringing and his working life he had accumulated a vast vocabulary of swear words. It was strange how he did not grasp the fact, that swear words would not be suitable reading matter for a small child. I found it extremely frustrating trying to read a page with him when every word he attempted to read that started with an 's,' a 'b' or an 'f' was uttered as a swear word. Did the sentence make any sense at all with every other word an 'expletive?' I tried to point this out to Bryan who thought the whole thing hilarious. Against the odds we did make some progress but on returning home in the evening from a hard day at work, he was often too tired to absorb anything. We struggled on regardlessly.

During this time, the project that Bryan had been working on at the Power Station was drawing to completion. He had often had to work weekends and I thought it might make a change for him to get a job where he had his weekends free. When he finally came home with 'his cards,' officially unemployed, I pleaded with him to try for work in the Morris Motor Car Factory at Cowley. He was not very keen as it meant working inside but I furthered my argument with, at least he would have his weekends free and the money at that time was very reasonable. He begrudgingly agreed to give it a try. He applied, and got a job in the Paint Shop. It meant working nights, but the good thing about that was, he would have from Friday morning until Monday evening free. He would be only working 4 nights a week. Perfect, or so I thought.

A minibus would pick him up outside the Flats and whisk him away each evening to start his shift. At first things were fine, he would come home and tell me tales of his work colleagues—how they had sprayed each other with paint or painted another's heels while they were inspecting the paintwork. Life for Bryan, at that time, seemed to be one long joke from beginning to end of shift. It was here that he 'forged' a friendship with 'Ginger.' Bryans reading skills had not improved to the extent that he could read the instructions that came along the line with each car. Ginger, soon realised Bryan's predicament, and discreetly helped him by reading the instructions to him. They became great friends, a friendship that was to last a lifetime.

As days turned into weeks, Bryan became more morose and moody. I had never seen him quite like this before. He would arrive home on Friday morning, go to bed and refuse to get up again until Monday afternoon. What a waste of a weekend! I would let him sleep until mid afternoon on the Fridays and then try to persuade him to get up. This was a big mistake!! He would pull the blankets (we did not have duvets in those days) over his head and refuse point blank to move. No matter what I did every weekend was the same. Through the week, he would go to work, but no longer would he come home full of chat, instead he would be tetchy and critical, moaning if a meal was not on time, grumbling if a shirt he wanted to wear was not ironed. Life became unbearable.

One Saturday morning I asked him what he fancied for breakfast. Over the past few weekends I had been ferrying food to his bedside when he refused to leave it. He said he would like poached eggs on toast for a change. I dutifully poached his eggs, buttered his toast, made coffee and took it all in on a tray. I called to him where he remained hidden under the blankets. I called to him several times wondering if I should leave the tray with contents on the bedside table. As I went to do this, he suddenly sat bolt upright in bed, snatched the tray from me and threw it up the wall shouting that he had not asked for poached eggs. He said he had asked for a full English breakfast. I was furious, this was not the Bryan I had fallen in love with. Was he ill or having a brainstorm? I did notice a bright red mark between his eyes, a sign I was to see many times over the next 30 odd years.

Trying to keep a still tongue in my head so as not to fuel his anger I tried my best to pick up the mess that was, until a few minutes ago, an appetising breakfast. Back to the kitchen I went, this time to cook a full English. Let me try again, bacon, sausages, fried eggs, tomatoes and mushrooms all assembled on a fresh plate complete with rounds of bread and butter and fresh coffee. I approached the bed for a second time. No response yet again so I told him, in no uncertain words, where he could stick his breakfast. Again he sat bolt upright, snatched the tray from me and with repetition of what had gone before, threw the whole lot at the wall, tray included. That was the final straw—I had suffered his moodiness for the last time, I was off. I grabbed the suitcases from the top of the wardrobe and threw them onto the bed. That caused a reaction. He leapt forward in the bed, snatched up each case in turn, tore them in half and threw each part at me, yelling for me to pack them if I could. I was so angry I called him every selfish name I could lay my tongue to and stormed out, snatching up Karl on the way. As at all times, when Bryan and I had disagreements, I made my way to my Parent's house. I am not sure what I thought my Parents could do as they had no experience of rows and upsets as they always discussed their differences sensibly over a cup of tea. They were dumbfounded as to what advice they could give.

After I had talked it over, I began to see the funny side of it and returned home, lighter of heart and determined to sort out the problem.

Bryan was still entombed in his 'pit' and I decided not to antagonise the situation any further. I just shut the bedroom door and pretended he was not there. Apart from rising for natural functions he remained there until early Monday evening, when he rose, showered and prepared for work. As he left I told him that on his return we would sort out the problem he obviously had, being at work would give him time to mull it over.

I then endeavoured to clear up the mess in the bedroom, change the bed and remove the halves of the suitcases which were destined for the dustbin. There, apart from a greasy stain on the wall, normality was resumed.

Over breakfast the next morning, Bryan explained that he hated working nights and would prefer working the day shifts. Would it not have made more sense just to tell me rather than go through all this drama? He spoke to his foreman the following night and the switchover was soon arranged. For a couple of weeks life resumed a normal pattern.

Time had passed and now Karl was old enough to go to 'Playgroup' and I had managed to get him several morning placements. It was good for him to mix with other children as being an only child, most of his contact was with adults. He loved it and I put his name down for a full time place at the local Council Nursery School. We did not have to wait long for a place and he soon left 'Playgroup' to take up his full time placement. There was so much more for him to do there as it was not only a play centre, they also prepared him for full time education. He would come home very happy but extremely tired.

I began to get bored at home all day. Bryan was at work, Karl was at nursery, and I did not know what to do with myself. Cleaning the flat, washing, ironing, and cooking did not tax my brain and I needed something more. What should I do? I did not have any hobbies, apart from reading, that I could absorb myself in, so my thoughts turned to work. Should I get myself a part time job? It had been a while since I worked but surely I could do something? I talked it over with Bryan, who I might add, was none too happy about it, (something about women's place being in the home.) Now more determined than ever, I scoured the 'situations vacant' in the local paper. I spotted a job that looked ideal. Jack O' Newbury Dry Cleaners were looking for a 'travelling manageress.' The job was part time so I would be back to collect Karl, it was perfect, I would apply. I had to go to Oxford for my interview where I was taken into a lovely café and treated to lunch. The interview obviously went well as I was appointed 'travelling manageress' the following week. The job, was more glamorous sounding than it actually was. It entailed covering for absent staff in the various shops. There were dry cleaning shops in

Didcot, Wallingford and Newbury. I had to cover all three.

I hated the job, as with my lack of understanding of anything mechanical with knobs, the machinery I was supposed to use was beyond me. Presses and steamers, commercial washing machines and dry cleaning units, all a complete fog, although in fairness to the Company, they had given me tuition on how to use them all. The instructress could just as well have been speaking to a brick wall, nothing sunk in and on my return to the shops it was as if they had sat me at the controls of 'Concorde' and asked me to fly. I did not mind the front counter work as I could speak to people and fill in their tickets, that part was not a problem. The actual dry cleaning part became a huge stumbling block.

I was not sure at the time if it was the chemicals in the air at the shops or the worry of not being able to do the job properly that made me feel so ill. At first, I could cope with it, thinking it would be a passing phase but very soon the pain became intense and I was forced to see a doctor. The receptionist was not at all helpful and refused to let me see one of the Practitioners. I was stood at her desk, gripping the edge with knuckles forced white by the intensity of the pain and sweat pouring down my face. 'Was it urgent?' I heard her saying as I was nearly on the point of collapse. A true gentleman, waiting his turn in the waiting room could see my plight and gave up his place so I might be seen. I will forever be eternally grateful to that man for possibly saving my life. Within minutes of seeing a doctor I was being whisked away in an ambulance with an ectopic pregnancy which was about to erupt. Fortunately with medical help I returned to full health but decided not to return to my job.

Chapter 20

Life and Death

*I*t was not long after this incident that I yet again, began to feel poorly. It was not the same but the sickness became quite a problem. At first, I thought I had eaten something that disagreed with me but when it continued I went back to the doctor for confirmation. Yes—I was pregnant. Bryan and I had never discussed having children, it was a topic that had never been raised. I was not particularly maternal, although I loved my son, with a vengeance, trying to make up to him for his own Father abandoning him. The ectopic pregnancy had been more like an illness so even then it had not been discussed.

Bryan and I, at that time, were both married to our previous partners, and probably for that reason, marriage had never been discussed, We were happy with our arrangement, although as week followed week, Bryan became once again, very moody working in the Car Factory. It was not entirely his fault as 'strikes' were being called on a regular basis and money was often short as a result. Due to this, Bryan and his friend 'Ginger' would often go hunting for a days work, just to make ends meet. They did a variety of work from labouring on a building site to laying turf on Golfing Greens, but it was an unsatisfactory arrangement as work was not always to be found.

When I broke the news of my pregnancy to Bryan I was shocked at his response. He told me he did not want anymore children (remember, he already had a daughter growing up in Shropshire.) and I was to get rid of it. I was horrified and upset at this and told him if it was a straight choice between him and the baby, he had better start packing. Did he not know me at all, even after all this time? I would not even consider an abortion. I later realised he had not meant it but under the strain of not being able to provide properly for Karl and I because of the situation at work, he was worried that another mouth to feed might be too much. It did not take him long to apologise and to look forward to the event. I did not like the ides of becoming 'an unmarried Mother,' even though I was already married to someone else but was not sure how to broach the subject. Bryan, always doing the right thing in the end, saved the day.

Over breakfast, one Sunday morning he looked across the table and said, 'Well, we had better get something done about getting married.' It was hardly the proposal that I had dreamt of but at least it showed his sincerity. Plans were put into action to contact both our estranged partners and divorces were progressed. Bryan's came through without any fuss, his wife had found somebody new but mine took much longer, when time was of the essence. The baby was due in January and by the time October came I was huge. Unlike some women who remain reasonably slim during pregnancy. I blossomed early and just grew in girth. I would hardly be able to disguise my 'bump' when walking down the aisle. The beginning ofNovember came and my divorce had still not come through properly. I began to panic. We had decided to get married at the local Baptist Church as that was the only church at that time that would marry two divorcees. I was adamant that I wanted to get married 'in the eyes of God' as the break up of my first marriage had not been of my doing. At last the necessary paperwork came through and we arranged to see the vicar. The first available date was the 9th December and we were asked if that date was soon enough. The vicar joked that our wedding car may have to be an ambulance and our bridesmaid a midwife but even so, he was very understanding and arrangements were put in place.

It was at the beginning of October that we had news from Bryans' Mother that his Father was unwell. We called down to see him and were both shocked at his appearance, He had been a strapping big chap when we last saw him but now we were looking at a shadow of his former self. His sleeves rolled up—his arms looked like 2 thin sticks, his face had lost it's chubbiness and his eyes looked dull and lifeless. Bryans' Parents had been told it was bronchitis with a touch of pneumonia. I was not a doctor, I had not had any medical training, but I could see immediately that it was no such thing. I was afraid to look him in the eye for fear he would see in my face what I thought it was. He soon tired and went up to bed, with Mother in tow to make sure he was comfortable. Bryan and I looked at each other. His thought was the same as mine—this was the Big 'C.'

Nothing else could have changed a man so quickly. We had seen him 3 weeks before and then he had appeared to be fighting fit. His only worry then had been what to do when he retired, a retirement which had been looming up faster than he had wished. He would have no worries about it now—his days were obviously numbered. Over the next few weeks his health rapidly declined and he was admitted to the cancer ward of the Royal Shrewsbury Infirmary. Almost on arrival Family were informed that he literally only had days to live. We spent as much time as we could travelling up and down, but it was heartbreaking to see the change everytime we saw him. He got worse on a daily basis. When we were finally summoned, as the end was near, we left Karl with my Parents and drove as quickly as we could to the hospital in the centre of Shrewsbury.

We parked up outside the church opposite and raced in, afraid we might be too late. No—although his breathing was very shallow we had made it, The whole Family was stood around his bed. We joined them and they spoke in hushed whispers. We had only been there a few minutes when I started to feel decidedly uncomfortable. My stomach was knotting and the wave of pain that followed made me cry out. Oh No—please it was too soon for me to be in labour, not now, not here of all places! All that kept going through my head was the saying ' one person dies to allow another to be born.' This was too close, too personal. 'Hang on Father, this child is not due yet.' I could not do this to the Family. I stumbled outside and down the front steps and made my way to the wall of the church. I felt physically sick and leaned over the wall—God forgive me—I did not mean to be sick in your garden. Bryan, on arrival at the hospital, had gone off to get a coffee but on his return was informed of my dilemma. He came running out of the front door hastily followed by a nurse and doctor. How embarrassing!!! I was told I would have to be examined and not wanting to exhibit myself to the whole of Shrewsbury's passers by I returned to the hospital. I was ushered to the next bed to Father's, where curtains were drawn and an examination took place. Yes, I had definitely gone into labour.

This was my worst nightmare. I wanted Bryan to drive me home. There was no way I wanted a child of mine to be born in Shropshire. To anyone who does not already know—Shropshire men all have little legs, big bodies, but extremely short legs by comparison. I did not want my child, be it a boy or girl, to have this affliction. I must, at all costs get back to Didcot. Nobody would listen to me. Of course, they did not understand—little legs to them was the norm!!!!. Why won't they listen?

Apart from the inconvenience of the situation, the locality of the Maternity Hospital was the other side of Shrewsbury. An ambulance was summoned and I

was whisked away. I told Bryan to stay with his Father,
as I would be fine. I tried to sound more confident
than I felt as all I wanted to do was return to Didcot.
On arrival at the maternity hospital I was carried in
on a stretcher and quickly transferred to the delivery
suite. God was looking down favourably on me that
day as once installed in the delivery suite, everything
just stopped. The knotting feeling ceased and the pain
disappeared. I was transferred to a normal ward and
left to rest. Several hours later, Bryan arrived asking to
see our daughter. I asked if it was all over and was told
Father had rallied. Maybe he had heard what I said after
all. He was not ready to go and our child was not ready
to put in an appearance, a perfect combination. I did
have to tell Bryan of course, that he had been given the
wrong information as our child was still tucked up in
it's nest. The next morning I was discharged but told
not to travel too far, so I went to stay temporarily at my
brother-in-law's house. I would not risk travelling to
the hospital again to see Father, one fiasco was enough.
I spent all day resting, not wanting to chance triggering
off the labour again. We had planned to return to Didcot
later that day but Bryan and his brother were once again
summoned to the hospital for the final time. It was late
evening before Bryan's Father finally gave up his fight
and both brothers returned in tears.

Thank you Father for giving up your place in order for
a new baby to be born but thankfully it was not your
Grandchild. I am determined that this child will have
long legs.

We returned to Didcot later that night. Bryan felt that there was nothing else he could do for the moment and myself, I was feeling utter relief to be leaving the 'Land of Little Legs' far behind me.

Chapter 21

Two Black Sheep

The journey home was uneventful, Bryan drove very carefully so as not to trigger it off again. We had arranged for my Mother to deliver Karl some time after lunch the next day, so on our arrival home went straight to bed. It had been a traumatic few days for one and all.

Father's funeral was arranged but I decided that I would not chance the journey again. Bryan understood and agreed to return to Shropshire alone. I felt fine when he left in the morning. I thought I would rest up in his absence as Karl kept himself amused now he was almost 5 years old. We had eaten lunch and I had just finished clearing up the mess in the kitchen when I felt a sharp pain in my stomach. Oh, here we go again! I tried not to panic, it was still too soon, the little blighter was just trying to unsettle me again. My Mother had said she would pop in after lunch and I hoped that she would not delay her visit as I was feeling very uncomfortable yet again. Fortunately, I did not have to wait long. On arrival, she took one look at me and raced off to a neighbouring flat to summon an ambulance. This 'little one' was certainly in a hurry to make an entrance. Once again I went through all the procedures of explaining what had happened the previous weekend. I was examined, confirmed, yet again, that I was in labour and transferred to the delivery suite. I had left Karl in the capable hands of my Mother and asked her to contact Bryan as soon as she could.

Bryan remained in Shropshire to see his Father buried and then left immediately after the internment to be with me at the hospital. After making enquiries, on arrival, he was told he had a beautiful baby daughter. He came up the ward, grinning from ear to ear, a proud Dad indeed. I was unaware of the information he had been given as once again it had been a false alarm. I had to stay in hospital for a few days rest but I was still as pregnant as ever, if a little tired of 'Juniors' antics. On the day I was discharged we went to collect Karl from my Parent's house. At least, now I might get a chance to be married properly before 'Junior' put in an appearance as December 9th was now not too far away.

As I have explained previously I was like a galleon in full sail. What could I wear to my wedding? A girl I knew, was a brilliant needlewoman, so I bought some rust coloured paisley patterned material (well, I could hardly have got married in white, could I?) and gave her the job of trying to make me look less fat. The material sounds revolting and looking back, it was. She made a good job of the dress, but during the last two weeks I had another growth spurt and by the time I got round to wearing it, it was slightly too short for my liking, but too late to do anything about it. My accessories consisted of a white fluffy hat and white shoes and I carried a small posy, hopefully to hide some of my 'bump.' The hat, I might add, was destined to cover the rather uncomfortable seat of my pushbike, where it did service for many years.

Baby held off putting in an appearance before the big day. The wedding, which was a very small affair went according to plan except for the point when Bryan had to slip the ring on my finger. We had not taken into account, my swollen fingers!!. When he looked into my eyes and tried to slip the ring over my knuckle, it got well and truly stuck. After two attempts he told me I would have to do it myself. I must be the only Bride who had to lick and suck her ring into place. Very romantic, I must say! We had the reception at our flat as there were only my immediate Family plus two brothers and his Mother from Bryan's side. Due to the recent death of his Father we thought a small discreet wedding would be more acceptable, especially in my condition.

At last I could have this baby with a clear conscience, I was now legally married to it's Father. Every day I waited with anticipation. Would today be the day? I waited in vain. Christmas came and went and so did New Year and still there was no sign. Finally with Toxaemia and swollen legs I was admitted into hospital on the 5th

January with a view to being started the next day. Bryan was very considerate and sat with me throughout the day and evening but we had agreed he would not be at the birth, so he returned home. I thought giving birth was women's work, he had already done enough, thank you very much!

The next day, around mid morning I was injected and the procedure began in earnest. At 1pm, our son finally put in an appearance. Oh, how I wished he had been born in November, when he first attempted his exit, he would have been so much smaller. He eventually weighed in at 8lb 12oz.

Instead of placing him on me straight after birth, as is the normal procedure, he was wrapped up and whisked away. Was there something wrong? I was told I had a son but why could I not see him? There must be something wrong? Did he have two heads or maybe limbs missing? Whatever was it?

I was taken to a side ward where several phials of blood were taken. I am needle phobic so this was a very big deal. I kept asking about my son but nobody would tell me anything. Upset and angry I demanded to see someone who could tell me what was happening. I remembered that during the birth his shoulder had got stuck, maybe it had dislocated.?

A doctor came and explained that it had nothing to do with his shoulder, it was his blood that was confusing everyone. In the normal course he should have been born a 'blue baby,' needing a blood transfusion at birth.

I was totally confused, had they muddled me with someone else? I was then told that I had rhesus negative blood containing certain antibodies that made it very rare. Women with my blood group, gave birth to normal first babies, without any complications but any further children would need blood transfusions immediately after birth. Doctors were confused as my baby was recorded as being my second child but his blood had been 'normal.' Suddenly I realised why this confusion had occurred, my records were still in my previous married name. I explained that I had re married and this was the first child by my second husband. The problem was solved and my son was returned to me.

Although this solved the problem of my baby's blood, it did leave me with an unanswered question. I had been told by the doctor that I had inherited this blood from one of my Parents. It must have been my Dad as Mum had had 4 children and none of those had needed a blood transfusion. How come it had never been mentioned., not even when I became pregnant? The mystery deepened.

Later that afternoon, Bryan arrived at the hospital, slightly under the weather from prematurely, the previous evening, celebrating the imminent birth. He brought Karl in to meet his new little brother. Bryan, having been told twice before that he had a daughter, did not seem disappointed that he did, in fact, have a son.

During the few days that I had to stay in hospital, I had time to think about the issue of 'my blood.' I was never aware of my blood group as because of my needle phobia, whenever blood was taken, I always felt queasy and it was always done as quickly as possible so I could get away. I never wanted to discuss it. Was this blood group something you kept secret? I would have to investigate this further when I got home.

I did remember, as I lay there, that my Dad's brother had 'special blood.' I could remember, as a child, asking him about his 'donor' badges and him explaining that his blood was very rare. I could remember him telling me that not many people in the whole world had the same kind of blood, it was that rare. Strange that, as I had just had a similar conversation with my own doctor about my blood. How strange that it was so rare and yet my uncle and I had the same blood group. What a coincidence! The penny did not drop. I needed to find out more.

On the day I was discharged, Bryan stopped on the way home so that I could do the week's shopping. He was not at all domesticated and shopping was not high on his agenda. He kept an eye on the baby in the car whilst Karl and I went off to do the shopping, not forgetting the milk for the baby. I did not naturally feed Karl and I was not about to start with this new baby.

Once home, Bryan said if I made up the bottle for the baby, he would feed him whilst I got on and cooked the tea. Not for me a restful homecoming to enjoy my baby in my own surroundings. I was straight back into harness. It was just Bryan's way, he was the 'breadwinner' and I was the 'homemaker,' and I was well and truly home!

I did not realise at that time, that I was going to be 'the black sheep' in my Family, neither was I to know that I had just given birth to a son who would become 'the black sheep' in my own Family. Such is Life!

Chapter 22

Prayers Answered

During my stay in hospital, Bryan and I had received a letter from our local Council to inform us that we had been allocated a 3 bedroom Council house. How exciting was that news? Bryan went to view it and I awaited his visit with growing excitement. What was it like? How big was the garden? What was the layout like? How big were the rooms? The questions just tumbled out. Bryan sat by my bedside and just grinned. He told me where abouts it was situated in the street but I got nothing else from him only that the lady who lived there wore a very short skirt that had distracted him from taking in much else. It didn't matter, a real 'house of our own.' We accepted the offer and awaited a moving date.

After arriving home after the birth, I soon got back into the routine of having a new baby around. I slept soundly during the night, probably from exhaustion, but when baby's crying disturbed Bryan, he would wake me, telling me that my baby was awake and needed feeding. I certainly wasn't married to 'a modern man' who felt it necessary to share in all the experiences of a new baby.

My Mother, Nan to her Grandchildren, was unlike most Grandmothers. I have mentioned before that she was not, by nature, maternal. Whenever any of her children had babies she would offer to baby sit during the first few weeks after the birth, so husband and wife could go out together for an evening without worrying about finding a responsible babysitter. It would be the only time she volunteered her services. On most occasions, unless it was an emergency, she would inform us that she had had to stay in to look after her own children, now it was our turn to stay in. She could not be expected to be at our beck and call It was odd really as my Parents never had a social life, in fact, they never went out at all. Still, that was Mum and we all got used to her strange ways.

On our allotted evening to go out, our son was just a week old. We went for a drink at our local pub and when we returned, Mum was looking worried. She told us that unless she was mistaken, our son was having 'fits.' I looked into his carrycot where he was sleeping peacefully, surely she must be mistaken, I had never noticed anything untoward. She went on to explain that it had only been very slight but she was certain all was not well. I watched my son sleeping for the next hour and saw nothing to worry me. When I later went to bed I did think I would mention it to the Health Visitor when she called early in the morning, just in case.

Next morning, I got my baby up and during his bath time I noticed him start to shudder uncontrollably. I took him out of the water and wrapped him loosely in a towel. The shuddering stopped, then almost immediately, it started again. I laid him on his side in his carrycot and called for Bryan. I was panic stricken. Fortunately, the Health Visitor arrived at that precise moment. She took one look at the baby who by this time was into his 7th fit and rang the emergency doctor on her mobile phone. A doctor was with us within 15 minutes and said he would call an ambulance. No need, car keys at the ready, we could not wait for an ambulance, we would leave now. Karl was quickly dressed and in minutes we were on our way, baby cradled gently in my arms.

The hospital notified of the problem had a doctor waiting for us, on arrival. The baby was taken away immediately for tests and treatment. We were stunned. We sat in the corridor unsure of what we might have to face. The next time that we saw our baby, he had been given a 'lumber puncture' and was in intensive care, wired up to monitors. All I could think was, thank goodness he had been born with a bit of meat on his bones so that he had something to fight whatever it was. It might give him a fighting chance. Bryan sat and cried. He felt that 'someone up there' was punishing him for saying he wanted me to 'get rid of his son' when I told him that I was pregnant. He felt so guilty. How could he live with himself? We prayed for our baby to get well.

We were shown into a doctor's consulting room for
the prognosis. It seemed that the baby had been born
without a 'soft spot' on his head. His body was seriously
deficient of calcium and the general thought was that his
body had used the calcium to fuse the bones of his skull
leaving him without a 'soft spot.' The doctors thought
this had caused slight pressure on the brain and that, with
the reduced level of calcium in his body, had caused the
'fits.' The outcome was that his diet had to be changed to
a 'high calcium' milk and he would be kept in hospital
to monitor his progress. They also warned us that our
son, possibly could be brain damaged, We sat in shocked
silence, our poor little baby.

We hardly spoke on the journey home. I was worrying
how I would cope with a brain damaged child and
Bryan, like most men would in the same situation, felt it
must be a reflection on his 'manhood.' We called in at my
Parent's house on the journey home, to break the news.
We were all devastated. All we could do was pray, and
pray we did, as we had never prayed before. Bryan, who I
must admit, had very little faith in anything but himself,
also prayed to a God he was not sure existed. We could
do very little else.

After a week of tests and treatment, our son was allowed
home. We had spent most of our time at his bedside and
all our prayers were answered. We had a normal little baby
back. We thanked God for the safe return of our son.

Chapter 23

A Step into the Unknown

Normality soon resumed and we were looking forward to Karl starting full time school. Everything seemed to happen at once. We got Karl's starting date, we were notified of our moving date and we had our baby son safely home.

Due to the time spent at the hospital, I never found time to visit the house that had been allocated to us, so the moving date was to be my first visit. The morning was manic, Bryan, as I have explained before, was not domesticated in any way and anything to do with the house or children was my domain. Bathing, feeding and dressing my baby son, sorting Karl out for school and getting breakfast for everyone was, prior to packing for the move, all down to me.

I raced off to school, looking as if I could not wait to get rid of my first born, but I knew how busy my day was going to be and every minute counted. As I walked down the school drive, that skirted the playing field, I looked at my angelic son in his new uniform and worried for his safety. All the other children looked so big and rough. How would my 'little cherub' cope? I needn't have worried, with hindsight, my worries should have been for the other children.

I settled Karl into his class and left at breakneck speed to start packing for our move. On arrival at home, I settled our son for a sleep. Fortunately the fresh air had done the trick and it did not take long for him to be in the 'Land of Nod.' Bryan, instead of doing something useful in my absence, was still sitting at the breakfast table waiting for his second cup of coffee having his 'perpetual' fag. I say 'perpetual' because Bryan smoked constantly. It was the first thing he did when he swung his legs out of bed in the morning and almost the last thing he did at night, roll a fag. He needed a fag to think, to go to the toilet, before and during any activity and definitely when he was stressed. These just about cover all aspects of his life, so you will understand that Bryan could always be seen, with either a cigarette in his mouth, or in the throes of rolling one. He may not always have had it lit, as it was constantly going out, but it was more of a comfort thing.

I made him his coffee and I got on with the task of packing. He had arranged for my brother to bring round a flat bed lorry he had borrowed, and when my brother arrived, yes, you've guessed it. I had to stop what I was doing to make more coffee, while they had a 'cigarette break' to discuss their plan of action. I have to admit that they did come in handy for moving all the large pieces of furniture. I saw dismantled beds, a dressing table, a three piece suite and a wardrobe disappear down the stairs to re appear loaded on to the back of the lorry, ready to go. This was like 'déjà vu' for me as it brought back memories of 'Fred Suttons Coal Lorry', a memory of my youth. It was quite windy on the day we moved and as I looked out of the bedroom window I noticed the empty wardrobe on the back, start to sway. I opened the window and called out a warning to the two men having yet another 'cigarette break' I was told not to worry as they had everything under control, they knew exactly what they were doing. Before their sentence was complete, a mighty gust took the wardrobe over the edge and off the back of the lorry to lay prostrate in the road. At least it had not smashed but the wide scratch down the door did nothing to either enhance it's appearance or my temper. Were men capable of doing anything at all? With the wardrobe back in place, tied down this time, after the damage had been done, they decided that this probably was a good time to take the load round to the new premises and rapidly disappeared.

In the meantime, I prepared a scanty lunch for Karl, once again fed my baby son and then raced off to collect my first born from his first morning at school. Luckily for the first few days he only had to attend mornings so it would allow me time to get on without watching the clock.

By late afternoon, the flat was empty. I had scrubbed it from one end to the other. I did not want anyone who might move in to doubt my cleanliness. I hoped the lady who was moving out of the new premises had my standards.

When all was done, I walked round to my new home with the pram piled high with last minute bits, anxious to see my new house, but beginning to feel extremely tired. At last I had arrived. The front of the house did not look too bad, all the windows were intact even if the front garden could do with a tidy, but not to worry there would be plenty of time to do that. I took a peek at the back garden, again it was a little untidy but with a rough lawn, a couple of fruit trees and a rockery I thought it had potential. I could hardly wait to get inside. What a shock I was in for!

I stepped into the kitchen to be confronted by one cupboard, high on the wall, painted deep purple and a Belfast sink minus any draining boards. That was the full content of my kitchen. The windows were thick with grime and the concrete floor equally filthy. As I made my way into the 'L' shaped lounge/diner, I noticed the word 'Michael' scratched into the glass of the dining room window. Separating the dining area from the lounge was a wooden partition partly made up of 'Raindrop Glass.' At some point the partition had been painted sunshine yellow but the paint had been allowed to run the full length of the raindrop glass. What a mess!

On into the lounge I went. Oh, it had an open fire, how delightful, but what was that all down the back wall? Somebody had obviously not liked a meal at some time as most of it was hanging from the wall. It did not look as if it was a recent event as it had gone green and mouldy. The stairwell also showed signs of culinary delights masquerading as pictures and the upstairs toilet was simply a joy to behold. It was a very tiny toilet, consisting of just a toilet, no room for a hand basin but decorated in 6 different patterns of wallpaper. Whoever were the people who had lived like this?

Bryan came with me to inspect the bedrooms and on entering the smallest of the three, I noticed 2 scaffold boards nailed to the wall with 'horseshoe nails.' I made some comment about those having to go and with one kick, Bryan took them clean off the wall. There, they were gone, but so was half the wall. I would have to get that re-plastered. What a help he was!

I was so shocked by the state of the place that I had failed to notice what my 'removal men' had done with everything that had been brought round. Downstairs and back in the lounge, I nearly had a fit. Instead of putting the furniture in the relevant rooms everything had been piled up in the lounge. I was appalled at the state of the house after having left my flat in pristine condition. I had no idea where anything was, it was January and very cold in the house and all Bryan seemed to be worried about was, when would his tea be ready?

I asked if he could find something to light a fire as the children needed to be warm and while he did that I hunted round for a kettle, cups and saucers and a means to making a drink. I very quickly realised that the electricity meter was faulty as I could not keep up with it's constant demand for more money. The fire lit, I thought we could at least be warm. Bryan had found some tar covered sleepers in the garden which had been cut up into lengths. Suddenly, as they got hot, they started to spit hot lighted tar into the room. I was terrified that the house would catch light so the fire was put out as quickly as it was lit. Bryan, still worrying about his empty stomach, was persuaded to visit the local fish and chip shop, at least we could be fed without too much hassle. I boiled a kettle and made my younger son his bottle. He may not be big enough to eat fish and chips but there was no need for him to go hungry.

I thought that once fed, Bryan would set to work getting our house straight for habitation. How wrong could I be? He no sooner finished his food, screwed up the paper and threw it into the embers of the dying fire and then informed me that he had had enough for today, he was off to the Pub. I looked round in dismay and burst into tears. I felt dead on my feet, I was so tired. Did I get any sympathy? Definitely not.
"Oh, if you are going to be miserable I am off," was his remark as he donned his jacket and made for the door. I was tired, angry and upset and hurled a few choice words at his disappearing back. I had never felt so tired and sat down on a box and wept.

I managed to find a suitcase with children's clothes in and a box containing some blankets. I would make it an adventure for Karl, he was confused enough. Starting school from one house, moving to another before teatime and watching me become more tired and tetchy as the day wore on, I would try to make amends. 'Find the mattress' became the first game and then once found, we dragged it up the stairs and put it into the second largest bedroom which was to become his. I managed to find, after several skirmishes through boxes, school clothes for the morning, soap, flannel and toothbrushes and clean clothes for Steed. With a bit of sorting out I managed to get both children settled for the night. It had been an exciting day for Karl, Steed was probably oblivious to it all, but to me, it had been a nightmare. I struggled to get the mattress of our bed upstairs and fell exhausted in a heap, to sleep, the sleep of the dead.

Door unlocked downstairs, I did not care, I was too tired to worry about anyone breaking in and too tired to care if Bryan came home at all. At that moment, I had gone off men altogether.

Chapter 24

An Apprenticeship in DIY

With renewed energy, I woke refreshed from a good nights sleep. It was dark outside so it was still early. I rose, without disturbing Bryan who had joined me sometime during the night, and made my way downstairs to make a cup of coffee.

Somehow today, things did not seem so bad. I realised that not everything had to be done in a day and made a promise to myself not to try too much, take it easier, to relax and enjoy the moment. My little chat with myself worked and when Bryan came down soon after, I was feeling far more placid than the last time he had seen me. We concentrated on getting Karl to school first and Bryan suggested taking him while I got the baby up, dressed and fed.

On Bryan's return we worked methodically through
the lounge and very soon it was straight, everything in
its rightful place. I have to admit that it was like living
in a goldfish bowl as none of the curtains from the flat
fitted these windows and I hadn't had the opportunity
to measure up for new ones. I did not care, I was now
in my new house and I would work hard to make it a
comfortable home.

The kitchen proved to be more difficult as there was
nowhere to store anything. A decorating table became
an essential part of my kitchen furniture and was used to
stack pots and pans at one end and food at the other. A
perfect solution.

This house became my apprenticeship for DIY. By
the time we moved out 14 years later I was a 'skilled
craftsman.' During that time I had plenty of practice. As
I have declared before, Bryan was the 'breadwinner' and
earned the money to keep his Family, anything else was
down to me. I decided to start at the top where nobody
would see my handiwork. The small bedroom was first
on my agenda.

My first job was to re plaster the wall. It proved to be
much harder than I first envisaged. I mixed the plaster
in a bucket and then Baby woke and had to be fed. The
plastering would have to wait a little longer. When I
returned the plaster was solid in the bucket—my first
lesson learned. When mixing plaster you have to apply
it to the wall as soon as it is mixed. New bucket, more
plaster and a trowel and I set to work.

On completion, I stood back to admire my work. It would probably have made a skilled plasterer weep but once covered in wallpaper, who would know? It was good enough.

The paintwork was disgusting, it looked like 'Jacob's coat of many colours. There were too many coats to be bothering with paint stripper, what I needed was a blowlamp. Bryan was very accommodating and next day produced that very tool.

My Mum came round the next day to help, thinking two people working might speed up the process. I have to say, at this point, that the windows were so dirty on the outside that I needn't have worried about anyone looking in, we couldn't see out. I decided to pay for a window cleaner to visit as I was not very happy about climbing ladders. The window cleaner appeared on the very day Mum and I decided to tackle the paintwork.

The blowlamp was an antiquated one that used methylated spirits to get it going. Novice that I was, I didn't realise how flammable methylated spirits was and spilt quite a lot as I was filling up the blowlamp. The window cleaner had just appeared at the window when I lit the match. There was an almighty 'whoosh' and most of the floor caught fire. I looked at the window expecting help from that quarter, but no such luck. The man in question, I loathe to call him a gentleman, slid down his ladder and instead of coming to our aid, was seen disappearing up the street with his ladder and bucket as fast as his legs could carry him. It is reassuring to know that not all people in our midst have so little conscience and my faith in human nature has been restored many, many times over during my life.

It was down to Mum and I to fight the blaze. Fortunately I had completely emptied the room before commencing so armed with wet towels which we threw over the flames we managed to thwart the 'raging inferno.' Lesson two, be more careful with methylated spirits. It is highly flammable!!

With the art of plastering, stripping paint and wallpapering under my belt, as well as renewing electrical switches and plug sockets, I stood back to admire my completed room. Bryan, of course, when viewing the room deigned to give me tips on how I should have done certain tasks. I can tell you now, those comments fell on deaf ears. If I was going to learn it was going to be by making my own mistakes, after all, where was my Mentor when the plaster dried hard in the bucket or when the floor was ablaze? You have guessed it—Nowhere to be seen!

Encouraged by my first attempt, I tackled both other bedrooms and totally transformed them. I re painted the bathroom and re papered the tiny toilet. It looked so much better with just one plain paper rather than six multi coloured ones.

I had to admit defeat when it came to the stairs, that was left to a professional. Downstairs and I was off again. I thought it would look so much better without the paint spattered partition. I did at first put ornaments on its shelves to try to make the best of a bad job but it was

horrid and would have to go. If I asked once I must have
asked at least 20 times for Bryan to dismantle and remove
it. One Saturday afternoon while he was watching horse
racing on the television, I asked again. It must have been
once too often as he jumped up, between races I might
add, grabbed a nail bar and a hammer and without
warning started to smash it apart. I had no chance to
remove my ornaments as the nail bar and hammer swung
into action. Within 10 minutes the partition was down,
along with my ornaments and half the dining room wall.
You could not imagine the mess! Glass, wood, plaster and
china completely covered the lounge carpet and amidst it
all Bryan had sat down to continue watching his racing.
When I started to grumble he said, "You wanted it down,
now its down stop moaning." I spent the rest of the
afternoon clearing up the debris and I had to admit the
rooms did look bigger and better without it.

Due to the two parts of the room being decorated in
different colours, the lounge/diner now looked neither
one thing nor another. Bryan, at this point, decided to
take charge.
He did not think I was competent enough to do this
room so he set about re-designing the fireplace. He
wanted a stone fireplace with a low wall extending to
a plinth to hold the television. My brother was quite
good at DIY and was asked to price up building the
new fireplace and to decorate the room. We looked
around locally for a quarry to supply the stone we
needed. It was not going to be an easy kit form for us,
we had to do things properly. We found one at Brize
Norton. Apart from knowing there was an air base there
we had no idea where it was. We had a Family trip out

there on a Saturday morning in order to purchase the required stone. Little did we know at that time that our Future was destined to be on the doorstep of Brize Norton.

The stone purchased and the wallpaper chosen, my brother set to work. He spent all day placing the stones in different positions before cementing them into place just before Bryan returned from work. I was pleased with the result and so was my brother but not so Bryan. He took one look at it and demolished it in seconds with his boot. I was furious at his insensitivity and my brother was none too pleased either. Once tempers had calmed they agreed the alterations and the following day my brother started again. This time all was well and the wall remained 'in situ.'

I had decorated all the bedrooms with Laura Ashley wallpaper which was very popular at the time but that was obviously not going to be good enough for the 'Gough' lounge. Bryan made his choice—the lounge was to be green and gold. The wallpaper, carpet and curtains were to be green with a gold coloured three piece suite. He chose the paper which was very rich looking and highly embossed. My brother warned him beforehand that it would take a couple of days to dry out due to the thickness. Bryan said he understood and the papering commenced. My brother worked all day to finish the room before Bryan returned from work. My brother explained to me that although the paper looked 'bubbled' it would go back to the wall once it dried out. I understood and couldn't wait for Bryan's return so I could show him the finished affect. The room would look grand once it dried out.

Bryan returned and I served him his dinner and as he ate it I could see him eyeing up the walls. I reminded him about the drying out period but he was getting more irate the longer he sat at the table. Without any warning, he jumped up and started ripping the paper off before my very eyes. I was horrified, all the work my brother had put in being destroyed by this 'mad man.' In the space of a few minutes the walls were almost bare again and the lounge looked a shambles. I broke the news to my brother later that evening. Bryan then had the cheek to ask him, if we bought more wallpaper, would he come round and do it again. He was a glutton for punishment as he agreed to do this but only on condition the paper was not embossed.

I cleaned up the room ready for the next attempt. This was a time when 'Novamura' wallpaper had just come onto the market. 'Novamura' was a type of paper that had a sheen on it and when it came to stripping it off, it came off in complete strips as we were to find out at a later date.

My brother completed the room in a day and this time it was to Bryan's satisfaction, no bubbles. A new 3 piece suite was purchased along with a green carpet that covered both lounge / diner and stairs. The room, now completed, now looked a picture.

The kitchen was the last room to do and Bryan called on his friend Ginger from the Car Factory. He was obviously better at DIY than Bryan and between them they set about installing a new fitted kitchen. Anything was better than the one I had and when it was finished I was more than pleased with the result. My home was now complete, a miraculous transformation.

No one will ever know the tears, tantrums, rows and bad feelings that went into getting that house transformed but now standing back seeing the difference. Everything seemed worthwhile. We now had a beautiful home to be proud of.

Chapter 25

The Biggest Drip?

*N*ow that we were established in our new home, Bryan's wanderlust for work returned. The car factory had caused us more problems than we ever envisaged and by this time I was even contemplating going back to work myself rather than have Bryan stay on in a job he hated. He was making life unbearable for us all.

My prayers were answered when he received a phone call about a new brewery that was being built just off the M4. They needed scaffolders and that was all he needed to hand in his notice at the car factory. I was so relieved, but this new job was to bring its own difficulties.

During the day, beer was 'on tap', so instead of having 'tea breaks' the men could have 'beer breaks.' I cannot explain in words the state he would come home in. Luckily, my brother was working with him at the time and used to drive him home. It would take, both my brother and I to get him out of the car and into the house. I thought he would soon get tired of the constant hangovers but no, he seemed to thrive on them. I could not understand how he could do his job, after all men's lives relied on the competence of his work? My brother then explained that Bryan would not drink any beer throughout the working day but when his shift finished all the men would hang on for an hour, chatting and drinking. That is when the damage occurred. How silly of me to think that he had been working long shifts! I soon got tired of that situation and more rows ensued.

Once again my prayers were answered when he received yet another phone call from 'the travelling man's network.' This time he was off to the Oil Rigs

This arrangement worked very well as Bryan was once again happy to be amongst his rough 'travelling fraternity' and I could get on with the job of looking after the house and boys without the rows and constant upsets caused by his permanent drunkenness.

It was a perfect solution. He would phone me most nights to make sure all was well and came home for a week once every 8 weeks. I have never been one to be depressed and kept myself busy in his absence with a constant round of activities for the boys. There were football matches to attend, football training, butterfly hunts across open fields and stickleback fishing in the stream that I had fished as a youngster.

There was always something to be doing and we fitted in our activities round such things as school and meals. During the week when Bryan was on leave it would be like a honeymoon period. We were both pleased to see each other and that week flew by. He was always too tired to discuss any problems when he first arrived home and didn't want to discuss them and spoil the last few days he was home so I am afraid nothing got discussed or done during his period at home.

An example of this was while he was away on one stint, the bathroom tap started to drip. You may think this very insignificant and I agree it was at that time. I tried to mention that I thought it needed the washer replacing on several occasions but it was never the right time. He had either just arrived home or was thinking about going back and if I mentioned it in the middle of the week, I was accused of trying to spoil his break. I decided to leave it. He knew about it and I guessed he would sort it out in his own time.

Weeks went by and nothing was done and the dripping tap got steadily worse. One day when I was working in the kitchen, there was an almighty crashing sound. Whatever had happened? I ran round the house looking for signs but could see nothing and the tap by this time was a constant flow. The bath was now marked with a long orange stain and no matter how I tried to stem the flow it got the better of me. I could not understand it, nothing seemed to be damaged but I had definitely heard a resounding crash. No matter, something would come to light later.

Later in the afternoon I went to the shed, which was integral to the house to get some potatoes for tea when all was revealed. The shed ceiling had come down and what a mess it had made. The plasterboard was soaked and it then became clear as to where the water on the side of the bath had been running.

The water had run back behind the taps and down into the cavity above the shed ceiling. Now Bryan would be forced to do something as the water was now cascading directly into the shed. Luckily he was due to come home and subsequently a plumber was called.

Now I had forgotten to mention that when Mrs Thatcher came to power and made it possible for ordinary people to buy their Council houses, we took full advantage of it and managed to purchase our house for the meagre sum, in comparison to today's prices, of £11,000.

It was at times like this that I wish we hadn't bothered. When the plumber took up the flooring in the bathroom to assess the damage he found the water had rotted the floorboards, not only in the bathroom but in the adjoining toilet and across the landing at the top of the stairs. It turned out to be quite an extensive job as all the floorboards had to be replaced. While all this work was being done we took advantage and had the toilet and bathroom knocked into one and had to replace the bathroom suite.

I am certain that Bryan wished he had changed the washer, it certainly would have been less expensive. I secretly was glad he hadn't as I got a lovely bathroom out of it without actually having to ask for it. There are some perks in keeping your mouth shut at times, although it is not something I am known for.

Chapter 26

Midnight Onions

Every now and again when Bryan came home, he felt obliged to return to Shropshire to visit his Mother. It was on one of these visits that I had an extremely eventful weekend.

We had recently purchased a Yorkshire Terrier puppy and felt that we couldn't leave it behind on this occasion, on account of it being so young., so the whole Family, complete with puppy, set off to Shropshire early one Sunday morning. When Bryan's Father had been alive we used to spend whole weekends down there but now it was only restricted to fleeting 'day trips.' We arrived mid-morning and made polite conversation until the pub opened. After a phone call to several brothers, Bryan did a disappearing act and left me at home to help with the preparation of dinner.

At 3pm, he returned for his dinner and then slept most of the afternoon blaming his tiredness on the journey. At 7pm he woke miraculously feeling better, had a bite to eat and once again disappeared to the local pub across the road. I had wanted to leave early evening as I needed to get the two boys home and I knew I would be called upon to drive. At 11pm he returned, merry but not drunk. His Mother asked him if he would like a sandwich before he left for home. The rest of us could obviously starve as the invitation was not extended to us. He decided a cheese and onion sandwich would be fine and that brought up the topic of 'midnight onions.' I had never heard of them before and thought they must be a new type, naivety being my middle name.

Well, I soon realised why they were so called as with instructions in mind, Bryan and I were soon in the car and heading out of the village to open country, children and puppy left in the capable hands of 'Granny.' Sack in hand, Bryan told me to drive down this dark road. Suddenly, I was told to stop. He got out giving me instructions to drive down this road until I came to a 'T' junction. I was then to turn round and when I arrived back at this bend, I was to flash my lights as a signal. It seemed simple enough and I drove off. I wound my way down this twisting road until I came to the 'T' junction. So far, so good. I turned the car round and drove back they way I had come. It was all so unfamiliar, here was a bend, I slowed right down and flashed my lights and waited. I flashed again and waited, and nothing. Maybe

I was at the wrong bend. I set off again, another bend,
maybe this was it—flash my lights, still nothing.
Oh my goodness, I am lost. How many bends are there
on this strange road?

At every bend in the road I slowed and flashed and I was
becoming more and more worried that I had taken a
wrong turning in the dark. Suddenly, out of the darkness,
Bryan loomed with a sack of onions, hurling abuse about
my incompetence and stating it had looked like the
'Edinburgh Tattoo' as I came up the road. Was I trying to
draw attention to us as I was doing a very good job of it
if that was my intention?

If these were 'midnight onions' I would rather buy
mine from the shop like everybody else I knew. These
Shropshire people are certainly a strange breed! I felt
like a thief and I suppose that is exactly what I was, an
accomplice to theft. What was this man turning me into?
I was not to know at that time that the night would get
worse, not better.

On returning to 'Granny's' to collect our offspring and
puppy we said a fleeting farewell due to the lateness of
hour and started on our return journey. I, as expected,
had to drive home. Karl and the puppy were in the back
and Steed was travelling in the front on his Father's lap.
It was not ideal but I thought the children and puppy
would soon drop off to sleep. Who went to sleep first?
Yes, you have guessed it—Bryan, with a few pints inside
him was asleep before we had reached Shrewsbury and
kept dropping Steed into the foot well. Karl complained
he felt sick and the puppy was trying its best to get

onto my lap as I drove. At traffic lights in the centre of town, trying to knock the dog into the back, push Bryan up into a vertical position as he slumped sideways and haul Steed for the fourth time out of the foot well, the inevitable happened. I slowly rolled into the car in front.

Thankfully, the lady driver was very understanding and even though I had slightly scratched her bumper realised the predicament I was in and wished me 'Good Luck' and a safer journey home. My faith in human nature restored I resumed my journey homewards. Eventually, all other occupants were asleep and I made my way down the motorway towards Northampton

I slowed as I approached the slip road where I was to leave the motorway and as I did so, I was confronted with a herd of black cows in the road. All I could really see were their eyes glistening in my headlights. I slammed on my brakes throwing everyone off their seats (this was a time before seat belts) waking them all up. Bryan was cursing my driving, the children were crying and the dog was yapping at all the noise. As quickly as they appeared the cows made their way back up into their field and I once again journeyed on.

I had travelled no more than half a mile when a fox, playing chicken, ran into the path of my car and continued to run down the centre of the road, seeing if I could catch it. Sadly I did. By this time I was so tired myself that my reactions were not as quick as they should have been and I did not brake in time. There was a thud and I saw it catapulted onto the bank. I stopped, got out and checked to see if I had just injured it but it was definitely dead or if it wasn't, it could have had an oscar for it's performance of 'playing dead.' I was the one now feeling sick as I tried to calm my passengers and once again we resumed our journey. I could not wait to get home. I was seriously contemplating never returning to Shropshire ever again. From the motorway I made my way homewards, the children and the puppy now settled back down to sleep but Bryan, now afraid for his life, stayed awake.

We had not travelled far when we came across an accident. One car was nose first in a ditch and another car, full of youngsters, was parked up on the side of the road. I slowed the car as the youngsters ran into the road, flagging me down, indicating that they wanted me to stop. Once I had stopped, they all jumped into their car and sped off. Bryan and I got out to see if there was anyone hurt in the other car. As we approached it we could see one man slumped over the steering wheel, bleeding quite badly from a head wound. As we are talking about a time before mobile phones we had no way of summoning help. We could not leave him so when he stirred, we offered assistance. Apart from the head wound he seemed to be alright but the wound certainly needed dressing as by this time it was bleeding profusely. We offered to take him to the nearest hospital that we assumed would be 'The Horton' at Banbury. He was extremely agitated about a small box that he had lost in the impact and would not leave without it. I thought it strange, in the situation he was in, to worry about a box but he was insistent that we find it before we left the scene.

We hunted around in the dark until we found it and with it safely ensconced in his pocket we started off towards The Horton. We had bundled him into the back of our car with a towel covering his bleeding wound. I had no idea where I was or which way to go so I had to rely on our passenger for directions. Instead of directing me straight to the hospital I was instructed to drive round through some seedy back streets. Suddenly I was told to stop whilst he jumped out and disappeared, presumably to deliver the box he had been so worried about. Box delivered, we were then allowed to carry on to The Horton where we dropped our strange passenger and bade him goodnight.

I was now on the final lap home. I was so tired by the time I eventually arrived home that I vowed it would be a long time before I visited Shropshire again.

It was not until we were telling friends about our escapade that it was suggested that he may have been delivering drugs. Why else would he have been so worried about leaving the aforementioned box in the car?

During an innocent day visit to see Bryan's Mother, I had become an accomplice to theft and subsequently a 'drug runner.' Was there no end to my criminal talents?

Chapter 27

A Point to Prove

Bryan's one leisure Interest in life was 'horse racing.' He was an inveterate gambler, not just with money but with life itself. He was always willing to take a chance and accepted the results whether good or bad.

During his weeks off he would invariably find his way to the local bookies where he struck up a friendship with the bookmaker, who coincidently was the publican of the hostelry where Bryan used to drink when he was employed building the local Power Station. They became very close friends and through their friendship I met his wife. The four of us started to go out socially together and we had some momentous evenings. He was tall, dark and immaculately dressed at all times and had a wickedly dry sense of humour. His wife, on the other hand was short, stocky and a bundle of laughs. It was through her antics that I learned to laugh at myself. I had always been very reserved and shy and disliked meeting new people. I had, at that time, a very large bust when the rest of the world resembled 'Twiggy.' I was extremely embarrassed and inhibited by it. I had been flat chested in my early teens but when my bust started to develop, it forgot to stop. I did not like mixing with strangers as my bust was the first thing that registered with them, not my face. These new friends helped to change my attitude towards myself. My confidence grew and I started to look forward to our nights out.

On one of our excursions to 'The Hare' at Hendred, we were asked if we would like to join a Ladies Dart Team that was being formed. I felt a little unsure as I neither played darts nor did I go out socially when Bryan was working away. The decision was made for me. My friend, who, by now, was an ex—landlady, immediately agreed and put our names down on the list. She thought it would be a great laugh. Her husband said it wouldn't be a problem to pick me up and drop me off on dart nights, so with these arrangements in place Bryan was persuaded. It was a decision that I never regretted but I have to admit, lead to many arguments and disruptions in our house.

On Bryan's return to the Oil Rigs, my involvement with the dart team took off. Weekly we would either play home or away matches and I met and got to know a variety of people. I found it great fun and soon I was voted in as 'Captain' of the team. After several months of being chauffered round to various matches it was decided that as I didn't drink, I could pick the team up and drive them myself. This worked really well while Bryan was working away but started to cause trouble on his return.

Let me explain further. While Bryan was working away, I was expected to fulfil the role of both Mum and Dad to both the boys—feeding, clothing and generally looking after as well as attending football matches, judo contests and any other activity that they wished to participate in. Alongside that role I was also expected to be general handyman, painter, decorator and gardener and if an emergency occurred I was expected to cope and deal with it, no matter how serious. I am not trying to paint myself as some kind of 'Superwoman' but those that knew me would say I did the job reasonably well. I had grown both in confidence and competence and knew my true value as a person in my own right.

You will now understand why I was so annoyed, on Bryan's return, to find that he now wanted a meek and obedient wife who would jump to his every command. Those days were long gone and the next two years were spent proving a point.

While Bryan had been away, meals had been planned around activities, arrangements had been made without asking permission and I returned home from dart matches at about midnight, having dropped off team members at various addresses on the way. Babysitters had never been a problem as I had a very good girl who lived across the road and if ever she could not do it, one of my brothers or my sister would be available. I had everything covered.

Life was expected to change dramatically on Bryan's return. He would demand that I have a meal on the table at 5pm, an impossible task as both the boys were involved in different sports at different venues at different times. It was a general merry go round of dropping off and picking up. 5 o'clock dinner!!! Was the man totally mad?

Dart nights also became nights of controversy. The 'beer' games were never played until nearly 11pm so it was an impossibility to meet the curfew hour of 11pm that Bryan gave me to be in by. I would drop the women off on my way home and arrive home myself about 11.45pm to midnight dependent upon where we were playing that night. Initially he would be sitting up waiting and there would be an almighty row about my not doing as I was told. This progressed, as he became more determined to make me obey him. He would then wait at the dining room window, which overlooked the drive, and once I had pulled up and got out of the car, he would draw the curtains and as I approached the back door he would subsequently lock it and go to bed.

I knew exactly what he wanted me to do. I was expected to make a fuss but I understood that would be playing into his hands so I slept in the car. It was fine in the Summer months but as Winter began to creep in I took to sleeping on top of the freezer in the shed where the motor kept me warm. In the morning he would get up, unlock the door and without comment from either side I would resume my duties. This went on for several weeks before he realised that I would not give in, so he changed his tactics. One night on my return from a match, as I entered our street I could see an orange glow in the night sky directly behind our house. As I got out of the car I could hear the crackling of a fire and smell the smoke. Whatever could be burning as I was not aware that we had that much rubbish? I was soon to find out. There was Bryan, standing looking quite triumphant, as all my clothing, handbags and shoes went up in smoke. His comment to me was "Now that you have nothing to go out in, you won't be able to play darts anymore." How silly he could be at times, thinking a 'funeral pyre' of my belongings would put a stop to my dart night. He obviously did not know this 'new' me.

Although I wanted to scream at him, I kept my cool and just went to bed determined to rectify the problem in the morning. Next day, the problem was solved. I maxed his credit card replacing everything he had burnt. He was very upset when he tried to use it and was told he was up to his credit limit. I pointed out he had nobody to blame but himself, I was not going to walk around naked for him or anybody else. The point was made.

He never did like the idea of my having a life of my own but being married to one very stubborn, obstinate woman, he was forced to live with it. It would take another two years before he accepted me for the person he had forced me to grow into and then only occasionally did his Shropshire chauvinism raise it's ugly head.

Chapter 28

A Very Sharp Learning Curve

During the time Bryan was working away on the Rigs he met another travelling man from Reading. They seemed to get on very well and decided to go into business together. They decided to form a scaffolding company as that is what they were both involved in. Bryan would be in charge of labour and the otherchap was to deal with the paperwork and contracts side, with me as his trustworthy sidekick.

I knew nothing about scaffolding at that time and never professed to but was willing to meet up with the other chap and his wife to discuss our roles. Although they made us very welcome, I came away feeling somewhat uncertain. I had not taken to his wife who, although liking the sound of her own voice, knew absolutely nothing about scaffolding or business in general. The husband, I had a gut feeling about and did not trust him at all. I decided to put those feelings behind me as after all, this was Bryan's project and Bryan's friend, I would keep a still tongue in my head. I was always a better judge of character than Bryan and my point was proved a few months later.

Money was invested in this new company. Scaffolding materials were purchased along with a very ancient manual typewriter and an old 'Bedford' lorry. Paperwork was printed and 'Rig Scaffolding' sprang into life. Bryan continued to work away to help fund the new company for the first couple of months and I tried to work alongside his partner. My 'Boss' as he thought of himself, would drop by about 4pm with a pile of paperwork to be typed and demand that it be ready to pick up early next morning to collect. It was an impossible situation. My two boys had to be looked after and fed and my typing skills were almost non—existent. I had whilst still at school, paid for one hours typing tuition a week. It had probably lasted a month before I realised that a typist was the last thing I wanted to be and ceased my lessons. I had not encountered a typewriter from that day to this. I did the best I could under the circumstances but was snowed under with pages of small print clauses and contractual rigmarole. I could hardly wait for Bryan's return home.

When the decision was made for Bryan to return to work on the small contract we had been lucky to win, I was delighted. It seemed that I was not the only one to dislike Bryan's new partner. The scaffolders did not like him and the contractors thought him arrogant and difficult to work with. Good old Bryan, everybody's friend, on his return he won over everybody, men and contractors alike. The company went from strength to strength, we seemed to be making a profit. The accounts side of the business were being dealt with by the partner and Bryan wouldn't get involved. He trusted his friend and that was the end of it.

During these early months of the business, Bryan's partner purchased a house in Reading in need of refurbishment. He told us very little about it but from time to time he would let slip that the refurbishment was well under way.

It had been decided at the formation of the company that neither partner would take more than was necessary from the account in order to get things off to a good start.

I learned to economise. I cooked inexpensive meals making enough to last for two days. We stopped having any treats and went out less and less as work commitments grew. We saved money by having the yard in our back garden, making it a little like hanging out washing whilst doing an obstacle course. Everything would be worth it long term—the profits should be accumulating.

Bryan never seemed interested in 'looking at the books,' his expertise was with the men on sites, not with his nose in ledgers. I urged him to check up on the money side of things as I was beginning to have a gut feeling that all was not well. On several occasions I had mentioned to Bryan's partner about how well we must be doing and never once did he give me a straight answer or look me in the eye. Finally I confronted Bryan with the idea that his partner might not be as honest as he thought, and asked him to request a look at the books. I did not think this unreasonable as we had invested most of our savings into this company, but all the same it caused an unholy row. We, were accused, of not trusting him and he did everything possible to prevent Bryan checking out our fears.

Eventually Bryan could not be persuaded otherwise, and sat down with ledgers, cheque stubs and bank statements. Lo and behold, our fears were justified as it was obvious what had been happening. Instead of the £5,000.00 profit we were expecting to find, the account was almost empty. The money had been filtered out of the account probably to fund the refurbishment project.

I can remember accompanying Bryan to a car park on the outskirts of Reading where, in no uncertain terms, the business partnership was dissolved amongst flying paperwork and flying fists. Justice had been done the travelling man's way. Bryan claimed the materials and lorry as his partner had had his share of the money and decided on the journey home that he would go it alone.

The idea of that panicked me as Bryan, although very good on site, was not into writing contracts or even reading the small print. I needn't have worried as Bryan decided to simplify everything and lose all the small print. This way everybody could see very easily what they were paying for and through a combination of safe scaffolding and amiable shrewdness the business thrived.

My manual typewriter was replaced by an electric one, bought from a nameless chap, no questions asked, and my book keeping skills improved daily. The administration side of the company grew from a shoebox to a box file and finally to a filing cabinet. We were now on our way.

Bryan's ex partner went into business with his wife and tried to compete with us but he was not a popular man and his business soon fell by the wayside. We were not to see him again for many years.

It was very surprising that although Bryan had the handicap of not being well educated it did not hold him back. Together we made a successful pair, Bryan doing the hiring, firing and manual scaffolding and me looking after the administration and accounting. It was not always a compatible working relationship but definitely a successful one that was to last for the next 23 years.

Chapter 29

Priorities

The company thrived and we began to take on bigger contracts. I can remember our excitement when we landed our first £5,000.00 contract. We went out and had a celebratory meal, we were so pleased with our achievements. Life became a little easier for me as I began to understand what people wanted when placing an order. This was mostly due to my many visits to see our scaffolding in various places.

On social nights out Bryan would do a detour so that I could see the erected scaffolding. He was not one of life's romantics but a man to be humoured.

I remember on one occasion, it happened to be our Wedding Anniversary. I had arranged a babysitter, bought a new dress for the occasion and made a special effort to look good for my husband as he had promised me a romantic meal at an Italian Restaurant in Oxford. I have to explain, at this point, that we had secured a rather large contract at the Morris Motor Car Factory in Oxford. It was necessary on this job to have men working both the day and night shifts.

All spruced up and ready for our romantic evening, Bryan decided that we ought to first call in to site to see if everything was alright. I did not mind as we were going to Oxford anyway. Bryan left me in the car and went on site as planned. He was gone longer than I had hoped but on his return he made no comment other than we would call into The Swan for a 'quick one.' I assumed that this was a 'quick one' before going onto the restaurant. I had hardly got seated when I was given a half pint of lager and lime, told to drink it as fast as I could as someone had not turned up for work and Bryan had to take his place. I asked him how he was going to scaffold in his best suit? I should have known as he had taken the precaution of putting a boiler suit in the boot of the car, just in case. I was furious. How could he do this to me on our anniversary?
It was a lesson that I learned very quickly, scaffolding came before anything else!

He explained that this was our livelihood and had to come first, before socialising. It was difficult but I learned to live with it. I was at least allowed to drive the car home, a small mercy, I was grateful for.

Life continued to be busy, working from home, as we didn't have office premises and looking after the boys.

I obviously wasn't busy enough as Bryan came home one day and told me he had got me a job, cleaning 'The Chequers' pub in Harwell, a village a couple of miles away. He explained that he had been talking to the Landlady who had told him that after a disagreement with her cleaner, the lady had walked out. It left her in a bit of a predicament as she was desperate to find a replacement. Bryan, being the Good Samaritan that he was told her to look no further—his wife would step into the breach. Like a fool, I thought I would be helping her out temporarily, until she found another to take my place.

I obviously did too good a job as she said she was more than satisfied with my work and would not be looking to find anyone else. I remained there for the next two years working beyond her retirement. The Landlady was very particular and the wooden bar had to gleam. I spent hours polishing it until I could almost see my face in it. On her retirement, a young couple with children took over and they had a Great Dane dog. I have nothing at all against dogs, especially Great Danes, as I have owned 3 in my life but when it jumped up with it's front claws scratching my polished bar, I cringed. No matter how hard I polished it I could not eradicate the marks left by those claws. It was so disheartening.

Marg, the original Landlady had been spotless in appearance, always very smartly dressed, even early in the morning and impeccably coiffured by 11am, ready to meet her public. The new Landlady would still be in her dressing gown at opening time and never once did I see her smartly attired. The situation got worse as the new couple's marriage faltered and I found it highly embarrassing when she took up with a young lad from the village and moved him in, whilst her husband and children were still in situ. I felt the whole place was falling apart around me. Repairs and upkeep were non existent as the marital situation worsened and eventually, enough was enough. I handed in my notice.

It did take the pressure off me a little as by now Steed had started school. Whilst I had been working at the pub I had been getting up at the crack of dawn, seeing Bryan off to work, then getting the boys up and ready for school before driving to the pub to do my shift. On my return I would do the housework, prepare the dinner and do any administration work for the scaffolding company as well as sorting out the messages on the answer phone before dashing off to collect Steed from school.

I never seemed to have much time for myself and crammed as much as possible into every day. It seemed to be a pattern developing as at 63, instead of my life getting easier, it seems to have got even busier

The scaffolding company was going from strength to strength and the paperwork was beginning to take over the house. It was time to take drastic action. The scaffolding materials had been removed from my garden a while back when we managed to find a farm that allowed us the use of some land to set up a yard. I thought it was wonderful to have my garden back, now it was time to take a stand with regard to my house.

Without too much trouble we managed to secure a Unit which consisted of, an office upstairs overlooking a huge warehouse type space which was undercover, complete with an outside yard. It was perfect, if a little dirty, when we went to view it. We accepted the terms of the lease and spent the next few weeks painting the office, having carpet laid and generally getting it ship shape and ready to move into. Wow, it was so exciting! We employed our neighbour's daughter to be my assistant in the office and everything else fell into place.

We all looked very professional. I took Claire to Oxford to buy red suits and boots to match and now with everything functional in the office we moved in.

It worked very well, Bryan would arrive there in the morning to organise labour and drivers. Claire would be there at 9am and I would arrive after seeing the boys off to school. I would leave in time to be home for the boys returning from school and Claire and Bryan would work until 5pm. We had everything covered. Claire and I had a very good working relationship in the office and became good friends. I cannot say the same about Bryan as our volatile relationship would often erupt in the office over a differing opinion of how something should be done. Poor Claire would be caught in the crossfire and learned to keep her head down. She was quick to learn and I knew I could trust her to do her job properly. She shouldered a lot of responsibility and it allowed me a little more free time.

Chapter 30

From Mighty Oaks to Little Acorns

I have mentioned previously about how my bust, once it started to grow, forgot to stop. It ruined my teenage life as I was rather shy and could not cope with the banter that it evoked. I hated my shape with a vengeance. I looked a bit like 'Humpty Dumpty' as I would wear big loose jumpers in order to disguise it but the reality of it was that it only over emphasised how small my waist, hips and legs were.

I tried everything 'on the market' to reduce my size and when I finally consulted my doctor I was told that once I had had children the chances were that they would reduce in size naturally. This unfortunately did not happen.

In desperation I spotted an advert in a paper for a 'Stephanie Bowman' sweat suit. Maybe this was going to be the answer to my prayers? I sent off for one and had a chuckle when it arrived. It was made from bright pink pliable plastic and consisted of a long sleeved round neck top and trousers with ties at wrists waist and ankles.

The idea was to wear them under your clothes and either go about you normal business or for more rapid results, exercise whilst wearing them and the weight would drop off. I thought that if I exercised and sweated enough maybe they would reduce in size. Nobody has any idea how many hours I exercised looking like a giant lobster, my face matching the pink plastic, but all to no avail, I never lost a single inch!

I returned to my doctor as the weight of them were deforming my back and causing huge ruts in my shoulders as the straps struggled to hold the weight. I was eventually sent to the hospital and told I would be put on a waiting list that was approximately 18 months long. I was overjoyed—the end was in sight. I was advised to ring up in a year to see how far up the list I had climbed. This was in a time when breast enhancements and reductions were almost unheard of. 'Twiggy' was the model of our day and everyone, bar me, seemed to resemble her straight up and down shape. Oh, how I wished I looked like that!

I patiently waited the year and then excitedly rang up, thinking I would not have to be suffering for much longer. I was horrified to be told, I was now at the bottom of a five year waiting list. Children with severe

burns needed cosmetic surgery more urgently than I
did and had taken priority over me. I was devastated and
distraught. Was there never to be an end to my misery?

Bryan, my 'Knight in Shining Armour' came to my
rescue and told me to have it done privately.

I remember making an appointment to see a consultant
in Oxford. I waited only two days for the appointment
and was elated when told my operation would take place
the following week. I was asked, "What shape I wanted
my breasts to be?" 'Flat' was my immediate answer. I
did not want a shape, I wanted to look down and see
nothing. I was asked to browse through a catalogue of
'boobs.' I wanted to screech with laughter—they came
in all shapes and sizes. I felt embarrassed, as I had never
seen so many. I could not take it seriously—was it April
Fool's Day? I settled for 'as small as possible' and 'no, I
would not regret it if they turned out to be too small.'
How could a man understand what it was like not to be
able to lay on one's stomach, to have a permanently sore
and blistered cleavage and have to pay inflated prices for
French bra's, specially made, at a cost of £12.00 each in
comparison to a normal bra which cost just over £1.00.
When all other teenage girls were wearing pretty lacy
bra mine looked like a Granny's bra and corset all rolled
into one as it came down to my waist and was made
from heavily stitched cotton. Would I regret being 'small?'
Never!

I returned home on cloud nine and looked forward to
the following week.

My day of admission to hospital, Bryan was conveniently, not around. He never liked having anything to do with hospitals and doctors, so his friend Clive from the Betting Shop took me in. He dutifully carried in my case and we waited to be shown to my private room. The 'Sister' who led us upstairs chatted and made me feel at ease until we arrived in the room. Clive put down my case and tried to make a quick exit. As he was about to disappear the 'Sister' said, "Surely you are not going to leave without kissing your wife?" I am not sure who was more embarrassed, Clive or me. He came back into the room and gave me a peck on the cheek and wished me 'Good Luck.' Afterwards he explained it was probably less embarrassing to just go along with it rather than have to explain that he was not actually my husband, but my husband's best friend.

The operation was a huge success. I had over 200 stitches but I never felt a thing. I woke up when the anaesthetic wore off and looked down by body. Lo and behold, through the gap where my cleavage used to be I could see my feet!! I cannot explain in words the feeling of elation. It was like being born again—this time 'normal.'

I was soon mobile, and couldn't wait to get home. Shopping for new bra's and clothes were very high on my agenda. From that day on I never looked back, my confidence soared and I, at last, felt completely happy with myself.

A couple of weeks later I was able to laugh when on a Family occasion, my sister came in wearing one of my old bra over her clothes. She had had to pack two terry towel nappies in each side to fill the cups. I felt so relieved that from now on I did not have to carry that weight round with me.

When today, I see the likes of Jordan deforming her body with enormous enhancements I cringe at the mentality of someone so vain. My reduction, was not done out of vanity, but of sheer desperation to be comfortable.

Chapter 31

A Gift from God

Everything was working well, my house was once again a home, my garden was recognisable once more and the Family were all settled and healthy. Life was great, or was it?

I had begun to feel poorly of late but could not explain why. I just did not feel right. I started to lose weight and my hair looked dull and lifeless. I was tired and listless which was not at all like me. I became irritable as worrying about myself took hold. Weekly the weight dropped off me and I began to look ill. People began to notice and ask if everything was all right. What could I tell them? I hardly looked a picture of glowing health.

One morning as I lay in a state of semi consciousness, my hand brushed over the front of me as I changed position. What I felt woke me up with a start. There was a lump on my lower abdomen as big as an orange. It was so prominent that I could put my hand over it. I woke Bryan in a state of panic. Whatever could it be? Maybe this was the reason I had felt so ill. I needed to visit my Doctor.

I made an urgent appointment and a hospital visit ensued the following week. I had tests, x-rays and scans and still I did not know what the problem was. Test followed test, I had several x-rays and still I was unsure of what I was suffering. I began to feel worse as my imagination ran away with me. I felt sure my days were numbered, as I could not feel worse. Nobody could explain my condition and by this time the lump had disappeared back into my body. It was suggested that it might be a growth but I needed more tests. I was convinced it was the 'Big C.' Why else would I have lost so much weight and feel so ill? As far as I was concerned there could be no other explanation and nobody was giving me any answers to convince me otherwise.

I decided I would be brave and go out fighting; I would tell no one and carry on as normal. My fears were confirmed when I was told that I was to be admitted at the end of the week for a full hysterectomy.

Oh well, I had not considered having another baby so if that is what it took to save my life—so be it. The sooner it was all over the sooner I could get back to normal. I was waiting for the final test results to come back to

finalise my condition. I needed to face this on my own.
I refused to let Bryan or my Mum accompany me to the
hospital and went in prepared to stay for my operation.

On arrival, after booking in, I was taken to a cubicle and
told to wait for the Doctor who needed to speak to me.
As I waited in suspense, several nurses poked their heads
through the curtains. Did I read looks of sympathy in
their expressions? Oh my Lord, maybe I did not have
as long as I had imagined. It was obviously worse than
I first thought. Maybe they had found out that nothing
could be done. All sorts of things raced through my
mind, Bryan, the boys. Who would look after them when
I was gone? The tears began to well up in my eyes and
at that moment the Doctor appeared. I stood up and
was told to sit down as I was in for a shock. The day
was getting worse by the hour, how much more could
I take. What the Doctor then revealed completely blew
me away. Never in a million years could I have imagined
what was coming. "What would you say if I told you
that you were pregnant?" Did I hear correctly—did he
say 'pregnant?' I sat in a state of shock and then the fears
started flooding in. What about the x-rays and all the tests
I had had done, all the things you should not have done
if you are pregnant? I had had more than my fair share
over the past couple of months. The Doctor shared my
fears as he went on further to explain that not only was I
pregnant but I only had 6 weeks to go. I was seven and a
half months pregnant!
How could I be, I was so thin, where was I carrying it? It
all seemed impossible.

The Doctor explained that very rarely did this occur but the fear now was that the baby may have been harmed by all the tests. The only test that was available was an amniocentesis. This is where a needle is inserted through the abdomen to take fluid from the baby—this could rule out Downs Syndrome, but nothing else. As I was too far into the pregnancy for an abortion to be considered, I just had to carry on and pray that the baby was healthy.

I left that cubicle in a state of euphoria. I was not going to die after all, anything else I could face. I would say my prayers for the next few weeks and put my trust in God. I went for a coffee to settle my nerves so I could sit quietly and take in this incredible news. How would the Family take it—having another child had never been discussed?

I had given away all my baby clothes, the cot, the pram. the baby bath, absolutely everything. It would be like having a first child all over again. Would Bryan be pleased?

I was not thinking rationally at this point. If he had a choice of losing his wife or having another baby, of course he would be pleased. Whatever was I thinking? With this thought in mind I thought I would soften the blow. On my way home I called at the butchers and bought the biggest piece of steak I had ever bought and topped it off with a good bottle of red wine. On his return from work he took one look at the size of the piece of steak and said it must be good news. He seemed very pleased to hear that I was pregnant and said it would be fine as we had nine months to get used to the idea.

When I told him the reality of how long we actually had to be organised it put him into a state of panic. I explained to him about how the x-rays may have harmed the baby and we decided that we would cope with whatever the future held. When I had the test for Downs Syndrome done I could have found out the sex of the baby but I decided to wait until the birth. I have always thought that that is half the excitement of giving birth but of course, many young Mums today would disagree.

When I broke the news to my Mum, who hated hearing of anybody becoming pregnant, she seemed to be genuinely pleased and said, "A growth with a hat on—a much better outcome than the one we were expecting!" I can honestly say that that was the only pregnancy that she was ever glad to hear of.

The next few weeks flew by in a haze of shopping and worrying. Once my body understood it was pregnant I seemed to explode. I grew enormous in the next few weeks. Claire took over the responsibility of work in the office as I tried to rest more. Finally, as the end of my pregnancy approached, toxaemia set in and I was admitted to hospital. I have to say, at this point, that I was more than a little worried, not just about giving birth but also about what we may have to face if all was not well with the baby.

I had secretly always wanted a daughter but when my sons came along I was not at all disappointed. I had always dreamed of building a good relationship with my imaginary daughter unlike the distant stormy one I had had with my own Mother. I always tried to be a good

Mum to my boys, taking an interest in all their activities, but what young boy wants his Mum tagging along as they grow up, certainly not mine. I could have done so much more if I had had a daughter.

Well, it was no good pondering on what might have been, after two boys, I had no doubt in my mind that this little one would also be a boy. What did it matter, as long as the baby was healthy? I was admitted to hospital on a Sunday and was scheduled to 'be started' next morning. Bryan spent the early part of the evening with me discussing imminent scaffolding contracts. Scaffolding was all he talked about these days and why I imagined today would be any different, God only knows! When he left he said he would be back in the morning to be with me at the birth.

After he had gone I lay reading my book and intermittently chatting to the woman in the next bed. I found it difficult to sleep when I settled down with all the unanswered questions going round in my head. Well, it would not be long now and all would be revealed. When I eventually dozed off I was awakened by a stabbing pain and then everything kicked off at once. I rang for a nurse and was quickly whisked away to the delivery suite. There were a few tense moments in the lift when I thought the baby was going to put in an appearance before I reached my destination. No, I hung on gritting my teeth, until I was safely on the delivery table and in no time at all, our child was born.

The nurses had been trying to contact Bryan, but instead of going straight home as planned he had called round to 'his local' to catch the 'last orders.' He had a habit of 'wetting the baby's head' before it actually ever put in an appearance. By the time he left the pub he would not have been in a fit state to drive, I would have to wait until the morning.

I was not brave when it came to giving birth, no epidurals for me as that meant needles and I am needle phobic. I stuck with plain old gas and air! It had worked twice before and I had every confidence in it this time. As I came back from 'my away with the fairies' experience I thought I heard someone say "a girl." I could not believe it—We had a daughter!

As I became more aware I was dreading asking the questions I needed the answers to. "Was she alright? Could they see anything obviously wrong?" As far as we could tell, she was perfect. As I cuddled her I felt so proud and said a prayer of thanks.

When she was taken from me for weighing, washing and some blood tests I lay thinking how lucky we were considering what the outcome may have been. Why it entered my head I have no idea but suddenly it dawned on me that our daughter had been born under the star sign 'Cancer.' Strange that!

I was so grateful that after all the worry we had had over the past few weeks, we had been blessed with not only a daughter but a healthy daughter.

Bryan arrived next morning, rather relieved to find it was all over. He was delighted to meet his daughter, his only comment being "Hasn't she got big hands?" It may, of course, have been something to do with him as his hands resembled 'two shovels.'

In the evening Bryan returned with our two sons, so they could meet their little sister. Karl, being the elder, took it all in his stride. He initially had not liked the idea of sharing his bedroom with his brother but did not mind having a little sister. Steed, on the other hand, had taken the news rather badly. He was nine years old and resented having to give up his own bedroom. He could not understand why the new baby had to have a bedroom at all. Why could it not sleep in the shed? On the Monday that I gave birth, he had been on a school trip to The Cotswold Wild Life Park. Whilst there he had purchased a yellow snake, a soft toy, not a real one I am relieved to say. He did not want to meet this 'little intruder' that was turning his world upside down and I could hear him arguing with his Dad outside the curtained cubicle that was my bed space. Suddenly without any warning at all, a yellow missile came hurtling towards the baby's cot followed by the words "I don't want to see it but it can have that." I guess that was a start. During the evening he was persuaded to look at our new addition but like most boys of his age he was not impressed. Time changes most things and as they grew up they became closer.

The problem of the shared bedroom was solved by allowing each son to choose the décor for their half of the room. It looked a little strange but satisfied both of them. The third bedroom was turned into a nursery.

As everything was normal and my Mum was on hand
to help I was allowed home the next day. I felt so much
love for this little one that I felt my heart would burst
and twenty nine years on I still feel exactly the same.
Ours was to be the perfect relationship that I had always
dreamed of. Of course, as she was growing up we argued
at times and had our differences of opinion but nothing
that could not be remedied with a kiss and a cuddle.
We have always laughed more than we have cried and I
thank God every day for the blessing I call my daughter.

We had not seriously discussed a name for this little one,
almost afraid to tempt Fate, but now we had to choose
a name that meant something, she was so special. I
trawled through Family names, nothing very significant
there. I thumbed through countless name books before
stumbling on the perfect one. It jumped out of the pages
at me, it could not have been more fitting for how we
felt.
KYLY—an Aborigine name meaning 'little boomerang.'
It was exactly what we hoped for the future of our
daughter. If she ever left home as she grew up, we hoped
she would always return. Our home would always be
her home no matter where life took her. Just like a
'boomerang', we hoped she would always return. Perfect!

With our daughter suitably named we settled back into a
normal pattern of life.

Chapter 32

In Limbo and Beyond

Once our daughter was born, we employed more staff to work in the office alongside Claire and that released me to stay at home and enjoy being a housewife, and Mother. I still kept my hand in by doing the wages and would go in on odd days if Claire were particularly busy.

As my daughter grew, she would happily sit at a desk 'scribbling' wage dockets or answering her toy phone with 'Rig Scaffolding, can I help you?' She pretended to take orders over the phone and sometimes, if she got a little restless, the yardman would take her down into the yard to paint fittings. There were many pretty dresses ruined by 'Rig red' paint.

My Mother was appalled that she was being brought up in this way and was forever telling me that it was wrong and that she should be allowed to play normally like a toddler. Kyly, on the other hand, enjoyed being with all the adults and I am convinced that it helped her develop. She had good social skills, knew how to answer a phone and learned very quickly how to read and write. She loved being part of the 'business' and it stood her in good stead for later in her life, when all her 'scaffolding skills' would be put to the test.

When Kyly was about 18 months old, I had a bit of a setback. I had not felt well for a couple of days and put it down to a bad cold. I was supposed to be playing in a 'doubles' dart match with my sister that evening but did not really feel well enough to go. We had done well to get through to this stage and I knew my sister would be disappointed not to go so I asked Bryan to pop along to her house and explain that I would go, but as soon as we were eliminated from the competition, I would return home. My sister, at that time, was not fortunate enough to own a phone so this was our only means of contact.

I told Bryan that I would get the tea in his absence. The children were all playing happily, Kyly in the sitting room and the boys in the garden. I got up and crossed the room and as I did I felt as if someone had hit me on the back of the head with a sledgehammer. I dropped to the floor and crawled to an armchair. I could not see! Whatever had happened had taken my sight. I stayed in that position until Bryan returned shortly afterwards. The pain in my head was excruciating. I had never felt anything like it before. On Bryan's return he realised something was wrong and carried me up to bed. Most people in the same position would have called an ambulance but as I have explained previously, Bryan had no faith in doctors or hospitals so he laid me gently on the bed where he expected me to heal myself.

As I lay there, the pain in my head subsided a little but my sight did not return. It was almost unheard of for me to be lying around doing nothing at all so unwittingly, Bryan asked, as I was not doing anything else, would I have a look at the accounts?
That was Bryan, totally oblivious to the obvious! Bryan managed to get the children ready for bed and settled. Later in the evening when he came to bed he said he hoped I would feel better in the morning, turned over and went to sleep. He had an early start next morning so got up to the alarm, said he was sorry he couldn't help but he was just no good with illness.

I was normally up and about first in the morning and when Karl got up and realised I was still in bed he came in to see if I was feeling any better. I knew I needed help as by now not only could I not see but I had lost some of the feeling in my legs. He knew something was wrong and ran round the corner to fetch my Mother. She took one look at me and rang for the Duty Doctor who in turn summoned an ambulance. The journey into Oxford was an arduous one—the driver carefully trying not to shake me about too much. We arrived at the JR hospital, where I was transferred to a darkened room. I was examined and given a lumber puncture. A decision was then made to transfer me to the Old Radcliffe hospital across town that dealt with head and brain injuries. The diagnosis was that I had had a brain haemorrhage. Many people die as a result of one of these, but I believe that Bryan saved my life by leaving me overnight to allow the blood to drain naturally away from the ruptured membrane in my head. I was being kept in a darkened room as my sight had still not returned. No one was sure what the outcome would be as I was very poorly and there was no guarantee that my sight would return.

Family visitors came and went but I was not aware of any of them as I had been sedated. On waking up, I was told that Bryan had angered close Family members because he had sat by my bed continuously telling me about scaffolding contracts he had managed to secure in my absence. Would I have expected anything else from Bryan at a time like that? Definitely not, as that was the only way he could cope with illness by carrying on as normal and not acknowledging it.

I lay in that darkened room for three weeks, unsure of my future prospects.

During that time, all sorts of thoughts went through my head. Could I have been a better Mum? I had always tried to do the best for my children—I loved them all. Could I have been a better wife to Bryan? Well, there was always room for improvement in that relationship but he would honestly have tried the patience of a Saint with his tempestuous behaviour and dire mood swings. I consoled myself that I tried to do my best under difficult circumstances and that was the best I could hope for.

As I lay there unable to see, it was like a 'Paul on the road to Damascus' moment. I suddenly became aware of an area in my life that could be improved. Up until the moment I had been struck down, I suppose, like so many other people, I looked after me and my own with little thought for others. Don't get me wrong, I was not insensitive to the plight of others, but did not go 'that extra mile' to help anyone outside my own Family.

I had always been very shy and retiring, never wanting to stand out in a crowd, but maybe now, if I was given another chance, and my sight returned, I would change. I prayed hard and promised if I regained good health I would not waste another moment of my life, I would live it to the full. I was not sure how this change would take place but I was determined that from now on I would find some way of giving something back to my Community.

Chapter 33

A Step in the Right Direction

During the time that Bryan had been coming to terms with his illiteracy, he managed to get a place on an experimental course run at Oxford College. It was organised by a wonderful woman who was appalled by the number of adults who, for whatever reason, had completed their education and emerged into the big wide world without any literacy skills.

I met this woman several times before Bryan was accepted on the course, as I too, had to be interviewed. During my interview I was asked about my education and she suggested that I might consider becoming a part time tutor. I dismissed it at the time because, if I am honest, I gave little thought to those less fortunate than myself. Maybe if my sight returned, this could be a starting point.

Fortunately, after three weeks, my sight gradually returned, and with my sight intact a new Irene was re-born. It took a while to get back into my routine, I was afraid I might have another haemorrhage but slowly my life returned to normal. I did not forget the promise I had made to myself to change and as soon as things settled down, I contacted the woman in question, to see if I could offer any help. She was delighted to hear from me and arranged interviews, assessments and trainings. I sailed through it all with my new inbuilt confidence and became tutor/organiser for this area. I was a little nervous at first but I soon got into my stride and I loved the job. During the day I looked after my Family, working at the office when needed and now my evenings were taken up with this new role.

At first, the job entailed interviewing adults who had answered adverts in local papers, offering individual help at evening classes. Other adverts, were run alongside the original ones, asking for volunteers to help adults learn to read and write. My job was to firstly interview the adults with the problems, then interview the volunteers and match them. I found this very rewarding.

I did have some 'moments' along the way. The Education Authority decided that a small number of adults suffering from 'Down's Syndrome' should be included. It was with a little trepidation that I went out to interview my first Down's gentleman. He was a youth of eighteen who lived in a town nearby with both his Parents. I was welcomed into the house by his Mother, a jovial, rotund woman, who pointed me in the direction of their lounge. I went through the door and was greeted by a large upright man who vigorously shook my hand and almost crushed it in his grip.

Most adults that found themselves in this predicament were highly sensitive about it and were always embarrassed to meet me. I therefore always intentionally tried not to look too confident. I was, after all, a visitor in their home and wanted them to feel comfortable so they were able to talk to me openly. I hovered just inside the door. The Father barked an order for his son to put in an appearance and shake my hand. Following this, the order 'Sit' was barked, and I immediately dropped onto the nearest seat. Did the Father speak to everyone like that? Then I realised that the order had not been for me but for his son who he ruled with a rod of iron. I found out later that the Father had been a Regimental Sergeant Major and I presume he could not change the habit of a lifetime.

Once students and volunteer helpers had been matched we met once a week at the local Senior School where other evening classes were subsequently taking place. I helped form structures for their lessons and advised volunteers when problems occurred. I found the work extremely interesting and came across some wonderful characters.

There was a woman in her 50's who had brought up her Family by means of watching the adverts on the television. She always bought Kellogg's cornflakes because she recognised the cockerel on the box. Her whole shopping list was made up of mental pictures. If boxes of produce had been blank except for the writing I dread to think how she would have managed.

There was also an elderly gentleman who was a very competent gardener. He knew the name of most flowers, shrubs and vegetables but could not recognise any of them if written down. He thought it was about time he made a concerted effort to learn.

Every student's lesson was designed around their interests in order to keep them keen. It proved to be a very successful class. We had all sorts within the class, from young adults with learning difficulties to intelligent people who for personal reasons had missed out on education at a crucial time in their lives. Ladies who had nursed sick relatives when they should have been at school, several farmer's sons whose strength when they were young was more important on the farm than their ability to read and write and sometimes those who had just wasted their schooling without thought for the future. A whole classroom full of individuals with their own stories to tell.

We would work hard with the students for an hour and then there would be a tea break when all the students, even those from other classes, would congregate in the Main Hall for a social chat. Students and volunteers would all sit together—it was a wonderful atmosphere. The 'Down's Syndrome' lad could sometimes, through frustration, get a little 'stroppy' so I had matched him with a well built man who could easily cope with these tantrums. He became infatuated with me and always called me 'Teacher.' I was constantly being shown his latest piece of work and I encouraged his enthusiasm to learn. We told him he had to earn his right to join the others at tea break by controlling his outbursts and his tutor worked hard towards this end. After several weeks his behaviour improved and it was decided to integrate him gradually. At first, he was to be allowed to just go and get the drinks for himself and his tutor and take them back to his classroom. If that proved to be a success he would be allowed to join the others as a matter of progression. He was always trying to please so we did not foresee there being a problem. I had underestimated his infatuation with me and was totally unprepared for what happened at tea break that evening.

The bell rang for the break and most students and volunteers made their way to the Main Hall. I got my drink and joined my class. I was seated on a low television chair between a disabled woman in a wheelchair and an slightly built elderly woman. Most of the classes had already taken their drinks back to their seats but there were just a few latecomers lining up. Suddenly the swing doors to the hall opened and in came our 'Down's' lad. He spotted me immediately and shouted out as he always did, "Hello Teacher" and waved. I returned his wave and told him to line up with the others to get his drinks and I resumed my conversation with my class.

Unbeknown to me, he walked round to the back of my chair where he grabbed a handful of my hair and threw me backwards, chair and all, on to my back.

He then tried to kiss me. To say I was shocked was an understatement, it completely took me by surprise. In fear I shouted at him and he immediately reverted back to being 'a little boy.' He sucked his thumb and kept repeating "I'm sorry Teacher, I'm sorry Teacher." I was helped back into a more respectable position by several males enabling me to once again take control of the situation. I pointed to the doors for him to make a rapid exit explaining I would take their drinks to their classroom and he was to go without further delay. At that precise moment his tutor made an entrance to see why his 'charge' had taken so long and was horrified by what had taken place. We thought it better, in future, that drinks were taken to them rather than risk another 'incident.' On reflection, I felt rather sorry for the lad, he led a very restricted life with his Father and was, after all, a 'red blooded' male with natural desires. It was just a pity that those desires were directed at me. I have to add that he was extremely sorry afterwards and drew me a picture for me to take home. We never had a problem with him again., I think he had at least learned that lesson.

After tea break the students had a choice of either joining in with a discussion group or carrying on working as individuals. The more senior, intelligent students usually chose to carry on working on their own projects but there were several youngsters aged 18-22yrs with learning difficulties who found it difficult to concentrate for more than one hour. These individuals always joined the discussion group. We covered all kind of subjects during these discussions. One such subject was 'The sea and the beach.' Not one of these students had actually been to the coast and seen the sea. They had, of course, seen pictures but could not envisage the size. I was asked, "Was it as large as a big pond? Was the beach bigger than a huge sandpit?" I could not comprehend how they could have reached their late teens and beyond and never been taken to the coast. I decided to arrange a day at the sea.

One of the volunteers was a coach driver by day so I approached the firm he worked for to see if they would allow us the use of a minibus as he had offered to drive us free of charge. The firm agreed and I then approached Bryan to see if 'Rig Scaffolding' would fund the day out. With transport and finances sorted I made up lunch boxes and drinks for everyone and had pocket money to make the day really special. It was a glorious day out.

We drove through The New Forest and stopped at a Nature Reserve on the way. When we reached the coast I can remember everyone removing their shoes and socks, holding hands, and running in a long line into the sea, screaming with delight.

I am not sure what the other holidaymakers thought of us but my bus load had the time of their lives. We visited a Fair during the day and finished off our day out with a pint in a pub overlooking the beach. What a day, etched in my memory forever! The students talked about their day out for weeks afterwards, writing about it, drawing pictures to capture the day lest their memories failed them.

During the class one evening, a young lad was frogmarched in by the scruff of his neck and thrown towards my desk. It was not the normal way I would have made contact with a student but it was obvious that the Mother was determined her son would join us. The lad was still of school age but had been expelled from full time education due to his bad behaviour. He so obviously did not want to be there but I had to try with him. I asked the boy if he would like to come into another classroom, away from his Mother, so we could chat uninterrupted, as his Mother was proving to be very volatile. He reluctantly agreed and followed me through. Before I could say a word, he told me he wasn't going to attend, he didn't want to learn and how it was all a waste of time. I just let him get all his anger and embarrassment out of his system before I started to talk to him about what he intended to do as a job of work now that he had been thrown out of school. It seemed that he had only a short time left in full time education and was nearing his 15th birthday.

Once he calmed down he told me he already had a job to start at the garage where he helped out on a Saturday. He went on to tell me that he had no need to be educated or learn to read and write as he was good with his hands.(This was a trait I found in many illiterate people) He was hoping to train as a mechanic.

I pointed out to him that a mechanic needed to be able to drive and how was he going to pass a driving test if he couldn't read the Highway Code. That thought had never occurred to him. I told him that if he agreed, I would bring in a copy of the Highway Code the following week and we could go through it together to see if he needed to read or not, the choice would be his. I was not convinced that he would return but he did, proving that with the right approach and the right materials, small miracles could happen.

The lad came every week and just stayed for the first hour but put everything he had into it and became our star pupil. He was intelligent and learned quickly once the decision to learn came from him. When he was 17 yrs he passed his driving test first time and brought in his pass certificate to show the class what could be achieved. On his way out he shook my hand and thanked me quietly. Another success story, no wonder I enjoyed the job.

Due to the success of the class, I was approached by a local residential home for young adults, some physically and some mentally disabled. I was asked if I could run a social afternoon combined with an opportunity for those that wished to improve their literacy skills away from the residential home itself. I said I would make enquiries and get back to them. Funding was found and put in place and we were offered a local Youth Centre where we could participate in all kinds of activities, billiards, snooker, darts, netball, dancing and table tennis. It was all made available to us. Upstairs there were rooms that we could use for literacy classes. Students were to pay a small entrance fee on arrival.

Prior to the first session I was invited to attend lunch at the home so I could meet the students in their own surroundings. I readily accepted the invitation but was unsure as to what I was embarking upon. With my new determination to meet all challenges head on I arrived with time to spare on the day in question. I parked the car and walked towards the huge front door. There was a circular drive fronting the house with a flower garden in the middle. There was a young man sat on the wall of the raised garden, a gardener I presumed. As I approached the front door he engaged in conversation. "Hello, what is your name, do you have a lorry?" I was a little taken back but said "Yes, my name was Irene and we had a scaffolding lorry." We then had an in depth conversation about lorries, if a little one sided as I knew absolutely nothing about them. He seemed well informed and didn't seem to require my participation. I thanked him for all the knowledge he had imparted to me and rang the bell.

If the gardener was like that, I wondered what the residents would be like? I was soon to find out. I was met by the Head of House, a charming, young man, who genuinely seemed pleased that I had made it. He introduced me to his assistant and then we embarked on a tour of the houses and gardens as he explained that all the jobs on site, with the exception of cooking, were covered by the residents. I realised that that explained my encounter with the gardener.

It was an amazing place, work clothes in certain drawers, best clothes in others, and everything colour coded for easy identification as each house had its' own colour. It was so well thought out and everyone seemed to be so happy. Well that was a good start. When the dinner bell rang I was escorted into the dining hall of the Main House. I was obviously a 'special guest' as everyone had been told to behave but everyone wanted to touch me or hold my hand or just talk to me. Why is it that the people who want to speak to me the most are always those with speech impediments that make it impossible for me to understand them? I think I made the right noises and I smiled inanely. Finally I was rescued as everyone was asked to stand behind chairs stretching the length of a huge dining table.

The meal was underway when I noticed a woman sat a little further down the table on the other side to me. She was sucking her thumb whilst holding a blanket and teddy bear, not unlike a small child, but she must have been at least 40 years old if not older. I noticed she was staring at me and I smiled at her and carried on chatting to the young man beside me who was very knowledgeable about music. I must have seemed very ignorant on the subject as I had not heard of the groups or songs he was talking about and he soon got bored of my lack of knowledge and turned his back on me. Suddenly in a loud, high pitched voice, the woman who had been staring at me said, "Lady, have you got any knickers on?" Well, I nearly died of embarrassment. Of course I had my knickers on but what did it have to do with anyone else? The Head of House realised my embarrassment, it must have had something to do with the crimson glow emanating from my face and reprimanded the woman. She just laughed and carried on eating. He went on to explain that the residents did that kind of thing to evoke a reaction and because I had blushed as I did, the woman would be quite content. It had worked, I am so glad she was happy but I can't say that I felt the same.

What is the expression? There is no such thing as a free lunch—What price embarrassment?

The social afternoons turned out much better than expected and those that attended seemed to enjoy the experience. On one occasion, unable to get a babysitter, I was forced to take my daughter along. I explained to her that some of the people would look a little strange, some would be in wheelchairs, others had long legs and short bodies and there were others that permanently 'twitched.' I thought I would prepare her as there were some odd looking characters amongst our visitors.

We arrived and prepared the hall for the activities. The bus from the home arrived and the students made their way to the pay desk. Mary, a young 'Down's Syndrome' girl took to Kyly and off they went together to dance. Kyly mingled with our visitors all afternoon and when the session had finished and all our visitors had gone she said, "When are those people coming Mum, those ones you told me about?" I could have hugged her. Maybe children do not see the imperfections that the adult eye perceives. What a wonderful world it would be if everyone was looked at as equal. How is it that from childhood to adulthood we are supposed to grow and learn and yet we lose so much along the way.

Eventually I had to resign this post as the Scaffolding Company grew and I was needed permanently back in the office. I had managed to get Kyly a place in nursery, which helped, but so much of my time was being taken up working, it was unfair for me to be continually working in the evenings as well.

I was sorry to say goodbye to both my students and my volunteer helpers but glad that I was part of the initiative that grew to be countrywide classes that are available today to help adults improve their literacy skills.

Chapter 34

A Day to Remember

Whenever I had a child it had always been important to me to have the child christened in the first couple of months after the birth. This was not to be with Kyly. Bryan and I could not agree on who should be her Godparents so the christening did not happen. Every time the subject was brought up we ended up at loggerheads so until such times as Bryan warmed to my suggestions I decided to let sleeping dogs lie.

When Kyly was almost five years old, Bryan had a health scare. He had a minor heart attack. As I have previously mentioned Bryan did not have much faith in the Health System, and believed illness was a case of, mind over matter. He fervently believed that he could heal himself. On this occasion it temporarily knocked his confidence, so much so, that he decided to arrange a christening for Kyly to resemble a wedding as he was sure it was a sign he would not live to see the real thing. He asked me to dress her up to look like a bride and The Shillingford Bridge Hotel was booked for the christening 'reception.'

It was a very grand affair, everyone came dressed in their finery. Kyly had a white Bo-Peep style hooped dress complete with Tiara and white net gloves. She looked stunning and turned many a head as she walked down the aisle towards the font. It was gloriously hot and we all had a memorable day in the grounds of the Hotel that swept picturesquely down to the edge of the Thames.

It was a very social occasion and everyone enjoyed themselves immensely. I was at last happy that my daughter had been taken into the Christian Faith and that we had at last agreed on her Godparents. Bryan had the satisfaction of seeing his 'miniature bride' so, all in all, a satisfactory outcome for all.

Chapter 35

Chasing A Dream

The business had continued to grow and make money and Bryan felt this might be time to fulfil his dream. He had often mentioned to me over the years that he would like to buy a farm and if he was ever lucky enough to get one whether I would be happy to run it with him. Of course, I agreed. I was only paying 'lip service' at the time as I thought the chances of it happening were so remote, I would never be put to the test.

Bryan set the wheels in motion. The 'Exchange & Mart' became our only reading matter as we scoured the pages for something suitable. Every weekend for a whole Summer season we took off to the depths of Wales in search of his dream. I have to explain that Bryan came from farming stock so he did know what he was looking for as I, on the other hand, just went along for the ride as my passion is viewing other peoples' houses.

We saw a huge range of properties, some within villages and other more isolated. There was one that was sat right on top of a gorse hill, their land a series of gorse covered fields resembling 'The Himalayas.' We viewed the house and noticed that some of the internal walls were actually made from hardboard sheets, a far cry from my bricks and mortar back home. Our search would continue

We viewed another that was built into a hill with the roof being part of the grass field above. It was very picturesque with its' stable doors and oak beamed façade but once inside a different story emerged. The kitchen was very basic without any modern units. A disgustingly dirty cooker, a Belfast sink which looked as if it had been used for growing potatoes in and very little else. The sides were littered with dirty enamel mugs and I wondered if cleanliness was a word this Family were familiar with? We were asked if we would like drinks but I declined for the health of my Family and we progressed through to the lounge. We were shocked to see that at some time an internal wall had collapsed, the huge boulders still as they had fallen. In fact, they were now being used as furniture as the children were laying on them as normal people would lie on a sofa. It was either that or they were trying to disguise them as furniture, whatever the reason, I was not impressed. We moved on through to what they called their 'Christmas Sitting Room.' aptly named as they only used it at Christmas.

I was astounded to find that the decorations still
adorned the ceiling. The Family may only have used
it at Christmas but the spiders obviously thrived in
abundance and used it all year round as the whole room
resembled a room from 'Great Expectations,' with thick
webs covering every space. I had seen all I needed to, I
was certainly not interested but Bryan seemed to be still
enquiring about the land. Did he not see what I saw?
He seemed reasonably impressed. I dragged him away
for consultation and he suggested that I might be able
to rebuild the wall. It was very pretty from the outside
and the land was good but had he seen the size of
those blocks that had come down? Forget it, we would
continue our search.

We did discover a beautiful house with 19 acres near
The Gower Peninsula. We were all excited about it, even
the children. We made a serious offer but it was not
meant to be. 'Gazumping' had just raised its' ugly head
and 'gazumped' we were, several times. We ventured
further into Wales where we came across another strange
property. The farmhouse looked alright from the outside
and there were flat fields surrounding it but we knew
from experience now that this could be extremely
deceiving. We met the 'Farmer' who turned out to be a
large eccentric woman. We were taken on a tour of the
fields where we met her animals, all with pet names, and
then back to view the house. As she opened the unlocked
door I thought about security, were people so honest
around this neck of the woods? The stench that hit my
nose was horrendous. I started to retch uncontrollably.
No burglar, in his right mind, would venture in there.
The woman apologised for the smell and explained

that she was cooking fish for her twenty cats that lived with her in the house, alongside six dogs and several chickens. I did not want to seem rude so I rapidly sped round the house, holding my breath. All I can remember about it was that it was very dark inside, but I did spot an Inglenook Fireplace as I hastily pushed the children back out into the fresh air. Once again a cup of tea was offered and declined as we hastily made our way back to the car explaining that we still had properties in the area to see. Bryan told her we would be in contact with her agent and added as we drove away that it would only be to ask him to put up a sign as a Health Warning to Prospective Buyers. I was beginning to wonder if all people lived like this in Wales?

We then travelled further north and viewed a property overlooking the Irish Sea. It had lots of character and although it was not exactly what we were looking for, it had something 'quirky' about it and we made an offer on it. Unfortunately, we had not noticed that the property only had one door and the Mortgage Company insisted that there should be two. On this basis they refused to lend us money on it. Oh well, another dream hit the dust.

There were several other properties, all lacking in one way or another, so we changed tactics and looked elsewhere.

One such trip was to Lincoln where we viewed several properties in a day. One had no running water and drew water from a well in the centre of the kitchen floor. That one was definitely out. Another that we saw, Bryan loved.

The land was good and clean, and it was situated on the outskirts of a pretty village but the bungalow that went with it was very ordinary and lacking in character. I was unsure but Bryan promised he would work miracles with it as everything about it lived up to his dream. He convinced me that it really was the answer to his prayers and we made them an offer that they immediately accepted. With the memory of the 'gazumping' still fresh in our minds' we decided to engage a solicitor from Lincoln to speed up the deal.

Everything was proceeding well until the day we received a letter informing us that they had changed their minds and had decided not to move.

That was the last straw for us! We had spent months dragging the children round the countryside in search of Bryan's dream, all to no avail. Enough was enough. We agreed that we would no longer look for a farm but extend the house we lived in and upgrade it, garden and all. We decided that we would not spare expenses and have whatever caught our eye as this was to be our home for a very long time. We would concentrate on building up the business rather than spend any more time chasing unrealistic dreams.

Chapter 36

The Transformation

With the decision made to stay put, Bryan engaged a builder who worked with his son and another young lad. We put a lot of thought into how we wanted our new home to look but did not have any plans drawn up. We decided to talk it over with the builder and leave it all in their hands.

Progress was slow, probably due to my keep changing my mind. A doorway put in here, a serving hatch there and then all change as it was not the overall look I was hoping for. Patiently they worked with us, never complaining, as over a period of time that they were with us extended into nearly a year. We almost began to think of them as Family they were with us so long. If the son was around, and Bryan nowhere to be seen, when shopping needed to be done, it was the son who accompanied me shopping. When my daughter hurt her leg and found it difficult to walk it was the son who carved her a crutch out of a block of wood. A cooked breakfast was always the order of the day before I went off to work in the mornings and yes, you've guessed it—breakfast time always included Bryan and the builders, all three of them.

Due to the long hours I was working, we engaged a local woman to keep house and generally look after Kyly. We were becoming busier and busier at work and I therefore felt justified in employing someone. She was a lovely lady who could not do enough to help. It was her job during the day to keep the builders happy with tea and sandwiches. My daughter adored her and that helped salve my conscience enormously.

Over the next few months a new kitchen and dining room were added and the sitting room extended through French Windows and onto a paved patio area surrounded by a low brick wall. The garden was laid to lawn and a huge shed erected to double up with one room a playroom and the other a potting shed. The house and garden were being transformed and the result would be magnificent.

Bryan was over critical at every point and the brick fireplace that was built and rebuilt in the sitting room was dismantled several times before he was satisfied.

Our 'lady' battled on throughout all the dust and chaos and we will always be eternally grateful to her for making sure our ever changing house remained a 'home' to return to each evening. She was marvellous and worth her weight in gold.

Eventually the sitting room, new staircase, new front door and porch were all completed to the degree of excellence Bryan desired and the carcase of the new kitchen and dining room was in place. The time had come to choose a new kitchen.

Through business, we had made friends with a Kitchen Designer and Installer. We paid him a visit and chose every aspect of our kitchen, settling for English Oak units, with small red tiles on the splash backs and work surfaces and Italian tiles on the floor. We sat back and waited for the transformation of our new kitchen to take place. Plumbers, electricians and plasterers arrived in abundance. Every night on our return from work, the house would look a little nearer completion. The floor tiled, the units all in place, the cooker wired in, we were almost there. A new pine table and chairs were delivered and all that remained was the surface tiling. Off we went to work just as the tiler arrived. Bryan stayed and had a few words with him and explained that he was expecting a perfect job. The tiler answered that he had tiled many kitchens and we were not to worry as he always did an excellent job. We went off to work with confidence. On our return, everything changed.

The red spot that often appeared on the bridge of Bryan's nose when his blood pressure was high was glowing like an ember as we entered the kitchen. Bryan took one look at the tiling and let out a yell of frustration, he was not a happy man. He grabbed the edge of the work surface and physically tried to prise it up. It would not budge so up with his boot and he tried to kick it off. Still no joy—so in temper he threw his bunch of keys at the new table, gouging a lump out of the pristine surface.

Something else ruined by his temper and this was less than 24 hours old. He grabbed the phone and told the Kitchen Fitter, in no uncertain terms, what he thought of his tiler. The air was definitely blue and Bryan's face as red as the newly laid tiles. A visit next day saw all the tiles removed and another tiler installed to try again. This time, thank goodness, all was well and they passed inspection with flying colours.

May peace reign but for a short time.

We said our goodbyes to all our builders and looked forward to Christmas in our new extended home. I am sure the builders had a brilliant Christmas too as it cost us a small fortune by not getting the job done on a fixed price. Never mind, we were all happy and looking forward to the festive season.

All the work was completed during the week prior to Christmas and although there was a lot of cleaning up to do everything was ship shape in time to entertain Family over the Christmas Period.

We had a wonderful time and I looked forward to many more Family occasions in our 'new' home.

Chapter 37

Uncertainty and Beyond

I was enjoying keeping house in my beautiful new home. I had every modern convenience making life so much easier and a lovely tidy garden to view from our rear windows I should have known better than to sit back and think how wonderful my life was.

The last of the brick dust had hardly settled when Bryan started to get restless. He had spoken to the accountant who had suggested that we might aspire to greater heights and look for a property beyond the Council Estate that we lived on. I have to admit that I was happy where I was but Bryan had loftier ideas.

I was given no more than a figure to work with and I hit the Estate Agents accordingly. They furnished me with details of grand houses with tennis courts, swimming pools and amazingly landscaped gardens. I would go home eagerly to discuss the properties with Bryan anxious to make appointments to view, lest they were sold. Not a flicker of interest would he show. There was no point in viewing houses on my own—he would never be happy with my choice. Weeks dragged on and we had not viewed one single property. I asked him if he had any intentions of moving at all as I seemed to be wasting my time. I was informed that when the right place came along he would know. I was pleased that he did, as I had no idea what he was looking for and he certainly would not divulge such privileged information to the likes of me. It was getting more confusing and frustrating by the day.

One afternoon, whilst at work, I visited the bank to deposit some cheques and decided by chance to call in at the Estate Agents situated next door. I was given a list of properties printed from a machine in the corner. I was not at all impressed as there were no photographs to gauge interest so I just folded them carefully and took them back to my office to peruse at leisure.

It was unusual for Bryan to stay in the office as he was never a 'paperwork' man—more a man among men 'action man' with the emphasis of action being on the other men, not himself. This afternoon was an exception and he looked over my shoulder as I sifted through the list of properties I had collected earlier. Nothing particular had caught my eye but something had certainly caught Bryan's.

I read and re-read the details that he was getting so excited about and I am afraid they did little for me. A 5 bedroom stone Farm House with acres of land. No, it did not stir me but I was asked to ring and find out more. I was informed that the Witney office had more details, as the property was just outside Burford.

We finished work slightly earlier than normal, made arrangements for my Parents to look after the children and found ourselves visiting the Witney Branch of Estate Agents to pick up further details.

I have to admit that I was not widely travelled but I did know my way to Witney having had to visit the Market Town on reasonably regular occasions to collect customer's cheques. Bryan discussed the property with the Witney Estate Agent and got him to ring for a viewing appointment that evening. Before I knew I was back in the car being propelled through open fields and unfamiliar countryside. All I could think was that our Yard and Office were in Didcot which seemed a very long way from where we now were. On and on we drove, wherever was this place? I only hoped it was worth all this effort.

'Burford'—the sign on the grass verge read—nearly there! Turn towards Swindon we had been told and it was along there on the right in a hamlet called 'Signet' (pronounced Sign—et). We drove left onto the Swindon road as instructed, past a Golf Club and more fields and then there it was, a sign for Signet pointing down a slip road.

I was beginning to panic as this seemed miles from anywhere familiar and certainly a long way from home (30 miles to be precise) I dutifully pulled up outside a farm gate and looked with horror up a farmyard. If it had been solely my decision I would have got back in the car and driven back to Didcot post haste but I took one look at Bryan and my heart sank.

What could he see that I could not? It looked like a scrap yard. There was rusty farm machinery everywhere, doors hanging from outbuildings at various angles and a rather aggressive looking dog chained to a heavy wooden kennel barking furiously, warning us not to steal anything. That was a laugh! There was nothing worth stealing, even the tractor had a wheel leaning at a precarious angle. What a dump!

Maybe I should explain that Bryan came from farming stock and many moons ago he had asked me that if he ever made enough money to buy a farm would I help him run it.? 'In love' and without a faint possibility that this would ever happen I had rashly said 'of course I would.' Suddenly I felt a chill in the air as the memory of this promise came flooding back.

I tried to persuade him to leave but he was leaning over the gate with a glazed expression, and I knew my pleas were falling on deaf ears.

Dressed in my office garb of high heeled boots and red suit complete with straight skirt, totally unsuitable for a farm visit, I followed Bryan to the front door. We were welcomed by the farm dwellers and their children and invited into their kitchen to have coffee before we were shown round. I had already decided that it was not for me.

As I sat there making comparisons to my ultra modern kitchen at home, Bryan was discussing land and outbuildings. The children had disappeared as we sat down and now returned with handfuls of fluffy chicks. They offered them for us to hold. Now, if there is one thing that I hate, it is the feel of feathered birds—feathered or fluffy! It took me all my time not to scream. They seemed so eager to impress and did they not think that they were in the company of a future farmer's wife? I gritted my teeth and briefly held their proffered charges. This has convinced me that I am not ready for this massive career change.

Coffee drunk, we were on the move again. This time to briefly see the rest of the house, which I was not remotely interested in as I had no intention of moving here. I made polite noises as I was shown round and then outside to walk the land. The first thing that I was expected to do was to climb over a locked gate which, I must add, in high heeled boots and a tight skirt was an impossibility. A key was found and I made a more dignified entrance to the back of the property. The land at the back sloped upwards away from the house and I found it extremely precarious trying to climb the incline in my totally unsuitable footwear. I decided to stay put and chat politely to their son.

Time was getting on and nightfall but a blink away. I looked up on the horizon where I could just see the outline of the two men in the fading light. Was that a handshake I just witnessed? I will physically kill Bryan when I get him out of here—it seems a decision has been made without any discussion with me. That is not the way we do things! We argue first and discuss later, that is the normal procedure for important issues. What has he done?

The men returned and the seller told his son that he was now looking at the new owners of Signet Farm. I have to say that no matter how I felt, I would never show Bryan up in front of anybody so I bit my tongue, smiled and followed the men back to the kitchen where great excitement broke out and a large bottle of whisky was un corked.

Several hours, and several tumblers full of whisky later, Bryan stumbled out of their kitchen amidst congratulations and plenty of hand shaking. I managed to keep up appearances whilst trying to fold him into my sports car but as I sped homewards I burst into tears. I cried all the way home, mascara and make up forgotten in my feeling of utter despair. Bryan meanwhile, totally blind to my misery raved on relentlessly about his plans for the place. Whisky and tiredness eventually took it's toll and he sank into total oblivion.

On our return to the beautiful house we had just transformed, he woke up long enough to realise that I had been crying. He was not sympathetic in the least and could not understand why I was not as excited as he was and said I would get used to it. The subject was closed.

I hated him with a vengeance. I got up next morning and went off to work without uttering a word to him. Our secretary, when I arrived, asked how we had got on and I could not trust myself to explain for fear of bursting into tears. Diplomatically, she knew when to keep quiet and the day progressed well until Bryan put in an appearance and informed me that he had already put in an offer that had been accepted.

I listened as he enthused about it to our secretary and a little of his enthusiasm rubbed off on me and I began to think that maybe it wouldn't be so bad after all. I am so glad that he took no notice of me as it turned out to be the best move we ever made.

I obviously had a lot to learn but wasn't variety the spice of life and I certainly was still young enough to learn some new tricks. Maybe I would get used to it and who knows I may grow to love it!

We put our house on the market with Estate Agents who were amazed when they ventured inside and dubbed the house 'The Tardis.' We had quite a lot of interest but it was a time of depression and people were afraid of taking on large commitments.
Bryan was desperate to move to the farm and equally so the sellers were anxious to move out. We seemed to have a stalemate as things were not moving fast enough.

Our eldest lad solved the problem. He decided he wanted to buy it with his girlfriend. An ideal situation you might think but we first had to reduce the price to something he could afford. We discussed a more realistic figure which was acceptable to him, and a sale was agreed. A moving date decided and I began to pack accordingly. A couple of weeks later our son came to us with yet another problem., the size of the house! Our house was much larger than the house he was leaving and worried that he would not be able to furnish it, he asked his Dad if we could leave behind a few bits of furniture to help him out.

Generous to a fault, Bryan decided we could start again. All we took with us was our bed, a television and a couple of garden loungers. I think we only were allowed to take those because our son actually owned his own.

The sale of the farm at Signet was anything but straightforward. There was a house next to the property we were buying and our property had a flying freehold over the top of one of their outbuildings. It caused all sorts of problems for us and caused bad feeling between our neighbours and ourselves before we had even had a chance to meet them. They lived in London and used the house as a country retreat. They objected to us wanting to farm the land and put one obstacle after another forward in order to delay the sale. The current owners had used the land to keep donkeys but we intended to farm it properly.

If Bryan was anything, he was persistent and usually got what he wanted in the end, especially when he wanted something as badly as this.

Several times we were given moving dates that were further delayed by our neighbours objections. I had even put my daughter into the local Primary School, we had been so close to moving at one point. Delay after delay meant a 120 mile round trip to school each day with my daughter and devising methods of keeping ourselves occupied on these tedious journeys. We would listen to story cassettes and squeak as we passed under certain bridges—anything to take our minds of the boring drive each day.

Eventually, Bryan ran out of patience and decided to move in without contracts being signed. Unheard of you might say and certainly against our solicitors wishes but Bryan was a law unto himself and a final moving day was arranged.

I have to say that although a little apprehensive of what the future was to hold in this new direction I began to get excited, swept along on the tide of enthusiasm Bryan exuded.

Once again it was not a conventional removal lorry that transported our worldly goods Burford way but our flat bed scaffolding lorry with everything we owned on display. I stayed behind to clean up after our move and to make sure everything was ship shape for our son to move into. As I walked round it did not seem very different as most of our furniture was staying put. I wished him well with his own move and drove off to begin my new life as a Farmer's wife.

Chapter 38

An Introduction to our New Surroundings

My journey through the Oxfordshire by roads heading towards my new life was filled with a mixture of regret for leaving everything familiar to a feeling of exhilarating excitement at the chance to do something different. We often dream of changing our lives but never really do anything about it but here was my chance to totally transform the way I lived. I decided to face the challenge head—on, after all there was not anything I could not do if I put my heart into it.

My resolve was shaken a little on my arrival as everything seemed so basic after the luxurious surroundings of my former home. Never mind, it was no good looking back—forward and beyond, that is where I should be looking.

The lorry with our few possessions had already been unloaded and I wandered round my new home to get a feel for the place. I climbed the stairs and wandered into the five bedrooms, my son and daughter having already decided which they had laid claim to. How odd, neither the walls nor the floors were straight, a fact I had not noticed before, but the old beams made up for it. The place certainly had a charm all of it's own. I looked through the windows as I visited each room and marvelled at the surrounding countryside. I made my way downstairs and up a level into the dining room and beyond into a vast sitting room. The sitting room overlooked the farm yard to one aspect and our neighbours paddock complete with Hilary the goat from another, and over one of our own paddocks from a third window. It was in this paddock that my washing line was situated, halfway up an incline. Hanging washing out there on a windy day would be fun!

The hub of every farmhouse is the kitchen and I hurriedly made my way back to mine to resume my duties. Cups of tea and coffee for the 'workers' and a pile of sandwiches hastily thrown together from the contents of a box carefully kept to one side. Fed and watered we set to work putting up beds in respective rooms, decided which corner our lone television would stand in and where best to situate the garden loungers, our only furniture.

The kitchen consisted of the bare minimum of cupboards that were quickly filled to capacity with everything from the spacious kitchen I had left behind. I was sure that I would never find anything again but come on where was my positive thinking? The kitchen had two steps leading from it up into a laundry room. Those steps became a vital piece of furniture at meal times as I will explain later. The kitchen was 'L' shaped, almost like a kitchen / diner with a door to one side. Through this door you went down two steps into a passageway that lead to the back door. Off this passage was a large room that housed a toilet and hand basin that was very handy when working in the farmyard. Through a doorway opposite there was another room that housed the boiler and a rickety staircase leading to the flying freehold over our neighbours outbuilding, that had caused all the aggravation prior to our move.

As the night drew in and tiredness overtook us we settled down in the sitting room for a relaxing evening watching television. Bryan and I were perched on the loungers and the children were sprawled on the floor. Everything plugged in, we switched the television on and nothing happened! We had not realised that we were in a dip that afforded us no signal at all. Yet another job to be done. The list of jobs to be done was growing constantly. We had left most of our food behind so finding a supermarket was a priority. Furniture also was a must. There was just nowhere to sit comfortably and thirdly Bryan was desperate to become a proper Farmer and so needed animals. A market visit was planned.

After an entertaining evening planning the next few days we all climbed the wooden hill and made our way to our beds, exhausted yet buzzing with plans for our new life.

The next day dawned and we were all up with the lark. The children wanted to go and explore and after a rather sparse breakfast we ventured outside to see what we could make of the place. As I have mentioned the previous owners had kept donkeys and these were still in situ until he could find time to move them to their new premises. At the sound of our voices they started braying so that was our first port of call. We walked the fields and enjoyed the fresh air but realised on our travels that the footwear and clothing that had been quite chic and trendy in Didcot did nothing at all to support ankles clambering over furrowed fields or keep out the chill winds of early morning March.

The decision was made, we had to get new clothes for our new Venture. As there was very little in the house to eat we decided to seek out a local hostelry for our Sunday Lunch. We had forgotten in all our excitement that this particular Sunday was indeed 'Mothering Sunday.' We visited a couple of places that were fully booked and ventured further a field. We happened to come across a Farm Supply shop which was open and we stopped off to see if they had suitable clothing for us. What a treasure trove of goodies we found. Barbour coats to fit us all (matching of course) and 'Hunter' boots. We looked fantastic, we were really 'country folk' now—dressed to the nines in our 'country attire.'

Hunger was beginning to bite now and the urgency
became finding somewhere to eat as time was creeping
on. Just up the road we found somewhere but because
of the lateness of the hour, they had sold out of much
of their fare. We were so hungry by now that we would
have eaten the Landlords 'leg' if it had been offered on
a plate so we were grateful for the sausage and chips he
could provide.

We sat around the table chatting and listening to the
'country accents' of the other customers. Suddenly an
elderly gentleman who had been sitting at a table directly
behind our daughter turned in his seat and handed her a
pound coin. He said he had been watching her since we
had come in and thought she was not only ' a pretty little
thing' but so well behaved and polite. We thanked him
for his comments but declined his kind offer. He insisted
that she have the money and we thanked him again as he
got up to leave.

What a lovely place this is, when total strangers give you
money for just being well behaved. I think we are going
to like living here.

Four platefuls of sausage and chips later, after thanking
the Landlord for stepping into the breach, we returned to
our farm in the knowledge that now we would be more
suitably shod and a darn sight warmer.

Chapter 39

A Rude Awakening

*N*ormality resumed the following week, Bryan and I went back to work and the children returned to school.

It took some getting used to, the 30 mile drive to get home, instead of the 5 minute it usually took, but I have to admit that I loved it. It gave me time to shake off my work mode and I looked forward to the peace and quiet of our new found countryside. Business seemed to be at a slower place in this 'neck of the woods' and everybody, with the exception of our immediate neighbours, seemed friendly and the local community welcomed us warmly. We knew that we had made the right move and settled down to our new way of life.

We found a local supermarket in a nearby town and stocked our limited cupboard space. Potatoes were bought in a sack, which came in very handy and Bryan promised us a vast array of meat from our local surroundings. He had acquired a shotgun on his travels (rules and regulations in those days were far more lax than they are today) and he talked of pigeon pie, rabbit pie and jugged hare. Out came my cookery books and I awaited the provision of these culinary delights with trepidation.

It was just as well that I had stocked up my freezer on my supermarket jaunts as we would have all starved to death if I had been solely reliant on my 'hunter.' Maybe with practice his aim would improve but in the meantime conventional meals were prepared and eaten, if not in a conventional seating area.

At meal times I would shout to the Family and there would be a stampede towards the kitchen. It was neither starvation on their part or the prowess of my culinary skills that caused this but the choice of seats. The two steps up to the laundry room served as the best seats 1 and 2 and then there was the potato sack which was choice number 3. The first two were at least stable but the potato sack altered shape every time I used any potatoes until eventually it was easier to sit on the floor. My position, as I was always last to get my dinner, was a permanent place stood at the work surface. It was strange but I never had to fight for my place.

Over the next couple of weekends we chose dining room and sitting room furniture to make our farmhouse look more homely but still had to live like squatters until it was delivered some 8 weeks later.

Bryan was still 'chomping at the bit' to get his farm up and running. He talked of fresh eggs so we found someone local to supply us with 'point of lay' hens. We wanted everything on our farm to be as happy as we were and being totally naïve to the predators of the countryside, wanted them all to roam free. We wanted proper free range eggs from 'happy' hens.

In the interim period between moving in and acquiring our hens I had tidied up the farmyard. Scrap had been disposed of and I had made a small walled garden complete with flowers that I viewed from my kitchen window. It was all very picturesque, and then the hens arrived!!

We had about a dozen to start with, complete with a beautiful Rhode Island Red cockerel which we named 'Reuben'. He was magnificent. He strutted the yard as if he was 'Lord of the Manor' and kept all his hens happy. In our ignorance we named all the hens and even though I was a little wary of getting too close to them I loved to see them pecking about the yard and enjoyed even more the fresh eggs which we had in abundance.

Two days after their arrival I woke up to find my flower garden completely destroyed. They had pecked and uprooted every single plant and scattered them across my pristine farmyard. How could they do that to me after we had given them such a lovely home? Somehow battery hens (even though I disagree with the principal of caged birds) suddenly became far more attractive! It did not take me long to realise that hens were a law unto themselves and my idyllic little garden was a waste of time and effort, especially in a farmyard. It was a toss up between flowers and fresh eggs and the eggs won hands down.

Bryan was a ' beef cattle' man as opposed to dairy or agricultural, so we found our local livestock market at Banbury and attended a sale. We donned our new jackets and wellies and set off with the intention of buying a couple of cows.

Not long after moving to the farm we had attended The Three Counties Agricultural Show at Malvern. Bryan had looked around the cattle on show and had decided that 'Limousin' was the way forward. The French breed produced lean meat which 'the powers that be' had decided was a healthier alternative to the established breed of Aberdeen Angus with its high fat content and tastier meat. It was with this in mind that we attended the Banbury sale.

Now remembering that we were all new to this,
we made our way to the seating area and watched
the proceedings from our elevated position. The
auctioneer took his place on the rostrum and
the sale began. A gate opened to the right of the
auctioneer and a drover walked a cow gently round
the ring. Bidding started almost immediately and
although we could not see who were making the
offers the auctioneer had reached fever pitch in
no time at all. What he was actually saying was
almost incoherent but the result was that someone
in the crowd had purchased the beast and then
he moved on to the next animal for sale. The sale
progressed with drovers walking round cows with
calves at foot, heifers and huge bulls in a variety
of sizes and colours. It was all very controlled and
straightforward.

Bryan had not seen anything that caught his eye.
Had inexperience made him miss the potential in
the cattle that had already been and purchased?

Suddenly there was a deafening din, as the gate
to the right of the auctioneer burst open, and the
drovers that had been in the ring, leapt over or
through the bars surrounding it, in fear of their
lives. Two fairly large beasts burst in and frantically
ran round crashing into the barriers in their fear
of unfamiliar surroundings. They disappeared
through the exit gate as quickly as they had
appeared. A hushed silence fell as the drovers
tentatively resumed their places in the ring and

the auctioneer resumed the sale. He explained to his audience that those particular animals were a couple of 'limousin' heifers just ripe for breeding.

Bryan's eyes lit up—this is what he had been waiting for, something with a bit of 'spirit.' He had hardly any competition in the bidding stakes and got them both for a bargain price. The 'Limousin' breed is known to be a bit on the wild side but I think these two had more 'spirit' than most farmers wanted to contend with. Not Bryan though, he was 'over the moon' with his purchases and after paying the auctioneer, arranged for a haulier to transport them back to the farm.

We returned home to await their arrival feeling that we had progressed one step further along the road to becoming 'real' farmers. A couple of hours later the lorry arrived with our new 'charges.' It reversed up the farmyard and stopped just outside the enclosed yard. The gate was opened and our daughter sat on the wall dressed in her 'Barbour' jacket and wellies complete with a stick ready to meet the new members of our 'Family.' The haulier advised us to remove her from the wall as he remarked that these particular beasts were pretty wild.

That was an understatement!!! Bryan had already bought some cattle cake and had a bucket ready to give them a feed as they came off the back of the lorry, a kind of 'welcome to our Family' treat. I was stood, all kitted out, with my stick at the ready to guide them into the stall that was to be their new home until they had settled down. Big mistake!! As the haulier dropped his tailgate they thundered down the ramp bellowing and snorting like the Devil himself was after them. They ran the length of the yard, turned and pawed the ground like a couple of cartoon characters. My immediate thought at this time was 'Oh my goodness, what had we done?' They were huge, they had looked so much smaller from where we had been sat in our elevated position at the sale.

The haulier wished us luck, returned to his lorry and drove off. We were left with these two manic animals contained in our enclosed yard.

Bryan and I looked at each other and he grinned. He was obviously still happy with his purchases and loved a challenge. He ventured into the enclosure with his bucket of cake and quickly disappeared into the stall. The heifers, seeing the movement, charged back down the yard with Bryan being their obvious target. Heads down they skidded into the stall and thankfully lost their footing on the cobbled floor. All we heard from inside the stall was a string of choice expletives and a resounding crash as Bryan threw the bucket in his haste to fall out the secondary door.

There was obviously more to this farming than we thought!

Over the next few weeks we acquired pigs and a couple of orphan lambs to complete our 'Family.' The next task in hand was to name them all. We were a proper farm at last.

Chapter 40

Over the Wall & Beyond

We thought our lives in Didcot had been busy but that 'prior life' had no comparison to the business of our lives in our new 'more relaxed existence.'

We would rise as dawn broke, wash dress and hurriedly down a coffee and some breakfast before starting our rounds of checking, feeding and watering our charges. The outbuildings were very basic with no electricity or plumbing to make our lives easier. There was a pond situated next to our neighbour's property and water had to be either fetched and carried in milk churns from there or hosed into churns from the house before being carried to the water troughs. Feeding was done by carrying feed sacks around and emptying them into the feed troughs. Who needed a gym to keep fit, we had a workout each morning for free.

When this chore was done, it was back to the house to raise the children from their beds and get them ready for school. By this time our daughter was well established in the local Primary and caught the school bus from the end of our lane. Our son, on the other hand, was still at school in Didcot completing his last year and had to be transported via our trip to work each day.

We still had our scaffolding base and office in Didcot, so from 9am daily we carried on as usual with our office jobs. Having worked all day, I would leave a little earlier than Bryan collecting our son on my homeward journey, arriving back at the farm just in time to retrieve our daughter from the school bus. I was grateful that she was the first one to be picked up in the morning but the last one to be dropped off at night, giving me enough time to return home without breaking the speed limit too many times.

Once home, the morning chores had to be repeated, this time with the help of son and daughter. A dinner had to be prepared and cooked and any other household chores outstanding needed to be done. Television and the likes became a distant memory as every daylight hour became crammed with 'farming activities'. When eventually time was found to sit down through sheer exhaustion, we slept the sleep of the dead.

We had a wonderful sense of achievement watching our animals grow, but as they grew they began to cause us more problems.

Our two sheep who we had named 'Mong' and 'Curly', could both have been 'stand ins' for Houdini, the escapologist. I would be getting ready for work in the morning and happen to glance out across their paddock. Sometimes they would be there and I would sigh with relief but more often than not they would be missing. At first I had not known where to look for them but soon established their escape route. They would jump on top of the walls (Cotswold stone walls are quite pretty to look at around fields as opposed to wire but they are of no comparison when it comes to containing animals.) and make their getaway. Invariably they would head along the verge towards the Wild Life Park, nibbling the wayside grass as they went. Was there not enough grass in the field they had escaped from?—obviously not and something comes to mind about 'grass being greener.' Did this phrase also apply to sheep?

Off would come my heeled fashionable boots and on would go my wellies, wax jacket thrown over my designer suit and off I would go in hot pursuit. I often wondered as I ran along that verge what people thought I was doing. I must have looked a dreadful sight with my red face, gasping for breath.

Did they think I was an eccentric, strangely attired jogger?

Taking my life in my own hands I had to cross the busy A361 in order to get in front of my escapees in order to drive them homewards. Once they realised that I meant business they would resignedly trot back to their field where they would carry on grazing leaving me in a lather of sweat, heaving my heart up trying to get enough breath to re-shower and resume getting ready for work. Lamb Chops, the very thought of them makes my mouth water.!!! Beware sheep!—you may end up on my plate sooner rather than later.

Eventually this morning work out became more than my time schedule would allow and I had to find a way of stopping them. I had a brilliant plan. The chain that had been used to restrain the previous owners guard dog was in an outbuilding where I had discarded it during my farmyard clean up. I found it and shortened it before chaining the two sheep together. What a novel way of solving the problem. The sheep had room for each to graze comfortably but the chain was not long enough to reach the top of the wall. Every time one of them tried to jump up, the other held it back, they were now each other's worst enemy. The problem was solved.

When we had viewed the farm, prior to buying it, the previous owner had showed us a couple of ponies that their children used to ride. One

of these ponies, a Shetland mare, was in foal at
the time and we had been promised the foal as a
moving in gift for our daughter. We thought it was
a lovely idea at the time and agreed to let the mare
and her stallion remain at the property until the
foal was born. Our daughter was to be allowed to
ride the stallion until the ponies were removed to
their new home after the birth. This became our
next problem.

Our property was situated on a road that was used
annually by the Travelling Fraternity on their way
to Stow Fair. This fair is widely known as the
largest gathering of its kind for horse dealers and
Travellers. On their way through one family in
particular always broke their journey and stayed
in the lay-by at the end of our lane. They were
of the Romany kind and were never any trouble.
On their return journey we would always ring
the Blacksmith at Lechlade for them to prepare
him that they would need his service on their way
through. We never had a problem with them at
all. Our problem was with Sonny, our stallion.
Whenever he smelt one of their mares he would be
off, over the wall and away. He was ever hopeful of
an 'encounter' with a willing mare. Once again,
my skills as an eccentric jogger came to the fore
as I raced after his disappearing haunches. Horse
Whisperers they may be but they were certainly my
Knights in Shining Armour as they easily caught
and restrained him long enough for a head collar
to be put on. He was then returned, not to the
field from where he had escaped but to the security

of the four walls of his stable where he had time to ponder on the futility of his actions, I, on the other hand, had another unscheduled workout that I could well do without. We very quickly learned to keep Sonny in a more enclosed environment while he remained our guest.

The two ponies that we kept in good faith waiting for the arrival of our 'gift' proved to be more trouble than enough as when the foal was born it was horribly deformed with a head almost the same size as it's body. An equine vet, who lived across the field had to come and put it out of it's misery. It was a hard lesson for our daughter to learn so early in life but it showed her the reality of irresponsible breeding. We learned later that Sonny and his mare were 'brother' and 'sister' and should never have been allowed to breed.

The owner was asked to remove his animals from our property that day as we did not want to be tarred with the same brush. We wanted to run our farm correctly so that our animals could be kept to the best of our ability in a responsible way.

It was a hard lesson that we all learned but it made us more determined than ever to be responsible farmers.

Chapter 41

An Experience of Life and Death

We soon got into a routine and really enjoyed our chosen way of life. At weekends when chores were done, a walk along the bridle path or a visit to a local Inn was appreciated and gave us time to plan ahead.

The children enjoyed the freedom to wander at will and were seeing nature in all it's glory first hand. Our son, nine years older than our daughter spent most of his time with his Dad, helping him at every opportunity. Our daughter, on the other hand, would spend hours paddling and fishing in the stream that ran along the verge to the front of our property or she could be seen hurtling down the lane at breakneck speed on her quad bike. She sensed no danger and felt no fear, as in her eyes, all her surroundings were one giant playground to be explored and experienced to the full. She wandered across fields and bridle paths without fear of abduction or attack and brought home armfuls of wild flowers to be identified, pressed and entered into her scrapbook.

What an idyllic childhood, no computers, I pods and the like, just fresh air and a world of magic and imagination. Were we naïve to let her have so much freedom?

The hamlet that we lived in seemed a million miles from the real world with all it's evil and our little bit of heaven was a haven to return to after a busy day in the office.

When the work was done and all the animals were checked and settled we would migrate to the sitting room to relax.

We had a pear tree, which carried fruit in abundance, just beyond the sitting room window. Bryan would often ask Kyly to pick him a pear as he relaxed in his chair. Nothing as simple as going into the garden in a conventional way to pick a pear. Not my Family! The sitting room window would be opened, Kyly would climb out, drop onto the top of a Cotswold Dry Stone wall, balance carefully along that, climb onto the tin roof of a rickety shed and finally climb into the pear tree. It would have been so much easier for me to pick them and put them in a fruit bowl like most normal people, but not us, this was far more fun.

The next animal that moved onto the farm was a huge sow, in pig. She was enormous. Watching her farrowing was our first experience of 'live' birth and it was amazing. Our son really enjoyed getting involved with the pigs and named the sow, 'Sally.' She had 10 healthy piglets and one sickly runt.

Never one to give up on anything, Bryan told me to wrap it up in foil and put it in the oven. At first, I thought, how barbaric, it had hardly any meat on it and it wasn't even dead yet!. He was right, of course, this was its only chance of surviving. It was given colostrums from the sow and then I did what I could., obviously not turning the oven up to 'roasting ' temperature but just to a gentle warmth. It did seem to pick up for a couple of days and I kept it in a box in the kitchen, fed it regularly day and night with a milk supplement and was hopeful of its chance of survival.

On the third day I noticed it was no longer rounded, it had lost weight and it's spine was stood up resembling a 'ridgeback.' It did not live to see the day out. This was our first encounter with death and it upset us all. Was there more that I could have done? I learned, after many more farrowings, that these runts rarely survived, it was nature's way of culling the weak.

When the piglets grew they were separated from 'Sally' and put into another stall. They reach a size when they harass the Sow constantly and never give her any rest. It is vital at this point to separate them in order for the sow to resume her previous good health and produce further litters. With this breeding programme in mind, a boar was purchased in the next few weeks and he settled in very quickly. We now felt that we were making headway to becoming a real farm.

The next animal Bryan needed was a bull to serve the heifers. Bryan made some enquiries about forthcoming 'Limousin' Sales. There was a 'Tanhill' sale the following week and Bryan attended, and bought our first bull. He was a fine beast, a proven bull by the name of 'Tanhill Capability. We set him to work almost immediately and true to form, the heifers were soon in calf.

Most of our animals acquired names and 'Waca' and Baga, our first two heifers, were no exceptions. They had now settled down and were used to Bryan standing watching them for hours on end. They were his pride and joy and were to produce the first calves of our Pedigree herd.

We pondered on the name of our herd as we thought it should be something relevant. 'Limousin' was a French breed of cattle so a French name would be very suitable. We had given our daughter a French middle name 'Chantal' because we thought it sounded 'classy' and now it sounded the perfect name for our herd. The 'Chantal' herd was soon registered with the 'Limousin' Society. We thought registering cattle was not unlike the registration of vehicles. Every year a letter of the alphabet was designated to represent that particular year and all cattle born in that year had to have a name that started with that relevant letter. The letter for that year was 'D'. While we were awaiting the birth of our first calves Bryan bought in a few more cows already in calf. They were not 'Limousins' but a mixture of Belgian Blue and Charolais and I hoped that they all calved down without any problems as I had never seen a cow calve and wondered how we would cope in an emergency?

Bryan always did a last minute check of all the animals before he went to bed each night and on this particular night he brought one down off the field and put her in a stall in the farmyard. I asked why he had done this and was told that she was going to calve around 3am and that she might need some help. He explained that it would be easier to help her in an enclosed stall rather than in an open field.

Well, I had never heard anything so silly in my life! Who ever did he think he was—Dr Doolittle? Even doctors cannot tell a woman what day precisely she will have a baby, never mind, what time! I laughed and said he was totally mad and made my way to bed remarking over my shoulder that if he needed me in the night he only had to shout. I was well and truly snuggled down and drifting off when he came to bed and set the alarm for 3am. Tiredness overcame me and I was soon in the land of nod. It seemed that I had only just gone to sleep when I felt him slide off the bed and open the window. He woke me to tell me that she was in trouble and he would shout if he needed me. I had drifted back off to sleep before he had even left the bedroom, convinced that he had taken leave of his senses at this unearthly hour—it was 2.55am. Suddenly I was awakened by "I, I (he was always too lazy to call me Irene) quickly, I need soap, towel and a bucket of warm water and get Steed up on your way down—I might need his help too!!"

I fell out of bed, clambered into some old clothes and shouted Steed on my way downstairs. 'Soap, towel and bucket!' I felt like an extra in the television programme 'All Creatures Great and Small'. What was I doing? I gathered these items together, grabbed a torch and made my way across the farmyard to the torch lit stall. Steed, sleepy eyed from his bed, padded along in his pyjamas and dressing gown, behind me, followed by Kyly who was wondering what all the fuss was about.

Bryan shouted to them to return to the house, to get dressed and to put on their wellies. Slippers indeed! What were they thinking of?

I handed over the bucket, soap and towel as Bryan rolled up his sleeves, washed from elbows to fingertips and then watched in disbelief as his arm slid into the back end of the cow up to his shoulder. What was he doing? This was a side of Bryan I had never seen before and I was amazed at his knowledge.

I was not sure what was going on in there but when his hand emerged he had hold of two tiny hooves. He shouted for me to put the calving ropes round the hooves before they slid back. I was all fingers and thumbs, trying to juggle the torch and avoid the heaving cow as she staggered from side to side as the next contraction took hold.

Bryan was not the most patient of men and Steed, Kyly and I were all in the firing line for our ineptitude. Between us we managed to get the ropes on but obviously not quick enough as Bryan lost his grip and the hooves slid back in and out of sight. Thankfully the ropes had tightened enough so that our efforts were not in vain. During the next contraction, as the cow's body arched and she pushed, the hooves re appeared and this time we knew what to do! Steed on one rope and Kyly and I on the other, shoulder to shoulder, we pulled when instructed and relaxed a little in between.

Finally when our arms felt as if they had been pulled from their sockets, faces red and sweating, a tiny head appeared and with one more contraction the body slid out. What a feeling of achievement, I mean for us, not the cow! She immediately turned towards her offspring and started to clean it. We moved out of the way of the blood and gore and suddenly realised how tired we all were. It was the middle of the night and suddenly the chill in the air began to bite.

Bryan looked on like a proud Father. I knew he was overjoyed with the result, a heifer calf, alive and well. We turned as one to creep back to our warm beds but Bryan had other ideas. We could not leave until the calf had suckled the cow and so we waited, and waited. We were all amazed to have witnessed the miracle of birth but now surely nature would take over and the calf would surely suckle when it was ready and not before? Obviously Bryan was taking no chances and ¾ hour later, much to our relief, the calf struggled to her feet and staggered to find her first 'breakfast.' Bryan was now satisfied that all was well and we had permission to return to our beds, a good nights work well done.
I made sure that the children were safely tucked up once more before I returned to our bed to find Bryan snoring

loudly, already deep in sleep. I carefully climbed in and tried to settle down as dawn broke through the bedroom window.

Suddenly, without warning, Reuben the cockerel, started to crow and it went on and on as he welcomed the new morning. What with this natural alarm going off continuously and Bryan snoring, sleep was impossible and I rose and went to make myself a drink.

I have to admit that nobody wanted to get up that morning. Everybody was so tired but glad they had experienced the action throughout the night. The children went off to school eager to tell their friends what they had seen.

No matter how tired we felt, the morning chores had to be done. We dragged ourselves round, watering, feeding and checking all was well. Our new addition was sleeping soundly curled up in the straw, her belly full and a proud 'Mum' standing guard over her.

We went off to our day jobs with a feeling of satisfaction albeit we needed matchsticks to keep our eyes open.

Whilst living at the farm it was more convenient to have our milk delivered as we were too far from the shops to just 'pop' out when it was needed. The milk delivery was usually first thing in the morning but by breakfast time there would be very little left in the bottles, if any at all.

The stalls, across the farmyard, which contained the piglets had lift up latches on the outside. As the piglets grew, if they rubbed themselves against the door, the door would rattle enough for the latch to lift up and lo and behold, the piglets would be on the loose! Talk about running amok! Dustbins would be upturned and rubbish strewn across the yard. Milk would be sucked up from the bottles or lapped up if the bottles toppled over and the chickens would run for their lives. Such was life on the farm—there was never a dull moment.

It was quite a task to round up excited piglets, just as you thought you had them cornered they would veer off in another direction, squealing loudly, enjoying their new found freedom. It was an incredible way of keeping fit but to us it was all in a day's work and we were often late arriving at our day jobs. We were extremely lucky that working in our office was a very confident lady who we knew would cover everything in our absence. Claire was our Saviour!

One weekend, all the Family were up on the fields behind the house when I happened to see movement in the sitting room. As we were altogether I feared that the unmentionable had happened, and we had been broken into. We raced as one towards the yard. We noticed that the front door was wide open and feared the worst. What we witnessed made us all laugh.

The pigs had escaped yet again, had entered the house (somebody must have left the front door ajar) and made for the sitting room. There were piglets everywhere, running round with fruit in their mouths (I was the proud owner of a fruit bowl by this time) and all the pot plants had been knocked over and soil was scattered from one end of the room to the other.

The thought of pork on our plates at this time was becoming more enticing by the minute. A full scale cleaning up operation was put in place as the men of the Family rounded up the errant piglets and herded them out of the house. It was time for action—bolts were put on the doors to replace the latches and hopefully the piglets would roam no more.

We decided to look round to see how we could make our lives easier. We contacted a plumber, and an electrician to sort out water troughs with running water in the stalls and electric lights to all the outbuildings. Torches were ok in an emergency but the light they afforded was very limited.

I think this was our next big step towards farming in the modern world.

Chapter 42

A Narrow Escape

Due to all the extra animals we had now acquired, household chores took a secondary place of importance and I would simply run out of hours and steam before I could accomplish everything that needed to be done. I decided to take some annual leave from my day job to enable me to catch up and maybe relax a little.

One morning, during my week off, I was sitting at the kitchen table having a welcome cup of coffee when I saw a tall respectable gent walk past the window and rap at the front door. I thought, as I walked to open the door, that possibly it was a neighbour I had not yet met come to introduce himself, maybe, but he did look rather official with a clip board tucked under his arm?

I opened the door and smiled as charmingly as I could, only to be told that he was an Inspector from The Ministry of Agriculture, as it was known in those far off days. He went on to explain that as we were 'new ' farmers, he was there to inspect our licences and movement book!! My heart sank—what was he talking about? Bryan had not mentioned any of these, what was I supposed to do? He went on to explain that there were hefty fines attached to the flaunting of rules and regulations and I began to panic. CALM DOWN AND THINK STRAIGHT WOMAN!—Invite him in, make him feel welcome and try to get him onside. Make him a coffee, offer him a piece of homemade cake and plead ignorance, after all ignorant I was. I didn't have to fake the ignorance but being so charming I did find more difficult.

I explained that in our eagerness to be up and running we had overlooked finding out about the paperwork involved. I went on to tell him that my husband was more a hands on kind rather than a paperwork man and therefore he had left all that side to me. I was a mere wife and Mother and had had no farming experience so it was all new to me. I think it worked, my innocent charm, as he explained in detail that in order to have cattle we had to register every animal in a movement book, where they were bought from and their destination when sold. He smiled and said," no harm had been done," so he would order me a book to be filled in with all the relevant details on receipt. I promised him faithfully that I would do just that but what he said next put 'the fear of God' into me.

He had obviously seen all the cattle out on the fields as
he had approached the farm and had assumed that they
were all the animals we had. He was unaware of the
50+ pigs that were across the yard in stalls or the orphan
lambs that were their neighbours. The conversation
turned to pigs and he became very serious. He explained
that to move pigs without a licence was a very serious
breach of the rules and there was a huge fine attached to
this. My heart went straight to my boots. Oh my God,
we would be bankrupted before we had even started! He
said I should not look so worried as it did not apply to us
as we didn't have any pigs. I smiled through gritted teeth
unsure whether I should come clean, but as I hesitated,
the moment passed. He said he would send me some
forms in case we later wanted to branch out into pigs.

At that precise moment, I don't think I had ever prayed
so hard. Normally our pigs were so noisy, squealing and
fighting, I was not sure how he could have missed them,
but miss them he had. They must have all been asleep.
Please God let them remain asleep until he had at least
gets back into his car.

With every finger and toe I possessed, crossed for good
luck, I thanked him for his visit, thanked him for his
advice and as quietly as I could, in hushed tones in case
the pigs should hear me, bade him farewell and watched
with bated breath as he returned to his car. As he drove
away I breathed once more and said a prayer of thanks
for such well-behaved pigs.

Half an hour later, all hell broke loose in one of the stalls.
I was washing up in between preparing the evening meal

when I heard the pigs squealing and snorting. Nothing unusual in that, but there was something else, another noise mingled with the squealing. I was unsure what it was and ran out to investigate.

There was the answer. One of the free range chickens had fluttered down amongst the pigs by mistake. What a mistake that turned out to be! The pigs had cornered her and were busy plucking her. Terrified and rightfully in fear of her life, she was squawking painfully as she tried to escape from her assailants.

As I explained at the beginning of my farming experience I do not like touching fluffy or feathered varieties so I raced inside to don appropriate clothing and footwear and to grab suitable utensils in order to rescue the unfortunate bird. On went my overalls and wellies topped by my wax jacket. Bryan's trilby was pulled well down over my ears, just in case (of what I am not sure) and a huge pair of gloves completed my Rescue En Semble. I was dressed in a flash and grabbing my eldest son's keep net, packed by mistake, I ran back outside collecting the basket from the front of my daughter's bike as I went. I was now ready to go to war with the pigs!

I threw open the door of the stall, shutting it as quickly behind me, and with feet kicking in all directions I just managed to reach the forlorn bird before it got plucked to death.

Pigs can be vicious animals once they get started and several tried to bite me as I waded through them. As

pitiful as the bird looked, I couldn't pick it up and had
to throw the basket over it and sweep the whole lot up
with the keep net whilst fighting off the hoard of open
mouths going in for the kill. I struggled back to the door
with the victim safely tucked in the basket, covered with
the net in order to stop it falling amongst it's attackers
again.

Once outside, I unravelled the net and pulled the
basket from over the traumatised hen. As serious as it
was, I couldn't help having a chuckle as she looked just
like a ready plucked oven ready chicken bought from
a supermarket. She was completely featherless. She
understandably was not moving, and I carefully poked
her back into the basket with a gloved finger and carried
her to the safety of a nearby stall where I tipped her
carefully into the straw to recover. I have to say that
recovery was not really what I had expected after her
ordeal but next morning she was up and about strutting
the yard in all her 'glory' more naked than the day she
was born. It took ages for her plumage to grow back but
she never made the mistake of paying a friendly visit to
the pigs ever again.

I was so grateful that the Inspector had gone—I am not
sure he would have been so friendly had he of known
what was lurking the other side of the yard.

When Bryan returned I asked him if he had known
about the paperwork that was necessary for modern day
farming. He, in turn, explained that when he was a lad
and his Father had been in farming, he had been unaware
of any paperwork, only hard work! I forgave him for

dropping me in it and was instantly promoted to farm Secretary in order to deal with the relevant documents as they arrived. It was a nightmare to start with as I was so unfamiliar with everything but through sheer necessity I mastered it all in the end.

Bryan was hardly any help at all writing down ear numbers and the like on scraps of paper, torn up cigarette packets or even feed labels, anything in fact that he could lay his hands on. These were usually kept for at least a week in his jacket pocket along with binding twine, handfuls of cattle feed, string and dog ends before he thought to give them to me in order for me to enter them in the relevant books. As you can understand rules and regulations were never one of Bryan's strong points!

Chapter 43

The Dawn of the Chantal Herd

Our pedigree heifers were blooming well and the births were imminent. Bryan was like an expectant Father, he was so excited. We came home from our day jobs one Friday and it was all over. Waca had calved in the field.—the result being a beautiful heifer calf. As this calf was the first of our own pedigree herd we named her 'Dawn.' This was the beginning. Baga followed shortly afterwards and had another heifer calf which we named 'Danika.'

Limousin cows make very good mothers but viciously guard their offspring from humans. Even though Bryan had spent hours talking to them and stroking them at close quarters, it made no difference, even he was not allowed near. If he approached the calves, the cows would put their heads down, paw the ground, not unlike bulls and charge headlong at him. With nothing but a stick in his hand to fend them off, he showed no fear, and stood his ground. Once he saw that the calves were thriving he would stand and watch from a distance, giving them the space they needed. Each day he would edge closer until they felt more comfortable with him again. When the calves were strong enough to run around, the cows settled down and normality resumed.

A week or so after the calves were born, Bryan had the ridiculous idea that he wanted to weigh them. It was complete madness as we did not own a cattle crush with scales or any other means of weighing them, or so I thought. Bryan was not put off by this mere fact—we had bathroom scales, they would do.

Bryan decided that he would weigh Steed first, and then weigh Steed carrying the calf. It seemed very simple but nothing with Bryan was that simple.

We had a major task just trying to drive the cows and calves down off the field into the enclosed farmyard. It took ages to accomplish this and Bryan's temper got the better of him several times when we were not in the right place at the right time or we let the cattle back through rather than be trampled underfoot. The cattle were never wrong it was always our fault. You would have thought that we were experienced drovers, not a mere wife, a son of 14 years and a six years old daughter. According to Bryan we should have known what to do and he exploded every time we put a foot wrong. I often thought what our neighbours must have thought when they heard him shouting at us?

By the time the cows and calves were safely shut in the enclosed yard, Bryans stressed out workforce, were all fed up with being shouted at and had no heart for the weighing process.

First, we had to separate the cows from the calves—a job easier said than done! The cows knew there was something going on and circled the calves protectively. Bryan tried to distract one of the cows so that Steed could snatch its calf. After many attempts, Steed did manage it, just managing to make it safely through the gate before the cow reached it, bellowing and snorting wildly. She rammed the gate with her head in an attempt to reach her offspring. She was not a happy cow!

The calf struggled, and Steed struggled, and it was anything but a true reading as he tried to balance precariously on the bathroom scales. Bryan seemed happy with the weight shown and the calf was returned to its mother via another gate, a much safer option for Steed. Once re-united they soon settled down.Not happy with just one weight, the whole procedure had to be done again in order to weigh the other calf.

Baga had watched the whole episode from the safety of a corner, snorting loudly, warning us to keep our distance. Bryan tried to draw her away from the calf, but Baga was not to be fooled so easily. She was far more stubborn until Bryan got close enough to her to slap her on her back. Startled, she ran forward leaving her calf behind.

Steed in a flash, grabbed it and made for the gate. She was faster than he was and trampled on his foot in her attempt to get to her calf. He screamed, let the calf go and hobbled to safety behind the gate.

Bryan was furious that we had been so close to succeeding, and showed no concern for the state of Steed's foot. The foot had swelled up almost immediately and was now turning black. Steed, against his Father's wishes, refused point blank to be involved any further. Bryan shouted in frustration that he would do it himself.

I tried to calm the situation down by explaining that Steed had done his best but failure was not a word that Bryan understood and I got the length of his tongue.

Bryan was always single minded and went straight for the calf without a moments thought for his own safety. Baga was waiting for him and cow kicked him sideways catching him square on the shin. Bryan normally felt no pain but he certainly felt that kick! He went down in agony clutching his leg. I told the children to get out of the way and I opened the gate to allow the cattle to head out back to their field. It was either that or have Bryan trampled on.

I examined his leg and once I had ascertained that it was not broken, we all burst out laughing, with the exception of Bryan. He was still furious that we had failed but we thought he had got his 'just desserts.' Maybe there was a God after all?

I helped both my 'wounded soldiers' into the kitchen where cold compresses were applied and plans were put in place to purchase a proper cattle crush complete with weigh scales.

It was around this time that our first litter of piglets, fully grown now, were ready to go for slaughter. We had made the mistake of naming them all as they were growing and now it was like losing members of our 'Family.' How could we possibly send them to their deaths? Although we felt uneasy about it—it had to be done.

The slaughter man's trailer arrived and we loaded them up for their final journey.
The farm gate slammed shut behind them as they disappeared into the distance on their way to becoming part of the food chain—the first of many more of our animals to go the same way.

Chapter 44

Tasty Meat with a Conscience

When these pigs returned to the farm they were in plastic bags, half a pig in each, jointed and ready for the freezer complete with their half heads intact. As our son was unloading them he was identifying each one as he carried it in. It made us feel quite guilty but the pork looked good and tasted even better. This was the moment of realisation—in future pigs would be nameless. It was the same with 'Mong' and 'Curly' our first two sheep. It was hard to stomach that we were eating what had virtually become our pets but the 'lamb' tasted 'out of this world' and future lambs were also to be nameless. Problem solved. We had to convince ourselves that that was what farming was all about—we were a farm, not a respite home for farm animals.

We had to toughen up!

Bryan bought in more cattle as we became more proficient. He would buy cows in calf (any breed) so we had a turnover of beef cattle whilst waiting for our Pedigree herd to grow in number. We had our own bull so it seemed silly not to work him to his full potential.

Most cows calved with ease, nature taking its course but occasionally a cow would be in trouble with a breach position calf or with a calf with an extra large head. Bryan was incredible; he always knew what to do and always had the welfare of the cow at heart. He would have made and excellent vet, he seemed to know instinctively what was wrong and how to solve it. We all admired his skills, if not his temper, and it was very rarely that we had to call in a vet.

Bryan was only ever interested in beef cattle but bought a group of cattle at market that contained one Holstein Friesian, in calf. The cow calved, without a problem, resulting in a heifer calf. The problem occurred afterwards when she produced more milk than her lone calf could consume. Bryan had an idea that he would milk her and feed the excess milk to the pigs. Many moons ago Bryans' Father had reared dairy cattle so he was capable of milking by hand.

This was something new to us, so we all gathered round in the stall to watch and learn.

First he needed a stool to sit on, he could not milk a cow standing up. We scratched our heads for a moment and then Bryan remembered that I had a bedroom stool that went with my dressing table. I was sent to retrieve it from the bedroom. I was sure this was not what milkmaids used with its soft, fluffy pink seat but it did have three legs! He was sure it would suffice so I quickly handed it over. A pail was fetched and Bryan, all 15+ stone of him, seated himself precariously on the stool placed carefully at the side of the cow. He explained that warm hands were a necessity as cold hands would make the animal kick. He set to work. We marvelled, as the white liquid squirted into the pail, but the cow was restless and kept kicking out. Maybe his hands were not warm enough? Once again he pushed his head into her flank and suddenly everything happened at once.

The cow kicked over the pail of milk, twisted herself round and sat on Bryan's lap. Fifteen stone of Bryan plus the cow was too much for my stool and with a resounding

'crack', all three legs splayed outwards and both Bryan and the cow found themselves sat in the straw. As the cow scrambled to her feet, Bryan rolled from under her mass expecting to find his legs broken. No, he was still in one piece, which is more than I can say for my stool! His legs were very badly bruised but we couldn't help laughing at our own stupidity.

The next time he attempted milking by hand a more solid box was found and hands well and truly warmed first. We did learn by our mistakes but had lots of laughs along the learning curve. We all had a go at milking but it was far harder than it looked. Bryan was the only one who really had the knack. It was tiring on the hands but he did persevere so that the pigs occasionally had a bucketful of fresh milk straight from the cow. The pigs loved it and after several bucketfuls their skin changed from pink to creamy white. Bryan soon found this too time consuming and bought in extra calves when the situation of a cow with too much milk arose. A much easier option all round.

Chapter 45

A Cow Named Racehorse

Summer time on the farm was idyllic, the days were long enough to get everything done and even though we were busy, somehow life seemed more relaxed. Due to our being in a 'dip', the heady smell of 'rapeseed' would hang in the air. It made a pleasant change from the cows' muck and pig slurry. We breathed in the perfumed air unaware that within days we would all have 'flu—like' symptoms that would make us all feel totally wretched.

Convinced that we had all contracted flu', I went off to the local town to stock up on relevant remedies. Whilst standing in a queue, I overheard a conversation that explained it all. It was not flu' after all but the effects of the 'rape.' I found out it would pass in a couple of days without dosing ourselves up with unnecessary medicine. It was part of living in the countryside so we would have to grin and bear it. Yet another lesson learned!

Having attended several other Limousin sales, Bryan had bought in another couple of pedigree cows. They were all pretty headstrong but it was their spirit that Bryan loved.

When the weather improved and it became dry underfoot we let the cattle out of the stalls to graze the open fields. Pedigrees and mixed breeds all driven up together, it was a spectacle that we all loved to watch. Young and old animals together, gambolling and frolicking in the long grass, racing this way and that, glad to have the sun on their backs.

They had only been up on the fields for a single afternoon when Bryan decided that he would check them before retiring to bed. He just wanted to make sure they had all settled down in their new surroundings.

He seemed to be gone ages, so I decided to go on up. I knew how he could get carried away watching them, losing track of time, so I was not unduly worried. Suddenly he burst in through the door shouting for me to get the children from their beds as all the cattle had disappeared. He had walked the length and breadth of the fields and could see no sign of them although he had noticed the wall down where they had got out.

We had no idea how long they had been gone or in which direction they had escaped? A phone call to the Police was essential—if they made for a road in the dark it could cause a nasty accident, after all, there were probably 30 head of cattle, a sizeable herd to be on the wander.

We threw on wellies and jackets and went off armed with torches into the blackness of the night. We stumbled along, over paths that were familiar to us in the daylight but now seemed uneven and strange. We could see no further than the beam of the torch allowed. It seemed a hopeless task. We made for the broken wall which lead directly onto the bridle path. Which way had they gone? In one direction was the A361, a fast busy road even at night and in the other direction was the hamlet of Holwell. If they went towards Holwell they would not cause too much damage if they all stayed together, but which way had they gone—that was our dilemma?

We hurriedly made our way towards the road, looking for clues (cowpats in abundance) but there were no obvious signs so we turned back, in the direction of Holwell. There were a few cowpats but nothing of any significance. It was difficult to see anything in the dark and we made our way back into our own fields and walked the boundary, flashing our torches this way and that, into neighbouring fields, hopeful that we might see or hear something.

In the field beyond ours, the 'rape' was shoulder high and it was by pure chance that one of the cows was facing towards us as the torch beam scanned the darkness. The light beam reflected in her eyes. We had them. Thank Goodness! There they all were 'hiding in the rape.' Bryan bellowed at Steed to get round behind them and try to drive them back towards the bridle path. Bryan was to stop them heading towards Holwell and Kyly and I had to go back down the bridle path and open the gate into another of our fields. We were to wait in the darkness, and as they came back down towards us we were to turn them into the field. We were told to turn off our torches until the cows were upon us so as not to startle them as they came round the bend in the path.

In the distance we could hear Bryan grumbling at Steed for 'playing' in the rape. At that time Steed was not very tall and could not see over the top of it without jumping up and down. Surely Bryan realised that he was doing his best? I am convinced that Steed would rather have been tucked up warm in his bed rather than leaping about in a rapeseed field in the middle of the night. The shout went up that the cattle were on the move and they were heading our way. We could not see them but we could surely hear them. The thundering of their hooves as they raced towards us—it sounded like a stampede. I tucked Kyly to one side lest they got past me and suddenly round the bend they came. Torches were switched on and I could see the reflection in their eyes. I waved my stick frantically, shouting and leaping up and down in front of them to make them veer off into the field to my left. Thankfully, they did just that but not before they had scared me witless. Bryan and Steed were right behind them for fear they may turn, driving them on towards me. As the last one snorted and thundered through, the gate was firmly shut behind them. This field had a barbed wire fence around its perimeter so we were sure they would now be safe for the night.

If they were not exhausted by their night time excursion, we certainly were as we hurried back to our beds, shattered but satisfied that they were all safely back where they belonged. A phone call to the Police to satisfy them that all was well and a phone call planned for the morning to our neighbouring Farmer to explain his trampled crop and then we returned to our beds for what was left of the night. You surely had to have stamina to be married to Bryan but at least I could not say that life was dull and boring.

In the light of day Bryan pondered as to why the cows had got out. There was plenty of grass in the field that they had vacated and we had never had problems with the cattle grazing the field before. What had caused them to break out?

We were soon to be enlightened. The last two Limousin cows that Bryan had bought were a little feisty and refused to be lead on a halter. Bryan, with Steed in tow, decided to train them in the enclosed yard. At first, he tied them behind the tractor and slowly drove up and down the yard with them tossing their heads and kicking out in all directions. They did not approve of this! The tractor was certainly a force, to be reckoned with, and they soon calmed down and trotted behind without too much fuss.

Bryan was now satisfied that they would walk quietly on a halter and with Steed dutifully behind him, each alongside one of these huge cows, they proceeded to walk the cows around the enclosed yard.

That done without a hitch, the cows seem to have been mastered. Kyly and I were called from the house to watch 'men folk mastering cows.' They continued to walk them round and round the yard until Bryan had the bright idea of walking them up the lane that ran along the front of our property, a lane that ran parallel with the busy A361.

I thought it a silly idea knowing the temperament of the cows but, as usual, Bryan knew best and out onto the lane they paraded, Bryan in the front, explaining to Steed what he should do. Suddenly a car on the road above, backfired and startled the animals.

It was like something from a cartoon film. The cows picked up speed as did Bryan and Steed. Suddenly Bryans' hat fell off as the gentle trot turned into a gallop. Bryan only had short legs and now they were a blur as he raced to keep up with the startled cow. Faster and faster it went, heading for a stone wall surrounding a neighbour's field. All I could think was 'please let go before you hit the wall.' Bryan was hanging on for dear life, as was Steed, as his cow was following on behind in blind panic. By now Bryan had lost his footing altogether and was being dragged along the track with Steed and his beast in hot pursuit.

Suddenly, at the wall, Bryan was thrown aside and the cow cleared the wall like a racehorse in the Grand National. What a flyer—it sailed over without any effort. I had heard 'the cow jumped over the moon' but thought this was just a nursery rhyme—here I had seen the reality!

Thankfully, Steed's beast was a more normal cow and shuddered to a halt at the obstacle. Not to be beaten (I have already explained how Bryan could never accept failure) Bryan, red faced and sore, limped off to get a bucket of corn to entice them back to the yard without any further dramatics. I have to admit that we ended up laughing yet again, at the spectacle that we had just witnessed. Bryan was always out to prove a point that always made his mistakes, more hilarious than ever.

We stifled our hilarity as he returned barking orders yet again at Steed. This time it was to tell him not to let go of his halter, as if he had! Bryan meanwhile, entered the field with his bucket of corn to retrieve his beast. Halter securely in place, once again, the cows followed Kyly with the bucket of corn, back to the safety of the enclosed yard, no worse for their little escapade. Bryan and Steed, on the other hand, had pulled muscles they didn't even know they had and were heaving for breath from the unexpected exertion.

Would Bryan never learn that he really was no match for a Limousin cow when it came to a battle of strength? The next day Bryan and I moved all the cattle back into the field from which they had originally escaped on that eventful night. Bryan and Steed had been in and fenced off the area with barbed wire as a precaution to stop the whole episode happening again. We watched as they trundled through the gate an raced around the field with one cow in particular in the lead. Which cow was it? You might have guessed it! The very same one that had led Bryan a 'merry dance' down the lane and over the wall. She ran straight to the area of wall that they had broken down previously, with her herd in hot pursuit behind her. She had well and truly taken over as 'boss.'

Due to her ability to jump walls so easily we named her 'Racehorse' and 'Racehorse' she was known as for the rest of her life. Who needed Pedigree names—this one was far more appropriate?

This cow had spirit and Bryan loved her. She proved to be a really good cow throwing off many excellent calves during her lifetime. Although 'Racehorse' was very dear to his heart and destined never to be sold, his all time favourite was a cow called 'Eloise.' We bred her, into our second year on the farm. She was an outstanding beast. She threw off many, many excellent bull calves and was a very good Mother. She produced an abundant supply of milk and Bryan would spend hours talking to her and making a fuss of her. If ever there was a female I could have divorced Bryan over, it was 'Eloise.' He was always far more concerned about her welfare than mine but sometimes he would throw me a morsel of hope when he compared my backside to hers. There was never a thing wrong with 'Eloise' so I felt sure it must have been a compliment!!! Romance and flowery conversations were never strong points of Bryan's. You had to understand him to love him and sometimes the understanding was impossible—I will say no more!

Chapter 46

Wily Fox and Friendly 'Hounds.'

By this time we had accumulated a selection of breeds of both hens and cockerels. There were Emma and Lady, my daughters favourites and as well as 'Reuben' our resident rooster we had 'King Cole' who only strutted his stuff when not in sight of 'Reuben'. We also had a pair of rogue cockerels who were identical to look at. We named them after a set of twins we knew—Norman and Billy. They continually fought with each other and spent most of their time racing headlong in pursuit of each other round and round the yard and fields. They were known affectionately as the 'Road Runners.'

Throughout the Summer months we had to continually search for our fresh eggs as the hens had taken to laying amongst the nettles that edged the fields. It was not too much trouble as our bacon was far more conveniently to hand. Hanging from two large hooks embedded in the beam above our bed was a huge side of bacon draped in muslin. On our bedside table, along with an alarm clock was a large knife placed for convenience. If we fancied a cooked breakfast, the bacon was close at hand and far tastier than anything bought from a local butcher or supermarket. Enormous rashers were hacked off and consumed with relish. The knife was wiped on anything to hand and put back for use next time. Unhygienic you might think in this modern world of healthy, germ free paranoia, but believe me, none of the Family ever suffered from sickness or 'dicky' tummies. Food tasted as we remembered it from our childhood, tasty and wholesome—not for us the 'junk food' of today

One morning, however, we awoke to our first setback. We thought it strange that there did not seem to be any chickens in the yard. We walked up onto the fields and there we found the answer. It looked just like a battlefield with bodies, some headless, everywhere. The fox had paid us a visit.

We all know that animals in the wild have to hunt in order to survive and what would our countryside be like without wild animals? This was not killing for hunger, this was brutal carnage for killing sake. The cunning fox had killed them all. It had eaten some, leaving their carcasses for the morning rooks to peck at. The rest had been left strewn across the fields. Horrified that our daughter may see the fate that had befallen her 'favourites' we hurriedly collected up the evidence and

stuffed the bodies in feed sacks to be burned at the
earliest convenience (whilst the children were at school)

Suddenly from down in the farmyard we heard a familiar
sound—the crowing of 'Reuben.' How has he escaped
when all the others had been so cruelly slaughtered?
He had obviously stayed in the shelter of the stalls that
night and had escaped the voracious attack. Although, at
times, we had cursed his loud raucous crowing, today it
was a joy to behold.

Several times we saw the fox during that day as it sat
either outside the front gates looking defiantly up the
yard or walking across the fields, intrepid as ever. By the
time Bryan had retrieved his gun the 'wily' fox had done
'a runner' and was nowhere to be seen, gone to ground.
We hoped that he had had his fill from our flock and
would move on. In the meantime, to explain the absence
of 'Emma' and 'Lady' to Kyly, we told her that they had
wandered off during the night, frightened by the fox. We
told her that they had found somewhere safer to live and
to think of it as if they had gone on holiday. We told her
that when Bryan eventually killed the fox, they would
probably return.

Lies, you may say, but how else was a little innocent
to cope with the reality. It was just to soften the blow
and when she got older, all would be revealed. She was
actually 25 before she found out but I think she was
more able to cope with the news by then! What do you
mean I was an over protective Mother?

Kyly was upset that her 'friends' had deserted her and each day asked if they had returned. She was disappointed that they had not come back but like all children she was soon distracted by our new arrivals.

We felt that the farm was not complete without a dog. We got together to decide what breed we should have. Bryan was not interested in a dog as he had already got his pet, 'Racehorse.' Steed, Kyly and I got our heads together to decide, but we could not come to a unanimous decision. I liked Great Danes, Steed wanted a Staffordshire Bull Terrier and Kyly wanted an 'Andrex' puppy. Our choices couldn't be more different!

I argued that I was going to be the one to be left looking after them when the children tired of looking after them, I ought to have my choice. Steed put forward his argument and Kyly just loved the Labrador puppy she had seen on the TV, dragging round a toilet roll. How could I argue with that kind of logic? I hated disappointing the children.

I mulled the problem over in my head. Maybe if I got them both what they wanted, it would be a companion for them as they each had to spend many hours at home amusing themselves as we were not within walking distance of any of their friends?

The decision was made after a Family discussion and we were all happy with the outcome.

I then scoured the 'Exchange and Mart' for respective breeders. First of all I found Great Dane breeders in

Kent. We had previously owned a Great Dane that was extremely destructive when left on its own and, with hindsight, had been told it would have been better to have two, to keep other company. With this in mind we visited the breeder who had several 'bitches' on offer. Our first choice was a light coloured fawn pup that was not as boisterous as the rest and then we looked around for another to catch our eye. They were all adorable and it was hard to choose.

Suddenly we heard it coming. It crashed through the open doorway and skidded into the kitchen romping over the top of the other puppies. It was half as big again as all the others but we were assured that it was the same age, just from a different litter.

The two litters, obviously with different 'Dames' had both been sired by the same 'Dog.' Once again, drawn by the spirited nature, Bryan decided that this was to be our second puppy. Deal done, we loaded them into the back of the car where we hoped they would settle down for the long journey home. They slept most of the way, for which we were grateful, but when they woke they snapped and snarled at each other continuously. We wondered if we had made the right choice as it was very obvious that they did not like each other. That situation did not change throughout their lives.

The more boisterous one was darker in coat and we named her 'Amber', the lighter one was 'Topaz.'

Having got my choice of dogs, the children were anxious that they should get theirs. Once again I was scouring the pages of the 'Exchange and Mart' with this in mind. Steed was very particular about his choice. I had stipulated that all the animals should be bitches to save any complications but he wanted a particular coloured Staff. He wanted a black Staff with a white blaze on it's chest. I rang several breeders before we located one to suit but just before this, the stories hit the headlines in all the National Newspapers that made me unsure we were doing the right thing.

Staffordshire Bull Terriers were classified, along with 'Pit Bulls' as being vicious and dangerous dogs. This unsettled me, as we often had young children to play from the local Primary School and the last thing I wished to do was to endanger any of these little ones.

Steed was extremely disappointed but I explained to him that I had not ruled it out completely. I would make further enquiries. I rang vets and several breeders and they all said exactly the same. Staffs, if treated right, were no different to any other breed of dog. Any breed of dog could be made to be vicious and some irresponsible owners were training Staffs to be 'fighting dogs.' As long as owners were treating their animals correctly—Staffs were no more a threat to other dogs or children than any other breed. This was good enough for me. Everybody, without exception, were of the same opinion. I located a breeder in Wales and Bryan took Steed down to collect one black puppy. I had to work that particular day so was unable to go. On my return, as Steed opened the gate, he said his puppies were fine and sleeping in a box in the kitchen. Did I hear right? Did he say 'puppies' not puppy.' I looked at him hard and he grinned at me. I had heard right after all. I parked up and followed him in to meet our new additions and find out why there were two instead of the agreed one. Curled up tightly together were the two little bundles, one black with a white blaze down its chest and the other was a brown and black brindle. How come?

Bryan explained that when they arrived at Towyn on Kinmel Bay, in Wales, the puppies were being kept in a shopping trolley and he had not been happy about how they were being looked after.

The breeder had reserved this black one for us and had only the runt of the litter left that nobody seemed to want. The breeder said it would be dead before the day was done as he wasn't going to keep it. A puppy with a death sentence—not if Bryan had anything to do with it. He would take the two of them home. We now had 2 Great Danes and 2 Staffs. We wondered if maybe Kyly would take to the second pup and forget about having her Labrador but we had no such luck. She was adamant that because we had got what we wanted she should have the same. I could see her point and I was back scouring the 'Exchange and Mart' once again.

I found a breeder in Middlesex and we made an appointment to pick up the last of her litter of fawn 'bitches.' We heard her before we saw her, yelping in her compound. We should have known that that was the reason she was the last of her litter to go. Kyly fell in love with her and we took her home. She was adorable but she just would not stop barking. It would go on, day and night. We had her checked out at the vets, as we had done with all our the others, and she was given a clean bill of health. As she grew she barked a little less but the only time you could guarantee any peace was when she was asleep and then she used to dream noisily.

Greedy! There was never a greedier dog in existence and she would upset all the other dogs by guarding her own feed bowl whilst raiding all the others. Although not an aggressive dog herself she would create bad feelings amongst the others and they would 'shun' her so she became a 'loner.' Whilst all the others would sleep together amongst the straw in the stalls, she would always be found a distance from them sleeping on her own. Not all the dogs got on, the two Great Danes treated each other with a distant distain having their own territory at either end of the kitchen when they were allowed indoors. If their paths crossed too closely a low growl or a throaty snarl could be heard warning the other not to take advantage. They were absolutely fine when apart.

None of the dogs were aggressive to humans although they each had their own character. Amber, was the largest and most boisterous. She loved humans and tried to talk to me in a variation of yelps and friendly growls. Topaz, was the strongest of them all, silent but masterful. She was second to only me, in the pecking order of the Pack.

Towyn (the black Staff) and Kimnel (the brindle), named after where they were born in Wales, were as different as chalk and cheese. Towyn was confident, inquisitive and hated other black dogs whereas Kimnel was painfully shy and a nightmare to take for a walk. As every dog approached she would plant her backside on the pavement and refuse to move. She was also very nervous around humans although we had never harmed her or even raised our voices at her. She would cower down when we approached her as if she were frightened and we often wondered if something had happened to her before we bought her to make her so nervous of humans. It was such a shame as she was such a gentle natured dog but she never altered no matter how much love we gave her. It was embarrassing when we were out and we often found ourselves explaining our actions to people when she cowered away from us. We later found out that this particular bitch had hidden talents that had to be seen to be believed, but I will explain this at a later date.

Kandi, the Labrador, did not have an aggressive bone in her body. Greedy she may have been but she was affectionate and loved to be made a fuss of. The only problem we had with her was her constant barking. No matter what we tried, it did not work. As we did not have close neighbours and those that we did have were either weekenders or were out working—her barking did not bother anyone but us. We hoped that she would grow out of it.

The Great Danes and the Staffs were marvellous guard dogs. Kandi, on the other hand, would have preferred to make friends, no matter whether friend or foe, and would have probably affectionately licked any intruder to death. It worked very well and we were never afraid to leave the property knowing only too well that anybody in their right mind would not tackle the pack of dogs, the Great Danes standing over 6ft tall at the farm gate or the yapping Staffs with their rows of menacing white teeth. I won't mention Kandi, who most of the time was too idle to walk that far down to the front gate. She preferred a much easier life.

Chapter 47

The Joys of Farming

*A*ll our spare time was taken up with farming—it was a full time job in itself as we were also running a scaffold company that employed 40 scaffolders.

As the number of farm animals increased we found it impossible to keep on top of things and decided the time had come to employ a farmhand to help. We put the word about locally and was approached by Sam, a middle aged local man who had plenty of experience of all aspects of farming. He proved to be a marvellous addition to our team. He had patience in abundance with the children and was willing to do anything to help. He always had a smile on his face and a cheery word for all. Nothing was too much trouble and he soon became like a member of the Family.

Kandi, from the day we collected her, always liked to sleep underneath the tractor. Sam loved Kandi, and she would follow him around as he completed his duties, never far from his side. Due to her habit of curling up under the tractor, Sam would always check her whereabouts before he moved it.

One evening, just as I returned home from the office, Sam was just about to start the evening feed. As I opened the farm gate, he climbed into the tractor and waved to me as he did so. Had I taken his mind of what he was doing? I am not sure to this day why it happened but Sam turned the key and pulled forward. I cannot describe the noise that Kandi made as the wheel went over her head, it was horrendous.

We leapt as one from our respective vehicles and went to the aid of the injured dog.
'Injured,' I did say—not dead as you would expect. She lay whimpering as Sam cradled her in his lap, tears streaming down his face. He couldn't apologise enough as he tried to wipe the tyre tread mark from her head. Accidents, just happen, we knew he would never have intentionally hurt her.

Once she had got over the shock of what had happened, Kandi, miraculously staggered to her feet, shook her head, wagged her tail and waddled into the kitchen to look for food and water. Incredible, you might think, but that is exactly what happened! I thought about calling the vet but she seemed none the worse for the experience—what an amazing dog! We kept an eye on her all the evening but she seemed to be acting quite normally, she was still raiding the other dog's food bowls so there didn't seem to be too much wrong with her.

I think it shook Sam far more than it shook her and even though she was only a puppy, her bones must have been made of 'rubber.' She carried on and lived to the ripe old age of 16 years but never lost the tread of the tractor tyre mark that was a constant reminder of what a miraculous dog she was.

Sally, our resident sow, did a grand job of producing many litters of piglets. She was a very good Mother and managed to raise most of them. As much as cattle were Bryan's main interest, Sally and her piglets was Steed's. One day after returning from school, he popped into the stall to see how she was doing, only to find her laid in the straw covered in purple blotches. She was obviously unwell and the vet, summoned. His diagnosis was that she was suffering from erysipelas and prescribed antibiotics.

We dosed her up and checked on her throughout the evening but there seemed to be very little change in her condition. Steed was distraught and insisted that he should stay with her through the night.

In the morning when we went to check on her, she was up and about, back to her normal self, which is more than could be said about Steed. There he was curled up, in the manger that ran along the back wall, fast asleep in the straw. He could not have slept very well, as he was very tired when he awoke but overjoyed to see the improvement in Sally. Sally contracted erysipelas several times during her lifespan, but Steed had learned his lesson and had enough faith in the antibiotics to pull her through. He never felt it necessary to sleep with the sow again. It was understandable though, as Sally was more like a pet to him, he could often be seen walking her round the yard on a lead. Usually when he took the lead off her, she would obediently wander back to her stall and make herself comfortable in the straw.

One Sunday, we had invited my Parents over for lunch. Dad loved it on the farm but Mum was a town lover and felt we were far too isolated and countrified for her taste. Steed had been outside with Sally when I called him in for his meal.

We had just sat down to eat when we heard her coming. She was grunting and snuffling as she made her way up the passage from the back door. The door always left open during daylight hours. Suddenly the door to the passage burst open and up the two steps, clambered Sally

We all knew what a stickler for hygiene my Father was, but nobody said a word. We all carried on eating our dinner as if nothing had happened. Sally, waddled round the table snuffling as she went—we all kept silent as if we had not seen her. Dad looked horrified and put down his knife and fork. He declared "In case nobody else had noticed were we aware that there was a pig wandering round our kitchen?"

We all burst out laughing and Steed ushered the offending animal out of the kitchen and back to her stall where she was securely locked in. Dad did eventually see the funny side of it but he did think it was a strange way of going on.

On another occasion, my sister had been visiting with her brood of young daughters. They loved looking round the farm and seeing all the animals at close quarters. We had, at this time, a very tame young heifer calf, that used to wander the yard. The girls enjoyed stroking and making a fuss of her and she would react by nuzzling them back. When the meal was ready, I called them all in and yes, you have guessed it—the calf followed them in. It was a lot easier allowing it in, than getting it out!

The children thought it hilarious having a calf indoors and it made their day. After a lot of pushing and shoving, we finally managed to manoeuvre her up the long hallway and back out into the yard. She got her own back on us by licking the windows much to the children's delight.

To other people, it might seem strange to have the animals in the house but to us it was quite normal to find a stray chicken on the kitchen table or to chase piglets out of the house. It may have had something to do with never shutting or locking doors—but we never found the need, as the dogs running the yard were deterrent enough to keep out strangers. It was a pity it did not work so well with the other animals!

Chapter 48

The Joys of Farming—continued

*M*y role on the farm was general dog's body, I was under no illusions as to my importance.

Bryan was the Master and I, a mere minion. When animals needed moving or separating, I was a necessary member of the team. On one such occasion, we had pigs in a lower field and cows in the top field. Bryan decided he wanted to bring a particular sow down off the field and put it in a stall. The logistics of this move meant driving the sow up into the field of cows, taking it through their field and then bringing it down through a series of gates into the yard. To actually say it sounds easy but the reality was a lot different.

It was always my job to do the running whilst Bryan held the gate, he was forever reminding me that every job needed a 'foreman.'

I spent the next hour herding this particular sow towards the gate only to have it veer off to either side at the last minute. I was doing my best amidst a torrent of abuse because I was either too close or too far away from the sow. 'Run faster—Slow down!' I was never in the right place at the right time. I was red faced and shattered when Bryan decided that I was useless and maybe I could do something less technical like holding the gate. What a relief—or was it?

Cows are very nosey creatures and because of all the activity in the pig field, they decided that they wanted to watch. They jostled each other on their side of the gate and when Bryan finally got the sow where he wanted her, almost at the gate—I opened it. Oh my goodness, was that a wrong move!

The cows gambolled through into the pig field and once again I was in the doghouse! He let out a shout that would have been heard all the way to the Main Road. I was everything useless he could lay his tongue to. His face was red with anger and he screamed at me to get out of his sight and return to the house. I am nothing, if not stubborn and I stood my ground. Who the hell did he think he was shouting and ordering me about? Again, he screamed at me and threatened that if I did not do as I was told—he would make me! I screamed back that I was going nowhere. The next minute he had grabbed an armful of stone from the top of the wall and started to hurl it at me. Well, two could play at that game. As quickly as he threw it, I threw it back at him.

We could easily be seen from the Main Road and certainly heard as Bryan was not the quietest of men and I was really fired up. We stood there for several minutes hurling abuse and rocks at each other until suddenly we realised how stupid we must look to the passing traffic. We burst out laughing and decided to leave the animals where they were until Steed and Kyly returned from school. I guess we needed more bodies.

A while back we had taken in some orphan lambs which I had bottle fed until they were old enough to graze the fields. When they had grown enough we let them loose to graze the field with the cows throughout the Summer months. When they were suitably fattened, the slaughter man, who was a friend of Bryans, came to help round them up.

Bryan and Paul spent all afternoon chasing the woolly critters round the field with very little success. Paul decided that the only way was, to get a shepherd with a dog.
That sounded far too sensible for Bryan! Who needed a shepherd and dog when he had his Family who could do exactly the same?

He bade farewell to his friend who said he would ring Bryan in the morning with the number of a shepherd.

Bryan determined, not to be beaten by a few sheep, told us that after our evening meal we would try to round them up again, all of us this time. He thought about it whilst eating and then came up with the idea of taking up onto the field a length of orange plastic netting such as we used on the scaffolding. In theory it sounded fine but the reality, like a lot of Bryan's schemes, was a different matter.

Steed and Kyly caught hold of either end and I was placed strategically in the middle. All we had to do was surround the sheep and drive them down into the yard. Where was Bryan, you may ask, while we were running our legs off? Yes, you have guessed it—he was the shepherd and we were his 'dogs.' This way and that, we ran as he barked commands—and the evening shadows fell across the fields. Soon it was so dark that had the sheep's wool been any darker we would not have been able to see them at all, but the chase went on.

By now it was pitch black and although we could no longer see Bryan, we could unfortunately still hear him. He was placed centrally in the field, barking commands continually. Although we were all doing our utmost, the sheep were always one step ahead.

At one point, unable to see in the darkness, I fell headlong over a feeding trough, falling into a heap of unmentionable. My shins grazed and covered from head to toe in smelly muck, sympathy was not forthcoming. I was reprimanded for fooling about when there was work to be done!

I am convinced that the sheep only allowed us to 'rugby tackle' them to the ground out of sheer sympathy for us.

They knew he would not give up until they had been caught.

We went to bed that night, aching and sore and Bryan's only comment was, "who needed a shepherd and dog?"

Next day when the slaughter man rang Bryan smugly told him that the sheep were all ready in the stall waiting to go. He went on to tell him that they had all been rounded up without too much bother! Who was he kidding? The only thing that he had used was his voice but the 'dogs' never thought they would ever recover, we hurt in places we never knew we had. Oh, the joy of farming!

Chapter 49

A House Warming!

I quite often ran out of hours during daylight to finish all my chores and would work until the early hours catching up with my paperwork.

One evening, I was working at the kitchen table where I had been since 9pm. Bryan had spent his evening down in Burford drinking with his cronies until late and arrived home at about 1.30am. I was still engrossed in my figure work when he returned and had not noticed the kitchen filling with smoke. He coughed and spluttered as he entered the kitchen and made his way to the boiler room to check all was well. There was a circular disc on the flue pipe that had a habit of slipping down allowing smoke to escape. This was the culprit. Bryan slid it back into place and we made our way to bed.

My routine in the morning was always the same. I awoke early, turned towards the window to check the weather (we had no need to draw curtains, we had no neighbours) and then I would rise ready to tackle a new day. This morning was no different. I opened my eyes, stretched and turned towards the window.

Oh my Goodness! What I saw shook me to the core. Huge red and orange flames were shooting past our window. I shouted at Bryan that we were on fire and as one, we leapt into our clothes. Now fully awake we could hear timbers crackling and falling and our first thought was for the children. Their bedrooms were located at the end of a long hallway, Steed's to the right, next to the airing cupboard and Kyly's right at the end. We banged on Steed's door as we raced past to get Kyly. The shouting had alarmed him and he sleepily opened his door. Kyly, sleeping peacefully, was snatched up and wrapped in her dressing gown.

We collected Steed on the way and made our way down the stairs unable to see where we were going through dense smoke. Bryan took the children out into the safety of the yard as I grabbed the house phone from the window sill to phone the Fire Service. It was only when I was trying to see the numbers on the phone that I realised I had left my glasses on my bedside table in the panic. Due to my terrible eyesight they are always the last thing I take off at night and normally the first thing I put on in the morning. Well, this was not a normal morning but thank goodness for my Girl Guide training that allowed me to find the numbers without too much trouble. I dialled 999, asked for the Fire Service, gave precise instructions on the whereabouts of the farm and felt a wonderful sense of relief. The Firemen would soon be here as they were only in Burford, just up the road.

Standing back in the yard we had a better idea of what was happening. The roof was burning the whole length of the house but the fire seem to be centred on the boiler room which was located behind our bedroom wall. Thank goodness the house had such thick walls or I may not be here today to write this story.

On getting the children out of danger, I realised that without my spectacles I could not function and without his wallet, Bryan also could not function. As soon as he realised the predicament we were in, without a second thought he raced back in, up the stairs to retrieve both items from the smoke filled bedroom.

With hindsight, we were aware of how stupid this was on his part, the slogan resounding in our ears, 'Get out and stay out! My need for my glasses in order to do the most basic of tasks and his need of money to sort out this huge problem were his only thoughts as he stupidly risked life and limb. Common sense seemed to go out of the window and distorted priorities seem to fill the void. Once more safely outside, his wallet tucked deep into his jacket pocket and my glasses perched firmly on my nose we were ready to face the trauma head on.

We heard the fire engine coming, blue light flashing and the siren disturbing the early morning birdsong. What a wonderful dedicated team they were. They immediately took charge of the situation and went into action. Hoses were trained on the building as more fire engines arrived from surrounding areas complete with a chemical tender to deal with all the stored chemicals that were kept in the boiler room.

Although only part time firemen, they knew their stuff and worked professionally to douse the flames. Being a typical young lad, Steed, enjoyed watching the firemen at work but Kyly was distraught. She was convinced that the house was trying to kill us and I had to take her to a neighbour to get her away from the vicinity. She was inconsolable. It took her many months to come to terms with the fire and she never entered our bedroom again. It had a lasting effect on her.

The dogs, on the other hand, could not understand what was happening and ran into the blazing house where they cowered in the kitchen and refused to budge. They had to be forcibly removed and we shut them in the stalls for their own safety.

We were very lucky to have woken when we did as the damage was contained mostly in the boiler room area, the flying freehold and the length of the roof. The living quarters downstairs, apart from the kitchen, although blackened by the smoke, had very little damage. A clean and a coat of paint would soon have those rooms back to normal. The kitchen was a different matter as the fire had severely damaged our bedroom. Sitting at the kitchen table, we were able to see the sky through the immense hole gaping above us. This was novel until it rained and we all had to sit in raincoats with umbrellas.

Eating egg and bacon breakfast under an umbrella is an unforgettable experience when you are doing it in the comfort (or in this case, discomfort) of your own home. The children thought it was great fun. We, on the contrary, found it a great inconvenience. It was bad enough having to remain there to feed and water the animals but it was a major job cleaning the smoke blackened rooms whilst trying to continue to run the business.

An investigation was done to try to establish the cause of the fire. You've guessed it—it was the boiler. We were told that it had not been installed correctly, which is why it had been smoking and now, this was the result. Maybe we should have got it tested when we moved in but hindsight is a wonderful thing.

We then began the mammoth task of pricing up all the work that needed to be done for the insurance company.

I am not sure where the loss adjusters were getting their figures from but it certainly was not from any builder in the 'real world.' Over the next few months many arguments were had and many loss adjusters were verbally 'thrown out of the house' as tempers flared. We sought prices from various builders tweaking the specification trying to come close to the insurance offer. It was impossible!

During all this time we were obviously not allowed to start the re-building and had to resort to putting a tarpaulin over the gaping roof as winter crept in. That in itself caused a problem as quite often when the new boiler fired up the tarpaulin could be seen smouldering on the roof and had to be moved. It was a good job that we had a scaffolding company which enabled us easy access to this or another major fire could easily have been on the cards.

We still had our main office in Didcot at this time and shortly after the fire, normal service resumed and I returned to work.

It was not uncommon, at this time, to arrive home to find a builder ensconced in my kitchen, plans extended the length of the kitchen table, deep in discussion with Bryan. This particular evening was no exception. I parked my car up in front of the kitchen window and although I had not noticed a car in the vicinity, I could see a couple of strangers in conversation with Bryan.

I bustled in with shopping I had collected en route, saying "Hello" as I entered. I pulled up short as before me were the strangest pair I had ever clapped eyes on. There was a young lad dressed very scruffily—holey jumper, frayed trousers legs but more surprisingly wearing only one grubby sock. His trousers had obviously been bought for another as they were far too short and exposed his worn over, worn out shoes. One foot covered by a red and green sock which had seen better days and one black, dirty foot.

The older man accompanying him was even stranger. He had long straggly hair which grew into a long straggly beard. He had on a brown overcoat that almost swept the floor, tied up in the middle with baler twine above long pointed toed shoes. His face was pinched and his hands were long and boney. My first thought was that Bryan had brought home a 'tramp or two.' There was no other explanation as our friends and acquaintances did not look like this.

I was stunned into silence and listened to the conversation that ensued. They were discussing the re-building of the house. Surely he could not be a builder? Where did Bryan find these specimens? As I turned to put the kettle on Bryan asked me to take down the 'gentleman's particulars. I grabbed a notelet from the side and asked his name. "I be Tom Fudge" he declared with a strong Gloucestershire accent as he got up to leave. I asked if he had a phone number and was told the name of a Public House where I could leave a message for him. What a strange procedure—it hardly instilled confidence in me. I went to show him out and walked down the passage to the back door. They followed me part of the way and disappeared into the door less boiler room.

I wondered what they were doing? I could not have guessed. They said 'Goodbye' as they climbed through the frame of the window (we were still waiting for the glass to be replaced after the fire) and disappeared across the fields. I stood and watched them go in amazement—had I imagined the whole scene—who leaves a property through a window? They were bazaar!

I returned to Bryan thinking that this must be a huge joke, but found out that this chap had been recommended. I am not sure who by but somehow he did not fill me with confidence and I persuaded Bryan to carry on with his search. I really did not want that strange pair in my house ever again. The search for a builder continued.

Chapter 50

Neighbours from Hell

We did eventually engage a builder whose price came somewhere near the compromised price of the loss adjusters. Materials arrived on site and work began. It was not an easy journey throughout the re-building as Bryan found fault at every twist and turn and finally threw the builder off site. Bryan came to an agreement on a settlement figure in order to engage his own craftsmen to complete the job in hand. It was an awful shame that in the rebuilding it had taken some of the character from the building. ie: floors were now straight not sloping and the old fashioned ' carter's games' carved into the wood in the flying freehold were now a distant memory destroyed in the fire, ashes to ashes, dust to dust.

We persevered with our search for more competent tradesmen and because of his contacts through the scaffolding Bryan was able to engage more suitable workmen who completed the rebuilding to our satisfaction.

This rebuilding caused more problems with our immediate neighbours than you could ever imagine. You would honestly think that we had set fire to the place just to inconvenience them! They complained at every opportunity and when it came to replacing the upper floor of the flying freehold we were refused access to their barn to enable us to place and fix the floor joists. How were we supposed to span such a large space when all we had was a gaping hole to work with?

They stated that it was not their problem and therefore they were not interested in helping us. They confirmed their unhelpful attitude by padlocking every access to prevent us entering the grounds of their property. I am afraid that it would take more than an awkward neighbour to prevent Bryan doing as he wished and we waited patiently until the 'outsiders' returned to their London home. They had no sooner disappeared from sight when a phone call was made to the carpenter and small scaffold towers were lowered into place for when he arrived. In no time at all joists were in place, towers removed and a new floor was laid. We would have liked to see our neighbours faces when they returned, padlocks all still in place, no forced entry, but a floor miraculously in place.

The one-sided feud with our neighbours continued. We got on very well with everyone else in the neighbourhood but for whatever reason they had taken

an instant dislike to us and there was nothing we could
do about it. We tried on several occasions to be polite
and friendly but our efforts fell on deaf ears. The lady, if
she wanted to complain about something would come to
our front gate, wait for Bryan to appear before shouting
"My man, my man" at him to draw his attention. To
start with Bryan tried to reason with her but there was
no reasoning and finally Bryan lost his temper and told
her in no uncertain terms that he was not 'her man' and
would she please address him by his name. She flounced
off in a huff. We tried hard to befriend them but there
was no pleasing them and Bryan decided that he had had
enough of their stupidity.

They had bought the front house as a country retreat but
surely if you choose to move to the country you have to
be prepared to put up with country ways. I remember on
one occasion in particular when we had been notified
that they were expecting friends down from London
for the weekend. We had just separated the cows and
calves and there was a lot of bleating going on as they
got used to being parted. As anyone in farming will tell
you this is always a noisy period but it only lasts a couple
of days while the animals get used to the separation.
There is nothing that can be done, it is part and parcel
of the cycle of keeping and raising cattle. That was not
good enough for our neighbours, they demanded that
we do something about the noise. Bryan obliged them
by going out into the field and shouted at the cattle to
keep quiet as they were disturbing our neighbours. He
tried but failed miserably. Due to the imminent arrival of
their friends we were also asked to do something about

the smell. Were they suggesting that we smell? No! They were referring to our pigs!

Bryan, tongue in cheek, explained that he had given them all a deodorant but could not force them to use them. He then added insult to injury by cleaning them all out and placing the slurry tank next to the wall beyond which was their patio area where they would be eating 'al fresco.'

Bryan got on well with most people but he was not a man to cross.

We heard car doors slam as visitors arrived but in no time at all, friends were being ushered back into vehicles and whisked away, no doubt to eat in one of the many hostelries of the Cotswolds. There really was no need for bad feeling but we were not going anywhere so it would have been better to come to some understanding rather than declare all out war.

On another occasion Bryan had taken his gun up onto the fields with the intention of shooting a rabbit or two for dinner. He was aterrible hunter and never actually shot anything. On this particular day he was game to shoot anything, he just wanted to prove himself. He aimed at passing pigeons, overhead rooks, the odd crow and several rabbits. All evaded him except one huge fat rook which had been perched on our neighbour's chimney stack. I am not vouching for the fact that Bryan shot it, not with his track record, but the gun went off and the rook disappeared down the chimney and into the room below. I am more convinced that it died of a heart attack or shock but in Bryan's eyes it was a definite hit. He thought the moment even sweeter when we ran to the neighbour's window to see how much soot the unfortunate bird had taken down into the room. Bryan was over the moon. The soot had hit the hearth with such force that it had slid across the rug in front of the fireplace and traces could be seen half way across the room. Not one to usually be smug he walked away saying, "That would teach them for looking down their noses at us." He almost had a schoolboy sense of of revenge and as I have said before, he was not a man to cross.

We began to see less and less of our neighbours from London. I believe their dream of an ideal 'getaway' in the country proved not to be so ideal after all.

So many people who buy cottages in the country have no idea how the countryside works, but what rights do they think they have to try to change things? We have now lived out this way for 25 years and have never fallen out with any other neighbours or acquaintances, that must say something in our favour. I think we were extremely unlucky with our neighbours at that time as I am sure they would agree, we must have seemed unwittingly to be their neighbours from hell.

Chapter 51

New Suites For Old

When we were furnishing our farmhouse we bought a black leather suite for our sitting room. It was not of a traditional style in keeping with the farmhouse but it was comfortable and leather and Bryan took a shine to it. We had been very satisfied with it until one day we had a visit from the son who had bought our previous house. He decided to move on to a 'yuppy' apartment with his girlfriend, stating that as he had decided he didn't particularly want children in the foreseeable future, our previous house was too big for the two of them. The 'yuppy' apartment was ultra modern and the red velvet suite that he had inherited from us previously did not suit the image he was trying to create. I was not sure where this conversation was leading but eventually the "punch line" was revealed. Could he do a swap with us, we to have the red velvet one back and him to take the black leather one in its exchange. Children—who in their right minds has them!!! Bryan, soft touch as usual, agreed and arrangements were made for delivery. I did manage to ask about the wall to wall wardrobe which I had had in our old bedroom. It seemed that this also was to be discarded so I asked for this to be returned to us. All was agreed and delivery was to take place the following week when the open backed scaffolding lorry was not being used.

I wonder why my belongings always have to be moved in full view of all and sundry when others revel in the privacy of boxed vans?

The designated day of delivery dawned and I was told the items would be delivered after dusk. I was excited about getting my wardrobe back as hanging space in the farmhouse was quite limited. We had our tea and Bryan decided that as he had been feeling unwell during the day he would take himself off to bed early. How fortunate for my son!!!

I had just settled down for the evening when the phone rang. I hurried to answer it expecting to hear my son letting me know an approximate time of arrival. No, that is not what I heard, apologies, why was he apologising?? Oh no, an accident!!!! Was he ok? Was anybody hurt? Amongst his garbled chat I heard the word wardrobe mentioned. What was he saying? Suddenly it all became clear, he was travelling along the road when the wardrobe fell off the back of the lorry and smashed to smithereens. My beautiful wardrobe!! What is it about me and wardrobes and backs of lorries? I had a feeling of déjà vu!

When our son eventually arrived at the farm it was the fastest delivery and collection on record. I had never seen my son move so fast, he was afraid his father would wake and then he would have some serious explaining to do. Now I was left to do the explaining as he disappeared into the night. Oh well, what are Mums for? We do, at times have our uses. It seems my son on his upwardly mobile spiral needed a black leather suite far more than we did, so we settled for our old comfortable red velvet suite and that did us proud for the next few years.

Chapter 52

Changing Times

We had all adapted well to our new way of life. We were kept busier but in a different way, we pulled together as a family and although we were not quite "The Waltons", we were all very happy.

We should have known better than to relax and enjoy life, that never seemed to be our way. Outside influences soon began to encroach on our idyllic lifestyle. Interest rates and mortgage rates soon began to climb in the governments' attempt to stabilise the economy. The construction trade hit crisis point as fewer contracts were being started due to all the uncertainty. At first we were lucky enough, with our wealth of contacts but as the economy took a nosedive so did our business. We struggled on regardless, everyday becoming a little harder to keep the wolf from the door. Our mortgage payments doubled and Bryan's blood pressure spot above his nose glowed like a beacon. We knew he was worried but he would never discuss his worries in case he worried us, but he went about things in a completely irrational way. He started to drink heavily and could often be found in the public houses of Burford, slightly the worse for wear. He got in with a drinking school and went from bad to worse. Unable to face the inevitable, he sank lower and lower into a depression which would manifest itself in two ways. He would either be sullen and moody snapping at every remark made or he would erupt into terrible rages when it was safer to run for cover rather than stand and try to negotiate. They were extremely difficult times, he began to sell everything that wasn't bolted down, even the Cotswold stone walls that surrounded our property were sold to help make ends meet. He tried everything to keep us afloat, he sold pigs, lambs and most of his cattle but still we struggled. The pressure on him grew daily. He spent hours sat up in the fields, back against the wall in more ways than one. We began to dread the phone ringing or the knock at the door which inevitably meant we had bailiffs visiting. It was a dreadful time for all, we laid off as many scaffolders as was necessary as contracts came to an end and felt dreadful for doing it as some of the scaffolders had become like family members, they had been with us since the beginning of our company.

We tried to keep it together for the children but as the noose tightened the pressure got to us and life seemed to be a continuous row about money.

One evening, after yet another row, Bryan stormed
out and did what had become natural to him, he went
drinking in Burford. The children went to bed and
I sat at the kitchen table trying to make sense of our
mounting debts. If only we could raise some money
from anywhere—I was past caring whether it was by
legal means or not. I was at the end of my tether trying
to keep up appearances but falling apart inside as I tried
to cope with Bryan's irrational behaviour and temper
tantrums. Don't get me wrong, I could understand
where he was coming from, he was slowly losing his
dream.

Suddenly I was woken from my reverie of 'robbing
banks' or 'inheriting from a long lost relative' by the
front door being slammed shut. He staggered into the
kitchen and I could immediately tell from his attitude
that the drink had done nothing at all to raise his spirits,
in fact, he was now quite aggressive. I asked him if he
wanted anything, thinking that my best plan was to
make a hasty exit to bed, if he did not require anything.
The comment that followed literally put the 'fear of
God in me'.

He remarked that yes he did want something, he wanted
me and the children dead! I was sure deep down he
didn't mean it, I know he loved us all dearly, but the
pressure had finally unhinged him and there was no
reasoning with him in this mood. At that time his
shotgun and cartridges were always kept down in the
boiler room away from the main house and boy was I
grateful for that fact. As he lurched towards the boiler
room threatening allsorts, I made a hasty retreat in order

to get the children to a place of safety as I felt sure on this occasion his threats were more sinister.

I woke the children, told them to throw on their dressing gowns and slippers and to follow me as quietly as they could. We crept downstairs and fled through the front door and into the black of night. I thought the obvious place for him to look for us would be the stalls opposite so I ushered the children through the side gate and up onto the fields. As we crept past the washing line we heard him stumbling across the yard, shouting obscenities as the torch beam moved this way and that in the night sky as he tried to search us out. When Bryan's 'head went' he was not in his right mind and I had no doubt in my mind that if he caught up with us it would be "curtains" for us all as I was sure he would then turn the gun on himself. He may have seen this as the only way out of the financial mess we found ourselves in but I was convinced that there must be another way. My children and I were not ready to meet our Maker yet, no matter what Bryan had decided for us.

The gate creaked open behind us as we ran further on into the next field. He was still screaming abuse as he stumbled up the slope hot on our heels. He fired the gun. I could not take any chances that the torch beam might just disclose our whereabouts so I got the children to climb over the wall between our field and our neighbour's vegetable patch. We lay flat to the ground. I am sure you are all wondering what the children were doing, were they not frightened by all this night time activity, being chased by a deranged father wielding a shotgun threatening to kill them and their Mother? You forget that the children had grown up with Bryan's raging temper and knew instinctively when to keep quiet. Kyly, bless her, had brought along her dolly in a Moses basket and now whispered to her "not to cry as Daddy was going to shoot us if he found us". The children remained prone on the ground as I ventured to peek over the wall to gauge where he was. I could not see him but I could still hear him and knew where he was only by the torch beam being shone this way and that as he scoured the field for his prey.

The gun fired again, but luckily not in our direction. A string of obscenities broke the stillness of the night and faded away as he made his way back towards the house. We remained where we were, after all a move too soon could literally be 'the death of us'.

I knew that Bryan's rages left him exhausted and that, with the combination of drink, once he sat down he would soon sink into oblivion. I could not chance him waking with the gun still in his possession so I explained quickly to the children that I would go down to the house, wait for him to drop off, retrieve the gun and cartridges and then return for them when it was safe. I had to warn them that if they heard the gun go off and I did not return they were to seek safety by knocking our neighbours up. With their whispered promises floating in the air I went forth on my mission to disarm my deranged husband.

I climbed the wall and keeping close to it crept slowly back towards the house, my heart in my mouth, in case he lay in wait for me. I stopped every few yards to listen. I could hear nothing so I crept on. When I reached the yard it was more difficult to be silent as I had to get through the creaky gate, I moved it slowly to one side and it must have realised my predicament as it hardly

made a sound. I peeked in through the floor length
sitting room window, so far so good, he was not in there.
The light was on in the kitchen as we had left it, so I
tentatively crept forward to peer in, hopeful of not being
seen.

There he was, sat in an upright kitchen chair, eyes shut,
mouth wide open, the gun propped up beside him. He
had managed to take off his wax jacket and that was laid
across the table with no doubt spare cartridges in the
pockets. I held my breath as I opened the front door and
stealthily made my way down the hallway, through the
gateway that spanned the double doors, a gate in place to
prevent the dogs having access to the rest of the house,
on into the kitchen. I froze as he mumbled something
and changed position. I·had to get to the gun, I moved
nearer to it hardly able to breathe for fear he might
hear me. So far so good. I reached out and yes I had the
barrel firmly in my grasp. I eased it from its position
and crept towards to table for the jacket. I decided it
would be easier to take that with me in order to empty
the pocket of the cartridges. I retraced my footsteps to
the front door and beyond. I buried the weapon and
its ammunition in an unused stall, deep in the straw. It
would at least be safe there for the time being. Now to
rescue my children. I found them exactly where I had
left them, flat on the ground behind the wall with Steed
reassuring Kyly that I would be ok. I explained that the
gun was hidden away where Bryan wouldn't find it but
we still had to creep back to our beds without waking
him, if he woke now we could still not be sure what
mood he would be in. Our homeward journey was made
in silence and once indoors the children made their way
quietly back to their beds and considering the upheaval

of the night, were surprisingly soon in the land of nod. I went to my bed but I could not sleep, I wondered where it would all end? What would the morning bring? From sheer exhaustion I eventually succumbed to sleep.

Chapter 53

The Way Forward

The next morning Bryan was up before any of us stirred. When I caught up with him he was feeding the animals, just as if nothing had happened. I wondered if he had realized what he had done or if he had even remembered. I helped him to finish feeding and then we returned to the house for breakfast, normality had resumed.

I could not forget the seriousness of what had occurred in the night and decided to tackle him about it when the opportunity occurred. I did not want to bring anything up before the children were away from the house in case it caused yet another row.

The children tired from their night time activities, came down for breakfast and after a shake of my head and a withering look, kept any questions they might have had

safely zipped behind closed lips. Bryan, unlike the rest
of us was chatting away quite normally, leading me to
believe he could not remember what he had done. If he
could not remember his actions of the previous night just
think of the devastation he would have felt waking up to
the carnage he could have caused if I had not taken his
threats seriously. Him and I need to have a serious chat!
Washed and dressed, the children were soon outside busy
making their own amusement, Steed driving my Suzuki
jeep around the fields, what young boy doesn't like to
get behind a steering wheel and Kyly playing in her
own world of wonderment and pretence. How adaptable
my children were they took everything in their stride,
I suppose it came with the territory of having such a
volatile Father.

With the children out of the way it gave me the
opportunity to tackle Bryan about what he had done. I
made us both a coffee and asked him to sit down because
I needed to discuss something with him. He was never
a 'discussion' kind of man and gave me several reasons
why he did not have time. I thought there was not going
to be an easy way round this so I came right out with
it demanding "Why were you going to shoot us all last
night? Whatever had we done to deserve it?"
Bryan looked visibly shocked and slumped in his chair.
He was staring at me with disbelief. He shook his head
and said he thought it had been a bad dream. I assured
him that it certainly was not a figment of his imagination
and if I had not had the sense to get the children to
a place of safety, today would have been a whole lot
different. He was horrified at what he had put us through
and after a long chat decided that we must do something

positive about the pressure we had been living under before it destroyed us all.

We got together everything that we owed, arranged a meeting with our Bank Manager and decided the only way to go was to put the farm on the market. We would take a step backwards to go forward again.

Chapter 54

Enticement

Once the decision was made we felt much better. It was not an easy path by any means but now we had decided to face up to things. We answered the phone with confidence explaining our circumstances instead of making excuses and forward planned our next moves.

Bryan was not a stupid man by any means and he started to plan for our future. We realised that due to this downturn in our luck, if something was not done, we would find ourselves homeless. We sold anything and everything that was left to sell in an attempt to get a deposit together for our future accommodation. We cut spending to a minimum and gave Sam notice, as apart from not being able to afford to pay him, once all the animals had gone, his job would be redundant. It was a sad day when we said goodbye to him as he had become part of the Family but thankfully he understood the predicament we were in and he wished us Good luck as he left the farm for the last time.

We were desperately treading water, fearing we would drown at any minute. It was no good, it was an uphill struggle going nowhere. We made the decision to sell the scaffolding company. We had several interested buyers and were hopeful that we might both at least, come out of this mess with employment.\

Some buyers faltered in the early stages but two stayed on regardless and our pressure lifted as one company, our preferred choice, were offering quite an attractive package, Our second choice of company waited patiently in the wings. Accountants were brought in and paperwork sifted through, ledgers poured over and already we began to feel that our business was slipping away from us. Claire, our PA soldiered on under the most difficult of circumstances accommodating them at every twist and turn. She was an absolute treasure and we both appreciated her enormously. She was a dizzy blonde, slim with a bubbly personality. Did I trust her with Bryan? Absolutely, without a shadow of a doubt. Sometimes he would take her to lunch and they would quite often banter between them but I never doubted that their relationship was platonic.

One day, one of the more important characters of the new company had a meeting with Bryan, a meeting to discuss our roles in the new company. Bryan was also concerned that Claire be part of the package, making her

job secure. The chap laughed at Bryan, suggesting that
Claire was his 'bit on the side.' Well, that was it!
The new company staff that were in the offices collating
everything were told to leave, the chap in question was
put in his place and Bryan, fuming at the suggestion,
demanded that they all get out and not return as the deal
was off. How dare he cast aspersions on both Bryan's and
Claire's good character. Well, after the showdown and the
dust had settled we were back to square one except now
things were getting even more desperate.

In the end we had no choice but to sell out to the
company waiting in the wings. Their deal by comparison
was rubbish but the expression 'Beggars can't be
choosers' springs to mind. They moved in, agreed that
Claire and I continue working in the office and Bryan's
role was to be overseer of the sites. What we were paid
was a pittance in comparison to the previous deal and
we went to an Abingdon Hotel to pick up the cheque.
We felt moderately rich on the drive home but knew,
even with this, it would not be enough to solve all our
problems.

As I have mentioned before, Bryan was not a foolish
man and had already put plans in place for our future.
He realised by the time everything had been sorted out,
he would end up being blacklisted and unable to get
another mortgage or credit.

We had, by fair means or fowl, managed to accumulate
a little nest egg and had also managed to filter away a
large amount of scaffolding which Bryan had used to
start a new company in our son's name. He could not

chance having his name on any paperwork, but that never stopped Bryan. He had already explained to all his regular customers what was happening re: the new company that he had started up but told everyone to keep quiet about it. They kept their word.

Bryan didn't particularly like the people taking over our company and negotiated a deal by which all the main and existing customers be treated to a weekend away as an enticement for them to remain loyal customers to the new company. It was a little underhanded of Bryan as he had already approached them all with a view to them coming over to our new company once it was up and running.

The suggestion was acknowledged as a very good idea and a coach was booked. It was a wonderful weekend away. We were taken to Sheffield on the Saturday where we were taken to the theatre on arrival to watch a show accompanied with nibbles and drinks. This was followed by a slap up meal in the theatre restaurant after the show. We were then all driven to a top class hotel to spend the night. Next day we were taken on a countryside tour of the Yorkshire Dales and finally finished up at a Grand Country House where we had afternoon tea. Everyone was very pleased with their trip, it had all gone like clockwork. The new owners of the company were very smug in the knowledge that the trip had been so successful and were feeling confident that they had wooed these customers sufficiently to ensure their future business.

Bryan, on the other hand, was feeling ecstatic. He had always felt that the new company had ripped us off and felt justified in this charade, calling it payback time. True to their word all the customers who had enjoyed the free trip to Sheffield followed Bryan and supported <u>our</u> new company.

Our buyers were fuming but business is business and sometimes good service and rapport pay off and I think the saying goes 'better the devil you know' I will certainly state that it was a 'devilish' grin Bryan wore as we returned home from our trip to Sheffield, tired but extremely satisfied.

Chapter 55

The Noose Tightens

*W*orking for the new company was almost the same for Claire and I, we were still doing what we had always done, except the buck did not stop with me so I actually found it less stressful. I no longer had access to the cheque book but was paid a specific wage each week.

Bryan was another matter. From day one he hated not being the Boss but was contracted to stay with the new company for a period of 3 months, longer if he wanted to negotiate a new contract. 3 months was far too long for Bryan and he would never leave the farm before 11am when he was supposed to be on site for 8am. When I was asked where he was I always said he was doing a tour of sites and was never specific, telling them I was not sure in what order he was doing them. We got away with it for a few weeks but never being able to catch up with him made the Bosses lose patience.

Having done a stock check of materials, completed after the sale, the Bosses had an inkling of what Bryan had done. They were now on a witch hunt! Private detectives were engaged to follow Bryan's every move, that meant he had to go to work, if a little late, but at least he was doing a 'little' in order to earn the wages they were paying him. He hated it. One morning, on stepping out the front door, the sight of the vehicle parked on the lane at the end of our farmyard instigated an immediate reaction. Bryan dropped his trousers and mooned at them. I am not sure that that was the picture they were looking for as the camera clicked into action, but Bryan was pleased to oblige.

Our combined earnings at this time were obviously not enough to cover the remainder of our debts and the astronomical mortgage payments. The noose was tightening daily.

I was no longer afraid to open the door to bailiffs after all we had nothing left they could take. I remember on one occasion I was confronted with a man with a clipboard on the doorstep. I was dressed in overalls and wellies and looked particularly scruffy. I had learned from experience by now to put on a sad miserable face when opening the door to these characters. I looked almost desperate when I faced him. At first he was arrogant and officious as so often they are. He did not frighten me, after all what could he do? He reeled off the debt he was there to collect and asked how I was to pay it. I burst into tears, an art I had perfected, and amongst stifled sobs explained that we were due to lose our home, already having lost all our possessions.

Hollywood here I come, what a performance!!! Suddenly his tactics changed and he put out his hand and patted my arm telling me not to worry, he would go away and recommend to the company that had sent him there would be no point pursuing the debt further. He then explained that he had been chasing a debt the previous week. After his visit the man had hung himself and he didn't want me feeling so desperate that I felt there was no other way out. The man's death lay heavily on his conscience, he did not want another one. Did I look suicidal, I was more talented than I had thought. Bless him, he must have kept his word as we no longer heard anything about the debt again and I feel that the gentlemen who sadly hanged himself, did not die in vain, he saved my sanity and I am sure changed the life of the bailiff, making him a softer character. May his soul rest in peace.

Having no longer got a business of our own we stopped paying for any of the work vans. We have owned several outright which had been sold as we had had to tighten our belts but we still had three lease hire vans. Two white vans had been used by the scaffolders, and one blue pickup which Bryan used on the farm. We received several letters asking us to return them but we were not in a position to do so. One white van was in a garage awaiting a new engine to be fitted, of course we could not afford to pay for it and the other had been involved in an accident and we couldn't afford the excess payment.

Both vans were still awaiting repair. The blue van had been used to move cattle and was severely dented. One day the inevitable happened a car transporter pulled up outside. Three burly men alighted from the cab and demanded the return of the three vehicles. Bryan explained that the two white vans were not on the premises but both in local garages awaiting repair and the blue one they could take it away if they could get it moving. He pointed to the battered heap that we had pushed up against the wall when it had refused to start one morning. It had been left there ever since under the trees in direct line for the birds to do what birds do naturally. I have to admit that it did look a mess. The men were astounded at the condition but Bryan had no respect for vehicles, especially work ones and to Bryan this was a work horse. As Bryan explained we were happy for them to take it back as we had no use of it anymore and gave them the address of the garages where the two white vans could be located. It was an understatement to say that the men were unhappy. We watched as they tried to load the blue van made more difficult by the fact the engine would not start. It was no longer our problem and we sighed with relief as we watched the transporter disappear in the distance, three vans less to worry about. I think the three burly men would have some explaining to do when they returned to base with their battered and bent cargo. Oh well, it was no longer our problem.

Chapter 56

From Home to Home

*A*lmost daily we were being harassed to pay something off our ever increasing mortgage. It was an impossibility to pay anything on the wages that we were being paid so we started to look round locally for a bolthole to rent. Remembering that we had 5 dogs to take with us, this was not an easy task. We made enquiries but there was nothing big enough, or anybody willing enough, to take on such a menagerie and who could blame them? We were once deemed to be the 'neighbours from hell' and now we seemed to be prospective 'tenants from hell'. In desperation we went to view a property in Bruern. It sounded perfect, wardrobes in every room a spacious garden and reasonably isolated. We hastily clambered into our Suzuki Jeep, they only vehicle we had left and raced to Bruern

for fear somebody might get offered it before us. At first
we had trouble finding it. There was no such thing as Sat
Navs in those days, patience was the order of the day as
we trundled up one track after another in pursuit of our
future home. Eventually, after an outburst of temper at
every dead end, we finally reached our destination. We
piled out onto the muddy track and stared in disbelief at
the run down hovel. It was semi detached, but neither
properties looked lived in. At the adjoining house,
windows were draped in dirty net curtains, all hanging
at different angles. The windows of the property we had
come to view were just hanging in cobwebs. The key
was enormous, far more imposing than the property it
unlocked and we tentatively crept forward into the dark,
dirty hallway. On the lower level was a sitting room, of
no significant size and beyond that was a kitchen and
scullery. Definitely no mod cons here then as we stared at
a Belfast sink and two filthy draining boards that clipped
on. There were no kitchen units and nothing but a pile
of rubbish in the scullery, it really was not doing anything
for me but Bryan insisted we look upstairs as it had taken
us so long to find it. Personally I think it should have
stayed hidden but I followed him up the brown painted
stairs. All the doors were shut on the landing making it
extremely dark and dismal. I think I exaggerated when
I called it a landing, it was a postage stamp sized square
at the top of the stairs. We worked our way methodically
through each room, looking for the wardrobes
mentioned in the details, there was not one to be found.
Surely we couldn't have missed them all, oh but wait a
minute. When you stood in each room and closed the
door, all was revealed. The wardrobes were there alright,
how stupid were we to miss them all, a hook on the back

of each door! Well, think about it, you hang your clothes in a wardrobe and you hang your clothes on a hook, is there any difference? Obviously there were not the restrictions on elaborating details in those days. Agents would certainly not get away with it today. Disheartened by the house, we checked out the garden at the back. Enclosed by a broken down brick wall the garden proved to be huge, it would have been ideal for the dogs but I am afraid our search would have to continue.

We returned home disappointed and discussed another option. We now realised how difficult it would be trying to find somewhere to rent so we decided to use our nest egg we had got together to buy somewhere suitable. It was obvious that we would not be able to afford too big a place as the next property was to be bought in our son's name. Bryan would never have been able to get a mortgage with the farm mortgage in arrears. We were very aware of that fact and looked around for somewhere appropriate. We were limited with the size of the property that a Building Society would lend money against as our son was a first time buyer.

Our criteria was not unreasonable, 3 bedrooms and a large garden. Most properties had minute gardens and very small rooms, would we ever find anywhere, the pressure was 'mounting' for us to leave the farm.

The first bungalow we went to view was in a local village. I did not get a particularly good feeling as we looked round and the garden was not really suitable for five dogs. It turned out to be a complete non starter when the seller explained that there was a problem with the people who supplied water to the property. There had been a dispute previously and the supply pipe had subsequently been filled with concrete. The seller, a young man living on his own, used the local village toilets and amenities. That may have been a perfectly logical solution and way round it for him but not something we wanted to get involved in. I knew there was a reason I did not feel comfortable in there. Call it women's intuition but we went hastily back to the car to continue our search. Some properties sent through to us were totally unsuitable and were discounted on sight but there was one out of a whole batch that vaguely seemed to be a possibility. We drove to Carterton, the place we normally shopped in and sought out the address. We parked up outside to get a first impression. It looked quite clean and tidy set back behind a waist high red brick wall. To one side lay a concrete drive leading into a carport that then lead on to a garage, so far so good. There we were, scrutinising the property from the road, when suddenly the inhabitants realised they were under scrutiny and immediately jumped up and closed the curtains. How rude we must have looked! We once again returned home but this time we rang the Estate Agent responsible for selling the property and arranged a viewing. It was quite deceptive from the outside because inside it was a reasonable size. The Kitchen was not huge, but it had room for a breakfast bar (which we mentally noted would have to come out if we bought it). It had plenty of cupboard space and flowed through into a reasonable sitting room with a huge picture window that overlooked the road to the front. This was the window we had been peering into the day before. I do hope the residents did not recognise us. Beyond the sitting room was a large hallway accessed by the front door that was situated just to the front of the car port. This property had a warm feeling as we progressed through the bungalow. It was not just the warmth from the gas fire alight in the sitting room but it had an ambience that was filling me with hope. I have always felt that a home should feel right from the onset and this one was certainly satisfying that role. The bathroom was very clean even if the bath and toilet were a startling salmon colour complete with gold taps. No matter, I could live with that. Onward into the bedrooms. The master bedroom overlooked the rear garden and had a fitted wardrobe, very nice. The smallest bedroom overlooked the carport to the side of the property and you actually had to walk through this bedroom to access the rear bedroom which had a small cloakroom en suite. There were French windows that lead out into a small conservatory with hanging vines overhead. Finally out of the conservatory and onto a small patio complete with fish pond and rockery. Our sellers were very quick to tell us that the price included all the fish in the pond. Just what we needed, a pond full of fish and five dogs. Great, I know there would be a drawback. Beyond the fishpond we began to make our way up the garden which was quite extensive. The gentlemen was obviously an avid gardener as most of the garden was one huge vegetable patch complete with a huge greenhouse.

I loved it, there was so much room for the dogs. We had planned to build a huge kennel and run for all the dogs as they had all been bought up on the farm and were used to being outside. Here, this was possible and we would still have plenty of garden left. We thanked them cordially for showing us around and said we would be in touch. We did not need to discuss it we were all sold on the property. The bedroom at the back would be ideal for Steed, it would mean he had his own entrance, he would not have to keep traipsing through the bedroom designated for Kyly.

Bryan made the offer in Steeds name which was accepted and we now had a future to look forward to.

Chapter 57

An Opportunity for a New Beginning

The new scaffolding company was well and truly underway but as yet not ready to take on the larger contracts. Bryan was still trying to keep things low key whilst he was still employed but he hated every moment of not being his own boss. The Company that had bought us out continued relentlessly in their search for the missing materials. Bryan had managed to secrete some away almost under their noses and with new paint, who could immediately tell. We had enough stashed away to get going again as soon as the time was right.

Eventually, the Company found a loose link amongst our chain of loyal scaffolders and they were told roughly in what area to continue their search. I think a monetary bribe was the incentive that broke the chain but we could never have proved it. The inevitable happened and Bryan was summoned to the office. A huge row ensued when words like 'grand theft' and 'being ripped off' were bandied about quite openly. It came to a head when the door was thrown open, Bryan stormed out telling them where they could stick their job and he told me to pick up my personal bits as we were leaving, never to return. I never even had time to say a proper goodbye to Claire, it all happened so quickly. Before I knew it we were homeward bound. Bryan was sporting a grin that went from ear to ear and the opportunity for a new beginning was upon us.

Chapter 58

Skills to Learn, even Holy Ones

During the next few weeks we planned our departure from the farm. The remainder of our cattle, pigs and sheep were sold together with any farming equipment and I spent most of my time at the bungalow in Carterton, decorating and preparing for the move. The inhabitants had wished for a quick sale and everything fell in to place perfectly. At last we were having some good luck, it was not before time.

I started at the rear of the property and worked my way forward. Steed's room, although a huge bedroom was completed quickly, I was keen to complete the whole project. Kyly's room was next. This was more difficult as it had polystyrene tiles on the ceiling. These I knew were a hazard if ever a fire broke out, so those had to be removed. Once removed they left glue marks on the ceiling, no matter, I would artex the ceiling to cover the marks. There was nothing I couldn't do if I put my mind to it.

I purchased the artex, a bucket, float and sponge and set to work. I made up a huge bucketful of artex to save time and decided that stippling was the easiest pattern as that really did not need much skill. It was much harder than I had at first imagined. I had watched plasterers before and they made it seem so easy. A scoop of artex onto the float, swirl it across the area you want to cover and a quick dab with the sponge to give the finished effect. Oh my goodness, it is not supposed to end up on the floor, how the hell do you get it to stay on the ceiling. This is not as easy as I first thought. Take a coffee break and give this a bit more thought. Coffee drank and a decision made to try to do a smaller area I returned to the bucket of artex only to find the broomstick I had used to stir the contents was set solid. In my absence it had gone off and hardened like concrete. I could not move the broomstick or remove the solid artex from the bucket. Back to square one. I, once again, purchased a new bucket, new artex, new broomstick and with a new found knowledge I prepared once again to tackle the job in hand. This time I was not so ambitious and took it more slowly, mixing and doing a small area at a time. My patience proved to be successful and even if I do say it myself I did a grand job. It maybe was not a truly professional job but I was pleased with the results and completed the room by wallpapering and painting to my daughters' satisfaction. Our bedroom, the bathroom and the hallway with all its' five doors, finished me off.

By the time these were all completed I wished never to see another paintbrush in my life. At this point we called in a scaffolder who did decorating in his spare time to finish the sitting room and Kitchen. I had at last run out of steam. When we got to the Kitchen the breakfast bar was removed and new units replaced the old ones. It was now beginning to feel more like our home. Bryan had always stayed at the farm whilst this transformation of the bungalow was taking place, he was loathe to leave the farm he loved so much. When all the work was almost complete I asked him to accompany me to help with a couple of jobs I couldn't manage on my own. I have to explain that at this time our surrounding area had been invaded by vast numbers of 'hippy' characters bent on attending 'illegal raves'. Farmers had blocked entrances to fields with anything heavy enough to deter the intruders. It had been broadcast in coded messages that one such rave was to take place in the nearby vicinity. The night I had asked Bryan to accompany me, the Police were out in full force to prevent this rave occurring. As we tootalled along the back lane, me, balancing a tray of milk, sugar, coffee, cups and snacks on my lap, the Police jumped out of seemingly nowhere and flagged us down. Bryan wound down his window and asked what it was all about. They were having none of it. We were told to vacate the vehicle and stand away from it. Whatever had we done? Was it illegal to carry a tray on your lap? May I point out I did have my seatbelt on!!

I know it was getting dusk but I am not sure what they thought I was doing in my lap to prevent easy disembarkment. Suddenly the door was thrown open and we were asked for an explanation of where we were going. Did they think we were the refreshments for the so called 'rave'? I know I am good and Bryan thought he was God but 2 cups, ½ pint of milk and a small jar of coffee complete with a couple of bars of chocolate would not go far amongst the hoards that attended these illegal raves. I must try harder with my miracle lessons, Fishes and bread seem to work much better than coffee and chocolate.

Never mind they did see the funny side of it and had a good chuckle as they waved us on our way.

Everything done, we finally locked everything up at the farm and moved to our new home. This was to be a new chapter adjusting to life on an estate.

Chapter 59

A Battle of the Boundaries

Once we had moved in we found there was still a lot to do. The kennel and run for the dogs was the most important issue that had to be tackled and scaffolders and labourers alike were brought in to help with the breeze block structure. The compound itself was to be surrounded by a 6ft wire fence. We did not wish to have any escapees.

The fish pond was the next big job as that and the surrounding rockery took up a lot of space. As none of us at that time were interested in keeping fish or had the time to sit and appreciate their relaxing qualities, a decision was made to get rid of them and fill in the pond. None of us were heartless so we part filled buckets with water and carted them all off to be released in a local village pond. I am not sure whether Koi carp and like survive in a village pond but we felt that was a kinder option than the one Bryan had in mind. I like to think they all enjoyed their new home. If they did not survive I expect the local villagers were puzzled where all the dead fish had come from "It's Raining Men" comes to mind but not "It's Raining Fish." Never mind, it is something we will never know.

The third job I had in mind to do was to clear all the brambles from the bottom of the garden. When we had initially viewed the bungalow I had not noticed but on closer inspection realised there was a further four foot of garden covered heavily in brambles. Four foot from the neighbours' fence I could just make out a paved path, the edge of which was just visible. Once I had removed all the offending brambles I would plant flower shrubs all across the back to hide the fence, a much prettier option, that was before I realised that I had a "neighbour from hell".

I duly cleared the ground and prepared it for planting my shrubs, I had previously been and purchased the plants eager to get on and transform my garden. I worked hard all morning and stood back and admired the transformation. I was very pleased with the results and crossed that job off my list of things to be done. I later went shopping and returned laden with food to fill my abundant cupboard space. I took a few toiletries into our bedroom and thought I would admire, from a distance my new shrubbery at the end of the garden.

I looked and looked again, something had happened. I was not sure that my eyesight was not playing tricks. The newly planted shrubs were strewn across my garden. Surely I was seeing things, no one had been at home when I left for my shopping trip and no one was in now that I had returned. How strange? Were the birds of Carterton super strong, had they pulled the plants out searching for worms in the newly turned soil? There could be no other explanation as everything else was in place just as I had left it and the dogs were all in their kennels and run. Oh well, I set to work replanting them all, puzzling at the thought of superior sparrows and titan like thrushes. The birds had all seemed quite normal when I was clearing the earth, maybe a cat had got into the garden. It must have been a very brave cat facing up to five dogs, none of which liked cats. Maybe I would never know, so I continued on indoors satisfied that my gardening was done for the day. I went into the kitchen to prepare the evening meal for my family who would shortly be returning from school and work.

Over our meal I discussed the strange phenomena of my uprooting plants and the family could not come up with a sensible explanation. The plot thickened the following day when exactly the same thing happened. Once again I replanted them all but enough was enough, there must be some feasible explanation, those shrubs were not uprooting themselves.

I decided to take up a position in our bedroom where I could see to the bottom of the garden. I waited for quite a while unsure of what I was actually waiting for and then it happened. Was I seeing things or was there a fence panel moving? Yes, my eyes were not deceiving me, the fence panel was being removed and an elderly gentleman was climbing over into our garden. I watched as he systematically went along the row, tugging out the newly planted shrubs and tossing them behind him onto the garden. So he was the culprit!

I was extremely angry at the cheek of the man and fled outside before he could conveniently disappear back behind his fence leaving no trace of his unwelcome visit except my discarded shrubs. "What do you think you are doing?" I shouted as I raced up the path. "They shouldn't be there" he replied. He then went on to explain that the brambled area that I had cleared belonged to him and he didn't want me to plant things in it. How absurd, he had a 6ft larch lap fence across the bottom of his garden. I asked why the fence had not been erected four foot further down incorporating the brambled area. He was not forthcoming with a reason so I told him in no uncertain terms that I was now claiming the garden to be my own as the fence line corresponded with all the neighbouring fences and I thought he was talking a load of balderdash!!

I went on to explain that I would be replanting yet again my shrubs and if he so much as looked at them again let alone remove them i would be paying him a visit to plant my spade neatly in the top of his bald dome.

I had no idea who this stupid gentlemen was but, I think he got the message, as my shrubs remained in situ without any further interference. It was strange though, every time we were in the garden we got a feeling that we were being watched, we could not see anybody watching us from the few houses that overlooked our garden but the feeling was definitely there. It was not only me, we all felt it. One day, quite by chance I was inspecting my shrubbery which was growing quite nicely now that it was allowed in the ground long enough to take root when I spotted an eye peering at me through a knot hole. It was a little unnerving but when I took a better look my neighbour had poked out all the knots in the fence at face height in order that he could spy on us. What a sad existence he must have had to find us remotely interesting.

It was even funnier when Steed brought home a friend that he had met since we had moved in, the lad was telling us about the neighbours from hell that had moved in at the bottom of his grandads' garden and yes, you have guessed it, for the second time we had been classed as the 'neighbours from hell!'

We all looked at each other in disbelief, and then burst out laughing, explaining as we did that we were those so called neighbours. We told the lad what had happened, he apologised on behalf of his grandad and joined in with the laughter, the easiest way to overcome his embarrassment. The lad in question, now a man, has remained friends with us throughout the latter years, so we can't have been too bad. I think as the saying goes it was a case of the pot calling the kettle black.

Chapter 60

A Means to an End

The bungalow although it had been a bolthole for us, was not really a happy home. There was a power struggle going on between Bryan and Steed due to the circumstances. Bryan had had to put Steed's name to most things! He was now 18 years old, and Steed felt for this reason that he should have more out of the company and Bryan was adamant that he should not. There was only one boss and Bryan was not about to give up the title, he was still the driving force behind the business, and kept Steed in check. There were many arguments due to this, and one day when I returned from shopping I found the sitting room door totally demolished, strewn across the driveway. There had been an altercation in my absence and Steed in frustration and temper had punched his way out of the sitting room, smashing through the closed door as he went. Such was family harmony at that time as Steed continued to struggle for more power and Bryan was trying to come to terms with living on an estate away from the farm minus all his bovine friends.

It was around this time that I began to find that I had time on my hands, don't get me wrong, I was still doing Brownies at Burford, something I had taken on when Kyly reached the age of 7. The business was a manageable size now and I had all the time that once had been taken up with farming activities. I was unused to being idle and looked round for something to fill the void. The senior school which Kyly had just moved up into was looking for somebody to join their learning support department. This was a paid position which I had experience in, so I attended an interview and got the job and had to work with the slow learners, with the more difficult pupils, and those on the cusp of being expelled. I loved it!! Every day was a challenge.

My first pupil was a girl from the travelling fraternity. She was a bright enough girl, if we could get her to school. She often did not turn up, so I was sent to persuade her to grace us with her presence. A task I did not always succeed in doing but if she did attend we got on fine. One day she just disappeared never to be heard of again.

My second challenge came in the guise of a tall, gangly youth in the latter years of his education. He was totally out of control and had struck several teachers before becoming my prodigy. My introduction to him was anything but formal. I heard him coming down the corridor verbally abusing the accompanying master. The door of the classroom was thrown open and he threw his sports bag at me. Not the best of starts I have to admit. The master looked for reassurance that I would be alright and left us to it. When I accepted the position I realised that difficult pupils who bucked the system would take little notice of me if I resembled the establishment, so I dressed a little eccentrically unlike all the other teachers. I wore long "hippy like" skirts with either, tassles or bells at the hem, large oversized jumpers complete with beads of various sizes and colours. Kyly was appalled as she was extremely conventional and did not wish to stand out in the crowd. I was a total embarrassment.

At the initial meeting with this challenging youth, I think my plan worked as he was not sure how to take me. I sat, not at the teachers' desk, but central to the room at one of the pupils desks. He paced round me but I would not make eye contact with him, so he found it difficult to intimidate me. He pushed all the desks and chairs over except the one at which I was seated. I did not bat an eyelid. He was trying to make me react, but I was a step ahead (although inside I was quaking) I showed no emotion at all. It was a very cold day outside and his next trick was to open all the windows, and try to freeze a reaction out of me. When this did not work, he continued to pace round me like an animal eyeing up its' prey. At this point, when he realised I was unlike other teachers I tried to engage him in conversation. I asked him to tell me a little about himself but he ignored me completely, so I changed tactics. I told him a little about myself, to see if we could find some common ground. It seemed he recognised the description of my sons' car, a pearlescent beetle, and then seemed to know my eldest son from his involvement with his football team. The initial meeting went considerably well knowing all the issues he was battling. He still refused to cooperate with any schooling that I might try to introduce. He was a bright boy considering he had fought his way through every aspect of school. It helped that I did not look like a conventional teacher and eventually, by a fluke of good luck, I had a break through.

My eldest son had always been involved with football from an early age and had always supported Manchester United. Due to the absence of Bryan, during his early years when working his way through the youth team, i had supported him by transporting the team, washing the dirty kits and generally attending the matches, both home and away, I soon picked up the rules, even the off side one, and this impressed my pupil as most girls were "rubbish" when it came to football, his words not mine.

It took several weeks to build up a rapport with him but eventually I could see a light at the end of the tunnel. It was by no means easy as he was as stubborn as a mule, but working on this football theme seemed to be working. He was very clever as never once did he divulge or give me a clue as to the major club he supported. One day when I felt we had almost exhausted all the talk of football he surprised me by giving me an ultimatum. If I could guess which football club he supported he would settle down and work for me. It seemed, that through all my hard work, i had earned a somewhat fragile respect. I really had no idea but suspected that it was either Man U or Liverpool, both very popular teams back then as they are now. I am not sure if it was divine intervention but I told him as far as I was concerned there was

only one team to support and that was Man U. He
punched the air and leapt up and down with glee. I
had chosen well, true to his word we worked together
well over the next few weeks on the run up to his
exams. He was obviously not going to take all those
that his fellow pupils were taking, he had wasted so
much of his schooling, but if I could get him through
Maths and English that would be at least something.
He attended the Maths exam and sailed through that
but I was away from school on the day of the English
exam. At lunch time I had a frantic phone call from
the Head of the department saying that unless I was
present he was refusing to sit the exam. I hastily
returned to school and promised him if he completed
the task in hand (write a poem and illustrate it) I
would frame his entry and hang it in my hallway at
home and include it in my 'Hall of Memories.' My'
Hall of Memories' consisted of special work the
children had done or memorable scenes from past
holidays. He took a bit of persuading but I promised
him that while he was taking the exam I would go
and buy the clip art frame and return to the school to
let him see it. He was sceptical at first but I explained
that he had kept his word to me and I would return
the favour. He completed the exam and I returned
complete with clip art frame, and framed the copy he
had done for me.

On my return home, I hung the poem and illustration
(two children climbing on a snowy gate to accompany
a poem called snow) as promised. Six weeks later he
turned up at my house to check that I had kept my word,
he was so sure that I wouldn't do it. Little does he know

that I still have the picture and poem nearly twenty years on today, be it that it is now stored away in my attic along with all those other memories that adorned the hallway at the time. O Ye of little faith!!!

Chapter 61

Festivities to Furore

$\mathcal{C}$hristmas was fast approaching and I was looking
forward to the festivities. Christmas has always
been an exciting time for me. I can ignore all the
commercialism and yet be caught up with all the fairy
lights and magic that surrounds the mystical visit of
'Father Christmas.' We had decorated the house and the
enormous tree that Bryan had brought in. He always had
to have the biggest and the best—no matter what and
every year we had to lop off about 3 ft so that we could
erect it in our sitting room. This year was no exception.
We stood back and admired the work of art that we had
created. With Christmas Eve upon us I was making a list
of the final few bits to get before the shops shut for the
Yuletide when the phone rang. It was my sister sounding
distressed. Apparently there had been some trouble with

her eldest daughter and her second husband. All I heard between sobs was that if I did not take her to live with me she was to be put in care.

She was my God daughter and I had a responsibility towards her—of course I would take her. It was arranged for my brother to deliver her to us and she arrived an hour later with literally what she stood up in. She had brought with her, no clothes and no Christmas presents so it looked as if I had a lot to do before those shops finally closed their doors. We tried to make Christmas as special as we could for my niece but it must have been a wrench away from her Mum and sisters at such a 'family time.'

Needless to say, I had always got on well with her so it was not as traumatic as it could have been if she had been put in care. She soon settled in, sharing a room with Kyly. When the new term started after the holidays I enrolled her at Burford School where she made friends easily and I could keep an eye on her. Fortunately she had seen Bryan fly into rages before she came to live with us so was not phased by his behaviour at this time.

I remember on one occasion 'The Colour Purple,' a film I wished to see was to be televised one evening. I had planned my day so that I could sit and relax and watch it. My plans had not taken into account Bryan's bad mood that day.

When he arrived home I could see quite distinctly the glowing mark between his eyes. We tip toed round him as we knew only too well how quickly he could erupt when this spot glowed. I made his coffee and dished up his meal trying to keep things on an even keel so as not to upset him. It was yet another example of my waking in the morning with my sole intention just to annoy him, or that was the way he saw it. I had so obviously not cooked his dinner to his satisfaction and the inimitable row broke out.

I am sure that some of you are saying to yourself that if I hadn't argued back there would not have been a row but I am afraid that was not the way that Bryan worked. If Bryan wanted a row, a row we had whether I joined in or not. The decision had been made, he flew into a rage and decided I was not welcome in the house anymore. I left without too much argument for my 2nd home, the neighbours bush a few doors down the road. He followed me into the street shouting abuse but I was nowhere to be seen—the bush hid me well. He stormed back in and demanded of the Family that no-one let me back in.

I waited until the coast was clear and he had settled down to watch television and then tentatively made my way back home keeping an eye on the big picture window to the front of the property lest he should look out. So far so good, down the drive walking on the lawn so as not to 'crunch' the gravel I crawled on hands and knees under the window, past the glass kitchen door, under our bedroom window and finally arrived outside my son's patio doors at the rear of the property. I could clearly see my niece and Kyly through the open connecting door to her bedroom. They had chosen to sit in there out of Bryan's way for fear of upsetting him further. They spotted me and I beckoned that they turn the television on and position it so that I could watch it from outside. I knew from experience that Bryan would calm down eventually but certainly not in time for me to watch my film. The girls quietly closed their door

365

leading onto the hallway and then passed me out a chair through the patio doors. They lay on my son's bed to watch the film and kept the patio doors slightly ajar so that I could hear the dialogue. As the evening air turned colder I began to feel the chill and they passed me out a jacket. My niece went to make me a black coffee on the pretence of her wanting a drink but Bryan was one step ahead of her and guessed it was for me. He followed her into our son's bedroom. I quickly moved, chair and body as one and disappeared round the side of the bungalow. He turned the television off and made the girls return to the sitting room. Fortunately he had not noticed the patio doors slightly ajar and once they had all left the room, I crept back down the side of the bungalow and quietly let myself in. I would be safe for the time being but would have to forego the end of the film. The last thing that I wanted at that time was for him to find me. I knew from experience that after these violent rages he would sleep and forget about what had happened previously. By the time he woke up normality (if you could call it that) would resume. I can honestly say that not once since that evening have I ever had the chance to see that film—but the title is etched on my memory forever.

Chapter 62

Treasure Seekers

*M*y work at Burford School continued for a while and I have to admit that it was both very rewarding and extremely varied. I was dealing with academic problems one minute and social and hygiene problems the next. Life certainly wasn't dull but the business at home was picking up and as much as I loved working with the pupils I had to get my priorities right and the time had come to leave.

Life at home was no easier although Steed had settled down a bit, realising how futile his arguments with his Father were. Bryan, on the other hand, was finding it harder and harder to re—adjust to living on an estate. He desperately missed life on the farm and this resulted in extreme bad temper and furious rages that seemed to be triggered at the least instigation. How long would we have to tolerate this dreadful behaviour? The signs were not good as the bright red pressure spot had never glowed so red or glowed so often. At one point things got so bad that he would erupt almost without warning and became so unreasonable that very often Kyly and I would race off at breakneck speed to hide in our friendly bush down the road. The bush itself was actually in a neighbours front garden and I do hope they did not mind us taking refuge there when he went out of control—but it really was the safest place to be. During those terrible months that bush became our second home we were in it so often and I am only surprised that our neighbour did not start charging us rent.

As the scaffolding picked up again and we got much busier it gave Bryan something else to focus on and he calmed down. I am not saying that he was an easy man to live with, far from it, but the rages became less frequent as he began to form a plan for the future.

It was around this time that my friend and I became interested in metal detecting. Armed with our metal detectors, presents from our bemused spouses, we joined a 'club' and became two of the 'Anorak Brigade.' On Sunday mornings, at the crack of dawn, we would head off 'into the hills' to meet up with our fellow detectors. We would 'sweep' field after field in search of buried treasure, to no avail. Our companions would find an assortment of ancient coins and daggers on fields that we had both covered but neither of us was destined to get rich on our pickings.

We did get excited over one 'dig.' Our machines had both 'bleeped' over the same spot and we both felt that this could be our lucky day. We scraped the earth away carefully so as not to damage our 'find.' Yes, there was certainly something buried here. We were now down on our knees, curiosity and excitement evident in our frantic soil removal. Oh yes, it was beginning to appear. Careful now in case we damage it. It was obviously caked in the heavy soil and who knows how long it had been buried? We pulled the soil away from our 'treasure' with our trowels and still it went deeper. Yes, I think this is the base of whatever it is as I can now get the trowel under it without any obstruction. Careful now, as we tried to clear some of the soil from its' sides and base. It looked very interesting, we wondered if it could be worth a fortune? Time will tell.

Should we call for more experienced members of our club or should we clean it up as best we could before we approached them with smug looks on our faces? We decided on the latter as everyone else seemed to find something exciting except us, so let us enjoy our moment of glory.

We spent the next 10 minutes poking and prodding at our 'treasure' which was, minute by minute, beginning to resemble ' The Eiffel Tower.' Finally we managed to clean off the base and "Oh no, what was that?" A HOLE! What we had found was nothing more than a metal table lamp complete with a drilled hole in the base to accommodate the electric cable. What a disappointment! We looked up at each other both mud splattered, our hopes of glory dashed, and laughed till we cried.

As treasure hunters, we were both a waste of time. We tried detecting in the Winter when we went out dressed in wellington boots, warm jumpers and scarves and dug about in thick wet mud. We tried it in the Summertime when the ground was rock hard and we ventured forth in sandals and pretty dresses but it was not to be. Treasure hunters we may be, but treasure finders we were not. We got disheartened when others went home with their 'finds.' What were we doing wrong? We watched their every move to see if there was a technique we were missing but no, they seemed to be doing the same as us, but were just luckier. Don't misunderstand me, we did find the occasional shell case dating back 200–300 years but they were plentiful, not the kind of treasure we were seeking. Well, where could we look next? We found a rope swing in a clump of trees close by and actually had more success detecting in the dip below the rope swing. I think we found about £1-00 between us in loose change that had fallen out of the pockets of the 'swingers.' Maybe there is something in metal detecting after all—a whole days work for less than the price of a cup of coffee. Not bad eh? At least we found something that day which is more than we found on any other day.

Chapter 63

A Thank You to All

I have to admit that the years we spent at Carterton were not the best. It was a strange place to live. If you were born and raised there you were accepted by the local community, but if you were an outsider that had moved in, that is what you remained, an outsider. I think, during the several years that we lived there we only ever got to 'nodding' and saying "Good Morning" to our immediate neighbours on either side. I suppose it may have had something to do with having RAF Brize Norton on its' doorstep. Locals resented the RAF personnel and included everyone else in that 'outsider' category.

Bryans' temper did not improve during this time and I often said "Goodnight" to Kyly through her bedroom window, her knelt on her bed and me stood on the driveway on my way to the garage. I had managed to stow away in the garage a surplus of bed linen ie: duvet and pillows for such occasions. It now took hardly anything at all to trigger off one of his rages and it quite often resulted in my being thrown out. It was a much easier option to walk away than to stand and argue with him as he could be totally unreasonable at such times. The freezer lid in the garage was a much better place to sleep than the option of walking the streets. The trouble with Bryan was that he was his own worst enemy. Even if I say so myself I am reasonably intelligent and have a vast vocabulary. Bryan, on the other hand, was brilliant at Maths but sorely lacking in the vocabulary department. He could swear his way through an argument but could never debate in a rational way.

Please do not misunderstand what I am saying as I am in no way defending his behaviour but he was not a 'wife beater' in the true sense of the word. He was frustrated more than anything and found it difficult to express himself. I have to admit that I was not the easiest person to live with (as I have now been told by 3 husbands) so together we made a volatile couple. Our relationship was a mixture of love and hate in equal quantities but it held us fast throughout our marriage. Love was to conquer all.

The business had now picked up and was doing well. We had a very good standard of living and Bryan was very grateful to all the contractors who had stayed loyal to us whilst we were setting up the new company.

Another Christmas was on the horizon and we planned to have a party for Family, friends, business aquaintances and scaffolders to say "Thank You" for their support through difficult times. We looked around and found 'The Farmhouse Restaurant' at Lew (sadly now turned into a domestic dwelling). They did us proud. We had a wonderful evening where all the guests mingled and had a super time. Although the drink flowed freely there was no trouble and the buffet was 'out of this world' for both quality and variation. The presentation was superb and the chefs that carved the meat were friendly and nothing was too much trouble. I cannot praise that establishment enough. Thank you to Wesley and his staff for the very best parties ever.

Chapter 64

A Family Celebration and a Family Rift

I t was at one of these parties that my Mum remarked that if she was ever to have a party in the future, this was where she would like it to be. I took that as a subtle hint as my Parents' 50th wedding anniversary was due the following January.

With this in mind, a meeting was arranged a few weeks later, to discuss all the options with my siblings. I knew where my Mum would like the party to be held but it was beyond the price range of my siblings and several other options were suggested. I knew that my Mother would be disappointed with any other venue so I offered to pay the bulk and split the rest between them making it more affordable. After much discussion and a few internal arguments I was asked to book the venue for the following year. I dealt with all the details of the catering and my sister took on the role of booking coaches and inviting guests, some of whom travelled from as far away as Yorkshire.

It was agreed that my siblings pay me as and when they could afford to. I did not intend to put pressure on them to pay over money they could ill afford. I was prepared to pay the bill and wait for their monies. I never had any doubt that each in turn would pay me in full when they could. One brother and my sister paid me in a couple of instalments but I knew my other brother was struggling financially. Out of the blue I had a phone call from his wife to tell me that she had secured another job on top of the several she already had and was willing to pay the wages from the new job straight to me if I was in agreeance. Of course I agreed, I was happy to help in any way I could and said that we would keep it between ourselves. I never told a soul about that agreement. The payments were not vast amounts but they were slowly decreasing the balance. I was happy with the agreement.

Due to the fact that so much money was being spent on the party itself and Mum and Dad did not want for anything, we decided to give them a large bottle of whisky (they both enjoyed a tipple), a bouquet of flowers and framed photographs of all their children and grandchildren. It was arranged for a Family friend, who was a competent photographer, to take these photographs in the month prior to the party. Unfortunately, something happened in the interim period that meant

that the photographs that were supposed to be taken
during Christmas had to be brought forward
My eldest lad, who had been in trouble several times
whilst growing up, was due a court appearance just
before Christmas. Don't misunderstand me but the
trouble he had got himself into was mostly down to
boyish pranks, nothing too serious up until now. He was
in a relationship with a young girl who we all loved. She
was an identical twin with a winning smile and a lovely
gentle personality. They had previously set up home
together and Karl had decided to go to Germany to earn
some extra money to help her through her final year of
College. Whilst he was working away, she bumped into
a car belonging to one of Karl's cousins. She asked that
Karl not be told as there was no serious damage and she
felt that if he found out he would pour scorn on her
ability to drive.

The cousin, an unsavoury character, took it upon himself
to make her life intolerable. He began stalking her and as
the window of his flat overlooked theirs would stare at
her menacingly, forcing her to keep her curtains closed.
He made her feel so uncomfortable that in the end she
was forced to tell Karl what had been happening. Karl
was furious and went hunting for him. He found him
in a local pub where a fight broke out. Unfortunately, in
temper, Karl lashed out at him with a pool cue which
was not acceptable. Although he did leave the scene at
the time, he did eventually give himself up and faced the
consequences.

GBH is frowned upon in all circles and we knew that
he would get a custodial sentence which would come

into effect before Christmas, hence Mum and Dads' photographs had to be taken early. It was the right thing to do as Karl was sentenced to 15 months on the day following the photographic shoot in the local park. Even though he missed the party he did at least make the photograph that adorned Mum and Dads' sitting room wall until the day they died. They would have been devastated if he had been missing as he was their first grandchild and they adored him.

Mum and Dads' party was a complete surprise. The week previously the whole Family went out for a meal except me. I phoned up on the night to say that I had broken down on the way and would not be able to attend the Family Celebration. It was a total lie but it gave me an excuse to take them out on the night of their real party. I made out that because I had missed 'their night' I had bought tickets for them to see a show but they would have to get themselves dressed up a bit as it was at quite a 'posh' place. I had to do this as Mum did not make much of an effort normally and would possibly have turned up in her indoor slippers.

We had several problems on the day of the party. First of all Mum rang about 11am to say they didn't think they would come as Dad had a problem and kept having to go to the toilet. I had to counter this by telling them that I had managed to obtain tickets especially close to the toilets with this in mind. She then rang a bit later to say thank you for the thought but that they were unused to going to shows and would probably fall asleep, they would prefer to stay at home. What—after all our plans! I had to get really upset and say that they were happy to go out with the rest of the Family but didn't seem to want to go out with me even though I had gone to great lengths to get these tickets even thinking of Dad and his problem. It worked. I made them feel so guilty that they really did not have another option than to get ready for me to pick them up later that afternoon.

During the early part of the evening I was awaiting a phone call from my sister to let me know that the coaches had arrived and everyone was in situ awaiting the arrival of Mum and Dad. The phone call came but not to let me know that we could leave the house, just to let me know that one of the coaches had broken down. Oh the joy of all this subterfuge! Can anything else go wrong? I shouldn't even have had that thought as that night was to see a change in my life that was to last for the next 14 years.

At last, the coaches arrived and all the guests were waiting for the Anniversary Couple. I set off to deliver them. The place was in darkness when we arrived and Mum was complaining that after all that, we must have the wrong night. Had she overlooked the full car park and the two coaches, maybe she hadn't noticed them in the darkness? We got out of the car and made our way to the door, Mother complaining bitterly about being dragged out unnecessarily and Dad just following in her footsteps as per normal. I touched the door handle and suddenly the doors burst open, lights went on and Mum and Dad were overwhelmed by the sea of faces that greeted them. We followed Mum and Dad in and were pleased by the number of people who had made the effort to attend. They were not the most sociable of couples so it had been quite difficult putting together a guest list. My sister had done a good job. We chatted briefly about the problems we had experienced throughout the day and then went our separate ways to mingle with friends and Family. My younger brother stopped for a chat on his way to the bar but my other brother seemed to be avoiding me. His wife and children were also avoiding me and he glared at me icily from the other side of the room. I had no idea what was going on and swept up in the party atmosphere I did not think too much about it. The party was going well and Mum and Dad seemed to be enjoying it immensely and were catching up with friends and neighbours from long ago. The time came for the presentation and I had put together some memories from my siblings hopefully to put a smile on our Parents' faces. I had previously been told that my brother who had been giving me a wide berth did not want to be part of the presentation and I accepted without question that he probably had his own reason for this and thought that I would take it up with him later. The last thing that I wanted to do was to embarrass him.

The presentation went ahead. I called my one sister and brother to present our gifts while I read my prepared speech with anecdotes. Everyone applauded and Mum shed a tear or two and then the party continued. During the course of the evening my immediate Family came and asked if I could have a word with my 'unsociable' brother as he seemed to be insulting them. This was not generally like him so I knew something was wrong and asked him to come outside where we could have a private chat. Once outside in the fresh air, he let rip! He called me for everything but I could not understand where it was coming from. I had not spoken to any of his Family since I had made the agreement with his wife about payment and at that point we had parted on good terms.

My son came outside to see if I was alright and I returned to the hall, angry at my brothers' outburst but still confused as to the reason. I was neither 'stuck up' or a 'snob', words that he had been bandying about and I certainly did not think I was any better than anyone else. What I wonder, was fuelling this bad feeling? Now was obviously not the time as he was too wound up and the amount of drink that he had consumed was not helping.

I tried to ignore what had been said and carried on making sure that everyone was enjoying themselves. My sister-in-law came down a staircase as I passed and I spoke congenially to her as we made eye contact. I was shocked by her response as she told me where to go in no uncertain terms. Whatever is the matter with them all? Have I been totally naïve and overlooked something so important that they have reason to ostracise me?

I could not understand any of it. I wracked my brain for a reason. We don't mix socially (we live in different areas) and hardly ever see each other at Mums so what could I have done that was so bad. We had an agreement over the payment plan which was acceptable to both parties and I had never mentioned it to anyone. I wish they would explain why they are so upset with me.

Never mind, it is Mum and Dads' night and I don't want anything to spoil things for them. I have to explain that the venue, apart from the bar area and the conservatory where the food was served, was made up of several comfortable rooms where guests could sit and relax. As I made my way through one of these rooms, I am not sure who threw it but I was suddenly confronted with the balance of the money owed by my brother. It was hurled into my face together with a load of abuse. I had no idea what it was all about and unfortunately did not find out until 14 years later

Chapter 65

Escape at any Price

*I*t was while we were living at Carterton that we realised that we had the equivalent of 'Houdini' in canine form.

One morning I went to hang washing out and could not find one of the Staffies. She was the most timid of all the dogs and possibly the one that was the least trouble. I called her, with no response, and then went into the run to investigate. She was definitely missing, but how had she got out? I inspected the wire and found no sign of breakage. The wire was intact and 6foot high and the door to the run, through which I had entered, was bolted. It seemed impossible for her to escape, nobody was allowed in the dog run unless I was with them, and I certainly had not let her get out.

I immediately started a search for her. Kyly and steed
ran around the immediate vicinity and I jumped in
the car to look further afield. She just seemed to have
disappeared into thin air. In desperation I rang the Police.
I was told that a Staffie fitting her description had been
picked up and taken to local kennels in Bampton. Thank
goodness for that! I rang the kennels to let them know
I was on my way and went in to retrieve my 'stray.'
How embarrassing did that visit turn out to be. I drove
into their yard and was shown to the caged area where
she had been put on arrival. I called to her expecting
her to be pleased to see me but she cowed down and
sloped away into a corner as if she was afraid of me. I
felt worse than she did as the owner of the kennels eyed
me suspiciously. I explained that she had always behaved
like that from the day we had got her but I suspect that
he did not believe me. Paperwork complete and fine
paid, I hastened home with my ungrateful charge. We
were all pleased to see her and, none the worse for wear,
we returned her to the run where the other dogs were
excited to see her.

A couple of days later the same thing happened. I
noticed her absence and rang the kennels once more,
after looking for her locally. Yes, once again the dog
catcher had brought her in. Once again I was under
suspicion as the owner asked me why I thought she kept
running away.? What could I say? She was well looked
after, watered, fed and walked across the fields daily with
the other dogs. What more could she want? She seemed
to be happy if a bit of a nervous disposition, but that was
normal for her. I could not give him a satisfactory answer
and left his yard once more under a cloud of suspicion.

I wouldn't mind, I was thinking as I drove away, but she had never even been shouted at, she was so good. Why was she behaving as if we had been mistreating her, the little bitch?

The big question was,'How was she managing to escape?' She could not get out through the door without being seen, the wire had not been tampered with and the wire was too high for her to jump over. Did she have magical powers that we were not aware of?

She remained in the run for the next week without incident, but then it occurred again. I looked around for her again, without success, but was hesitant about ringing the kennels. In desperation I contacted the owner, only to be told that this time she was not there. He suggested I might ring the 'Blue Cross' as sometimes, when an animal is picked up by a member of the public they sometimes end up there. It was good advice as when I rang them a Staffie had been handed in but they would not give me any details. I was sure it must be her and headed off to identify her. I arrived in reception and after giving a full description of Kimnel they went off to get her. She took one look at me and raced off and hid under the counter, cowering as she did so. What a little drama queen! I had to explain all over again why she behaved the way she did. Once again I had to pay a fine to retrieve her and I think they were very reluctant to allow her to go with me, it was against their better judgement.

I had a serious 'chat' with that canine on our homeward journey. She had not only cost me a fortune in fines but had cast aspersions on my good name, cowering like that. I was now looked upon as the local 'dog beater.' I hope now she was to be a reformed character but I had my doubts from the gleam in her eye. If she wanted to be put up for adoption she should have said but as we had had her for about 5 years, we had grown very fond of her even if the feeling was not reciprocated. She was staying with us, I would make sure of it. I was intrigued to find out how our 'Houdini' was managing to escape so I decided to keep a closer eye on her. When I went out next morning to feed the dogs I noticed that she was patrolling the wire like a caged lion. I could see the run from my bedroom window so decided to watch and wait. Nobody could have prepared me for what I was now to witness. I would never have believed it had I not seen it with my own eyes.

As I sat on my bed, I saw her start to climb the wire just as a young child would. It was just as if she had been trained by the 'SAS' as she never faltered once. First her front paws followed by her back legs, up and up she went until she reached the top. A little bit of an untidy 'up and over' the top and a leap onto the soil that ran alongside the concrete path. At least it was a soft landing. Well, at last, I knew how it was done., the little minx. Before she had time to collect her thoughts I shot out of the back door just in time to prevent her escaping once more. She looked a little downhearted to be captured so quickly before her adventure had begun and I brought her into the bungalow from which there was no escape. I realised it was no good returning her to the outside run before we had adapted her escape route so she remained indoors with me for the rest of the day.

We stopped her, once and for all, by fixing brick guards
(something used in scaffolding) to the top of the wire
at right angles to the original fence. It did not stop her
trying but it prevented her from going over the top.
Once she had fallen back onto the concrete run a couple
of times she thought better of it and settled down once
again. The ungrateful little 'hobo' and there we were
thinking she was the best of the bunch—I have her card
marked.

Chapter 66

A Last Farewell

Next morning I went out to hang washing that had been in my machine overnight and noticed that something was not quite right. Always when I went into the garden, Amber, the largest of the Great Danes, would appear from the kennel and talk to me in a series of soft growls and whines. On this occasion she did not appear even when I called her. The other dogs were all there excited to see me but there was no sign of Amber. I then noticed what appeared to be blood splatters around the pen. Oh no, what could have happened?

I immediately went in search of answers and nothing could have prepared me for what lie inside that kennel. There had obviously been a fight of huge magnitude as my faithful hound lay in a pool of blood, ears torn half

off and bleeding profusely from several deep wounds
to her head and body. She looked up pitifully as I went
towards her, exhausted and beaten. I burst into tears and
ran back into the house for help. I needed to get her
away from the other dogs and into the house so I could
treat the terrible gaping wounds.

Bryan helped me to get her onto her feet and we half
carried her into the kitchen. I got a clean blanket from
the airing cupboard and made her as comfortable as I
could and then called our vet. Whilst waiting for him to
arrive I attempted to bathe her wounds and never once
did she growl at me, she knew I was trying to help.
The vet arrived and checked her over, injected her and
left some cream to apply to her wounds. He told me
that although the wounds looked horrendous they were
not life threatening, but she did seem to have lost a lot
of blood. I nursed her throughout the day as she lay
on her new bed in the kitchen but she hardly moved.
I guessed she was nursing her wounds so apart from
bathing the bites as I had been advised to do I tried
not to disturb her physically too much but chatted to
her as I went about my daily chores. It was a Tuesday
and I had to attend a 'Brownie' meeting later that day.
I went to 'Brownies' but was uneasy about leaving
Amber as she had slept most of the day but showed no
sign of improvement. I could not wait for 'Brownies' to
finish so I could return to my injured pet. As I opened
the back door she attempted to lift her head as a way
of acknowledging my return. She looked pitiful and it
broke my heart to see her like that. I knelt on the floor
beside her and cradled her head in my lap. She looked
up at me with her sad, doleful eyes and spoke in a series
of growls and whines as was her way, the closed her eyes

and slipped away. I think she had been waiting for me to come home in order to say her final goodbye. I was absolutely distraught, she had been such a gentle giant.

I will never know what caused the other dogs to turn on her the way they did, they had lived together all their lives but it left a huge void in my life for a long time. Bryan was sorry that it had happened but to him, a dog was simply a dog, and I hated him for his casual acceptance of her passing. That morning there had been a sharp frost and the ground was rock hard. I needed to keep her close so had decided to have her buried in the back garden. Steed was selected to be the gravedigger as Bryan wanted the vet to collect her body and be done with it, which I had vehemently disagreed with.

Steed cursed me as it was a task and a half trying to dig the frozen soil but he understood how I felt and set to work. When the job was done I needed help to carry Amber to her last resting place as she was extremely heavy even in death. I reverently wrapped her in an almost new duvet and we as a Family attended her burial. By now it was quite dark which was just as well as the size of the grave may have made the neighbours suspicious that we might be burying a human member of our Family I was extremely upset throughout these proceedings but Bryan continued to grumble about it being ridiculous having a burial service for a dog. He did nothing to endear himself to me as we struggled to carry my 'canine friend' around the garden to her resting place. We had no lights in the garden and so it was a treacherous path we trod across uneven soil. Suddenly, Bryan disappeared with a howl as he found the grave in question. He had walked backward straight into it. 'Just reward', was the thought that ran through my mind at that very second. He was cursing and swearing at my so called stupidity as we lay Amber gently into her grave and the Family left me to say my last farewell. Steed then returned to the garden to complete the job.

The dogs throughout this scenario, kept unusually quiet, as if they knew they had done something wrong but the secret of what went on that night will always remain a secret for eternity.

The following day I spoke to the vet to inform him of her death and he explained that sometimes, after a traumatic experience, dogs can lose the will to live and he thought this had been the case with Amber. It made me feel even more convinced that she had waited for my return that night to say farewell to me for the last time. Humans and dogs are not that different in some ways, as I was to find out later in life.

Chapter 67

Death and Beyond

t was not long after Ambers' death, that Topaz, the surviving Great Dane, succumbed to a disabling condition which caused her to lose the use of her back legs. When we first noticed the condition, it was treatable with tablets but within a short space of time, we knew that a heart breaking decision had to be made. It was terrible to see her struggling to get up and down for the most basic of necessities. The time had come and I rang the vet to arrange for it to happen in our home rather than at the surgery, a place Topaz hated with a vengeance. An appointment was made and the day in question arrived. I looked for signs that she had improved to delay the inevitable but sadly she was still struggling and looked in pain.

The vet arrived and administered the lethal dose and left. I had her laid in the kitchen on yet another new duvet and nursed her during the few minutes it took for the drug to take effect. I once again broke my heart when she looked up at me with her big brown sad eyes but I knew I was doing this for her benefit and certainly not for mine. I gave her a cuddle and then she was gone. I was desolate but tried to console myself with the fact that I had had no choice, she did not deserve to suffer. She had been looked after to the best of my ability all her life and this was my last act of kindness towards her, may she rest in peace.

I made myself a cup of coffee and tried to come to terms with the fact that I had lost both my beautiful Danes in a matter of weeks. I had to get out of the house. I showered, changed and went shopping to help take my mind of things, leaving Topaz discreetly wrapped in her 'burial duvet' on the kitchen floor where she had breathed her last.

I was gone a couple of hours and on my return, lo and behold, a miracle had taken place. Topaz had gone. There was no one about and no sign that anyone had been home, but the body was no longer where I had left it. Well, Jesus had risen from the dead, could not my dog have done the same? I looked around but I could not see any sign of her. I stupidly called her name expecting to see her run in from who knows where, but nothing, no body and no sound. Something very strange had happened, had she taken her duvet with her, wherever she had gone?

I ran to the dog run in the garden, but of course, she was not there and then I ran round the house searching in every room but I could still see no sign of my missing pet. I was mystified.

Suddenly I heard a car pull up onto the drive and was relieved to see Bryan striding past the kitchen window. At last I could share my grief at her passing and my bewilderment at what had followed. I blurted out the full story interspersed with tears and sobs. He brought me down to earth again with a resounding crash when he explained that he had called in earlier. He had found me to be out and the dog dead on the kitchen floor so he had dragged her out to the conservatory. My grief turned to anger, had he no heart! I was horrified, he had dragged her out to the conservatory! How dare he? She at least needed to be carried out reverently, what was he thinking of? Whatever had I seen in this hard hearted monster?

All my pent up grief and anger came pouring out as I vented everything upon Bryan. I cried, I screamed, I shouted until I had nothing left inside and subsided into a resentful silence. Bryan took it all in his stride, as to him a dog is just a dog, and nothing more as I have said before.

On their return, Kyly and Steed were upset, but youngsters being youngsters, they were soon distracted, after all they still had their dogs.

As evening fell, a new grave was dug and Topaz was laid to rest on the opposite side of the garden to Amber. They did not particularly like each other in life, we thought it only right to give them their own space in death. Gone were my two magnificent Danes but I like to think of them racing around the fields of 'Doggy Heaven' as they had done when on the earthly plane.

For many months, Bryan had had his eye on a property plus farmland and buildings that were owned by two different people. It was his dream to buy both and combine them. When the farmland and buildings had come up for sale several years before, it had not been the right time and he had had to stand back and watch his best friend purchase it. Although he did not own it, it did not stop him spending many hours helping his friend look after cattle on it.

Bryan was absolutely dedicated to his cattle when he had owned a herd and could not understand how his friend could live several miles from his cattle, having other commitments which did not allow the time to commit fully to his herd. Over a period of time many calves were lost and this disheartened his friend. Finally the decision was made to sell up and Bryan jumped at the chance to buy it. I have to admit, that on the few occasions I was asked to help up there, I hated it as it was several degrees colder than the local village of Fulbrook which was nestled at the bottom of Burford Hill.

Bryan, as usual, had an idea in his head and neither hell nor high water would dissuade him. He was convinced that once I lived up there I would love it as much as he did. What a forward thinking chap he was, as at that time, there was no house attached to the land, this was the reason his friend had had to live so far from it. I thought I was safe ensconced in my bungalow in Carterton with everything on my doorstep but I should have known better. When Bryan had an idea, he made it happen and I don't know why I even doubted that he could! It looked like we were on the move again.

Chapter 68

In Search of Utopia

The sale of the farm buildings and land took quite a while to complete as there was a complication over water which had to be sorted out and agreed with several parties. Everyone seemed to be dragging their heels, much to Bryan's annoyance. Several times he lost patience and I was asked to get information about other properties with land in the surrounding area.

Once more we were off 'farm hunting.' We ended up looking at several, all with their own drawbacks. All three were on the A40 heading towards Oxford, an area none of us wished to live in. Needless to say, Bryan was so desperate to get back into farming he was willing to look at anything that he thought fitted the bill.

The first one we visited did not impress us at all. We could not get past the smell of dogs. As you are by now very much aware that I do love dogs but this was something else! We knocked the door and were greeted by two middle aged ladies, who we later found out were judges in high 'Doggy' circles. I am afraid that I took very little in as we were shown round. I was concentrating on breathing as little as I possibly could in an effort not to pass out. The smell was horrendous. How could the sellers not have noticed it? My only thought was how quickly we could vacate the premises without seeming rude. I did not care what the land around it was like I certainly could not live in that house.

On to the next which was literally 'up the road.' This property fronted the main A40, an extremely busy road. The house was lovely, a bit quirky, which I found interesting but the land adjoining it was totally unsuitable, there was simply not enough. It had a beautiful landscaped garden plus a huge purpose built games room. This would have been ideal for the children but certainly not suitable for a herd of cattle. Our search continued.

The third property sounded ideal with more land than we had contemplated, several outbuildings and a huge house. I couldn't wait to view it. We made an appointment as the property had 'sitters' in it looking after it for the current owners. They were a jolly homely couple who made us very welcome with cups of coffee and homemade cake. During the conversation it was revealed that the gentleman in question had previously been working in London alongside a carpenter by

the name of Phillip Gough who just happened to be
one of Bryans' brothers. This seemed to bode well for
the viewing, and we eagerly started the tour of the
'farm.' The fields were generally flat and fertile, this was
good start. The outbuildings were huge and plentiful
and mostly in good condition. Everything was falling
into place, now for a tour of the huge house. What a
disappointment! A renovation project had been started
on the property with the intention of turning into a
hotel. There were 17 bedrooms with all the room doors
numbered. The project had obviously run out of funding
as nothing had been completed. There were wires and
pipework hanging from half plastered walls, bathrooms
and toilets only identifiable by sewage pipes protruding
from floors, and the main kitchen had been stripped of
all cupboards and electrical items obviously with a view
to it being upgraded. We got more and more depressed
as we wandered round, Bryan tallying up mentally what
he thought it would cost to complete the venture. By the
time we had seen the last room we were both suicidal
at the surmounting costs. The property was already
on the market at a price that would sorely stretch our
budget, but with all these added costs it was an absolute
impossibility. There would, of course, have been a certain
amount of flexibility in bartering the price due to the
amount of work that needed to be undertaken but it was
too much of a project for us to take on both manually
and financially so our search continued.

Chapter 69

Que Sera Sera

By this time I was extremely disheartened and Bryan was getting more and more irritable as the search continued, despairing that he would ever find what he was searching for. Eventually, at the point where we thought we would never find anything to suit, a series of events happened which we could not have contemplated. A solution to the original water problem on the farm buildings and land at Shipton had been found and agreed by all concerned parties and the sale to us could move forward. Bryan was overjoyed. We still had the problem of the house to overcome but Bryan was convinced that that would prove to be no problem at all and his mood swung to convivial and euphoric.

Every spare moment was taken up with planning where to put what animals and what we would grow on each field. It was exhausting and we hadn't yet left the comfort of our armchairs. One evening Bryan did not arrive home at his usual time for his dinner. This was not too rare an incident as he quite often went for a drink with his scaffolders after a particularly hard day at work. I covered his dinner for later and tried to ring him just to make sure he was ok. His phone was switched off! Oh well, it was obvious he did not want to be disturbed so I settled down to watch television taking full advantage of the time to put my feet up. The time got later and later and still no sign of Bryan. Surely I would get a phone call soon to go and pick him up from ' who knows where' due to his inability to drive. I was just starting to get a bit worried, having tried his phone several times to no avail, when I heard his car pull up onto the drive. I was just about to begin a lecture on the illegalities of drinking and driving when he bounded in with a grin on his face that would have done the 'Cheshire Cat' proud. I had no idea what was going on as he shouted "we've got the house, we've got the house!" Had the drink addled his brain as I had no idea what house he was talking about? On reflection he did not appear to be drunk, just intoxicated with excitement. I made him a coffee and asked him what the heck he was talking about and where had he been all evening with his phone switched off?

He then went on to explain that on his way home he had reason to pass the house adjoining the land we were now in the process of purchasing. The owner's car had been on the drive and he thought it would be an ideal opportunity to make her an offer to move out and to sell the property to us. You may think that this was a bit of a cheek but Bryan was not one to let the grass grow under his feet and always did what he thought was necessary.

He had knocked the door and introduced himself as her prospective neighbour and asked her if she would accompany him to the nearby 'Masons' to have a friendly drink. She, of course, had seen him before when he had been working up there so he was not a complete stranger to her. She readily agreed and he then treated her to dinner in order to sweeten her up so he could go in for the kill. Bryan always knew he would have to pay over the top for the house in order to combine the two adjoining properties but he was no fool and not one to be taken advantage of. He had a figure in mind and after much discussion she agreed for the sale to go ahead at that price.

I was, of course, delighted for him and naturally asked what she was like as I had never set eyes on her before, neither had I ever taken much notice of the house. I was a little perturbed that once again, he was agreeing to buy a house without any consultation with me. He went on to tell me that she was 'an old sheep dealer' and there was nothing at all to tell. It was just exciting to be able to turn the two adjoining properties into one working farm. Who was I to burst his bubble as I had never seen him so ecstatic since he had initially set eyes on the farm at Signet? I would, once again, go along with what he wanted and try to make the best of it. We went to bed that night and I had no doubt at that time that Bryan's dreams were of nothing less than cows and pigs. Had I known what I found out a couple of days later—I may have had a few doubts about the content of his dreams that night.

In my head I conjured up a picture of this 'old sheep dealer.' I imagined a greasy lank haired old crone of about 70 with grubby clothes and equally grubby hands. I have no idea why this picture came to mind as my knowledge of sheep dealers was very limited but I felt quite happy that my husband had taken this old lady out for dinner. Poor old soul, it may have been the only proper meal she had had all week. The following day I drove up past the property and have to admit that I was not impressed by the exterior of it. It was pebble dashed and small and it looked as if it had been dropped onto the side of an overgrown field. The garden resembled a mini jungle.

I returned home to discuss this minor detail with Bryan. He countered me with "but the inside is very nice." He then went on to tell me that Claire had suggested that I might like to take a look around. 'Claire'—that sounded a rather modern name for my 'old crone.' This needed further investigation. He said that I should ring her to arrange a viewing. Armed with her number I went in search of the phone. She had a very young sounding voice for her age, I needed to see her post haste to allay my creeping doubts.

She was very accommodating and Kyly and I set off almost immediately to view my husband's 'dinner date,' oh sorry to view our future home. Nothing could have prepared me for the shock when she opened the door. I was stood facing a Lady Di look alike. Blond, petite and lovely teeth, I took everything in with one sweeping glance. Just wait until I get home, I will give him 'old sheep dealer!' She greeted us warmly and said she had been shocked to get Bryan's proposition, (I hope we are still talking about the same one,) but it did make sense and he had made her a generous offer. (I bet he did!). He will certainly have some explaining to do—no wonder he had his phone switched off!

The house consisted of a galley kitchen with a small 'Stanley' cooker (similar to an Aga), a fair sized sitting room / dining room leading onto a postage stamp sized hallway with stairs leading up to 3 small bedrooms and an equally small bathroom and toilet. Throughout it was painted white and looked clean and airy. The one thing that sold it to me was the French Windows in the sitting room. The vista was amazing. Beyond the overgrown garden, the fields swept away to where the spire of St John's church designated the rise of Burford Hill. It was breath taking. The only drawback was the busy A361 which fronted the property with its constant stream of traffic. It seemed noisier when outside but once inside all was silent, the house was obviously double glazed.

I thanked her for showing us round and on leaving did not feel quite so bad about the exterior as the interior certainly surpassed expectations. The house may have passed with flying colours but Bryan certainly hadn't. He certainly had some explaining to do!

The next few weeks were a bit hairy as Claire changed her mind several times, going back on her original deal and resorting to asking for more money. Bryan was not

to be taken for a fool and stood his ground resolutely.
I have to admit now that I had got used to the idea of
living up there and did not wish to lose the house. I
discussed with Bryan about increasing the original offer
but he was adamant that his offer had been fair and
more than generous and that was the end of it. He was
convinced that given time she would see sense and come
round. How right he was—AGAIN! After a few weeks
of hearing nothing at all, a phone call confirmed that she
had found somewhere else to live and was willing to sell
at the original price offered. A solicitor was engaged and
the sale was set in motion.

We did not bother finding a buyer for the bungalow we
were living in as it had already been decided that Steed
would take it over and make it his 'first home.' He had
great plans to change it all so that it did not resemble
'Mum and Dad's house and he could not wait for us to
move out in order to start the alterations.

Combining the two properties had stretched us just a
little too far when it came to the financial side. We could
afford the repayments but the Bank was a little hesitant
about lending that amount of money to one person,
especially as Bryan had previously been bankrupt. Bryan
knew the Bank manager well and he was aware that we
could afford the commitment we were taking on but
the Policy of the Bank prevented him from giving us the
go ahead. All was not lost though when it was suggested
that maybe we split the financial paperwork and let Steed
technically take on one of the commitments. This was
to be a paperwork exercise only and Bryan and I would
commit to paying the full amount. The agreement set
up, the contracts were drawn up and everyone happily

signed. Who would have known that that 'Family Agreement' signed confidently by Father and Son would see me made homeless a few years later when my own son's greed turned him against me. (Needless to say that is another story, another time.)

Everything was now in place, the house deal was ready to complete and the adjoining land contract had been drawn up to complete concurrently.

Success at last! We were now ready to resume farming.

Chapter 70

A Roller Coaster Ride to Our Dream

On the day of the 'big move,' the scaffolding lorry was once more loaded with the furniture we had decided to take with us and I stayed behind in the bungalow to clean it thoroughly before handing it over to our son. I sent Kyly and her Dad ahead to the new house to try to sort the incoming furniture into the relevant rooms.

I worked like a 'trojan' scrubbing and polishing in order to leave the premises spick and span. I was not sure, knowing my son, when it would next be cleaned so I had to give him a head start. Exhausted by my efforts, when all was complete and satisfactory I made my way to my new home. I was dismayed on arrival to see that little had been done in my absence. What had Kyly and her Dad been doing all day? Well, it did not take much working out. They had been checking out the local inn for lunch and the rest of the time had been taken up by walking the fields and checking out the outbuildings. Why was I surprised?

I have to admit that Claire had left the property scrubbed and polished just as I had left the bungalow, for which I was very grateful. It did not take long to get straight ' in a fashion.' Bryan, on the other hand, was less interested in the house but far more interested in contacting the local market for information about future cattle sales.

It was only a matter of weeks before the sheds were full of cattle, some pedigree and some just for fattening. Pigs were next on the agenda and a sow and boar were purchased. I then contacted a friend who reared sheep to make myself available to take any orphaned lambs. We were now up and running. What was a farm without chickens and fresh eggs? An orchard area was fenced off and several chickens were obtained from a local landscape gardener who had befriended us. He had a glut of them and was looking for a good home for several. We certainly fitted that bill so as soon as the area was ready, complete with huge hen houses for them to roost in and keep them safe from predators at night, our new residents moved in. There were about 40 in total including several cockerels that used to fight over their territory and their hens. We had eggs in abundance! It was glorious and I loved it. It was several degrees colder up there on top of the hill but we soon adjusted to it and the views from the sitting room were stunning no matter what the weather.

Of course, we still had the scaffolding company to cater for so we set about turning an area behind the outbuildings into a working yard. A huge square of concrete was laid so the racks could be built on a solid base and boards, fittings and tube were transported from our hired yard to our purpose built one. It was very convenient as it could not be seen from the road so everything was hidden from prying eyes, or so we thought. Huge conifers ran the full length of the front of the property hiding the house from passing traffic but also taking most of the light from the kitchen. We made a mental note of all the things we would like to change but Rome was not built in a day and some things would have to wait.

The first thing we had to do was to construct a kennel and run for the dogs. They had absolutely no road sense and caused havoc on the busy A361 that ran alongside the farm. Weaving in and out between the vehicles they were totally oblivious to the danger they were in. We were more concerned that they would cause an accident so their new home was erected before we tackled anything else. Dogs safely caged in, we turned our attention to more pressing matters. We ordered water storage tanks for the cattle so they never ran out of water while the new pipes were being laid across the fields and all the cattle sheds were cleaned and painted. I knew all the animals would come before me in the pecking order and I waited patiently on the side lines for the plans to go in for the new house Bryan had promised me. We found a reputable architect who designed our new farmhouse but the plans were refused outright by West Oxfordshire District Council. We had thought long and

hard about what we wanted by the time Bryan had got
all his animals sorted., so we were sorely disappointed
with their decision. We decided, after chatting to others
in the area, to try an architect who was more familiar
with the workings of the District Council. He submitted
the same drawings but drew vines growing up the
exterior stonework with a little man in the foreground.
This seemed to be all that was lacking from the original
plans and we achieved one step closer to getting our
dream house.

Bryan was not a patient man, by any means and all
this dithering about with the Council annoyed him
tremendously and the red spot on his forehead glowed
threateningly. Several times during this period he lost
it altogether and vented his frustration out on me. He
could not be spoken to. It would have been easier just
to agree but that was not my way, I could not keep my
mouth shut.

On one occasion he had been extremely tetchy all day
and had got the whisky out to drown his sorrow. I hated
him drinking whisky as this often turned his head and he
would lash out in temper. He would grab my glasses as
he knew I could not see without them and handicap me
in this way. It used to infuriate me and I would go back
at him verbally. I never knew when to shut up and on
this occasion he chased me upstairs where I tried to lock
myself in the bathroom. He was in too much of a temper
to let this stop him and before I could lock the door
he had punched a hole straight through it. That was no
longer a safe haven and he grabbed me and threw me the
length of the landing. I bounced off the wall and landed

in the smallest bedroom which doubled up as my office. I grabbed the phone and touched the 999 button. Before I could say anything he was upon me and had ripped the phone from my hand and hurled it across the room where it lay shattered into many pieces. He hurled abuse at me, completely out of control, his eyes like someone possessed. Almost as quickly as he had fired up, he calmed down and took himself off to bed, no apology, nothing. Right at that moment I hated him with a vengeance and crept downstairs to 'lick my wounds.' He had upset me dreadfully, rough handling me the way he had and I felt safer keeping my distance from him. I curled up on the sofa where I intended to remain for the rest of the night. I had no intention of going upstairs for fear of disturbing him and setting him off again. I have to admit that I was feeling particularly sorry for myself at that time but suddenly I had other things to think about.

My attention was caught by several powerful lights being shone around my back garden. Whoever could be prowling round the property at that time of night? Suddenly the back door was thrown open and several burly policemen ran through. The emergency call that I thought had not gone through had obviously set off alarm bells when they could not call me back. There was a total of 8 policemen in all. They must have heard Bryan before the phone was smashed as they asked where the man was. I told them he had now gone to bed. Three policemen raced upstairs, one stayed by my side and the others stood between me and the stairs.

Upstairs Bryan was oblivious to all this and had snuggled down to sleep. He was suddenly awakened by our 'visitors' and told to get up and get dressed. He was being arrested for assault. Bryan in his drunken stupor told them where to go and refused. He was given one last chance to come quietly or they would drag him from his bed and take him away as he was. I think Bryan thought better of this and agreed to get dressed. He was then handcuffed and escorted from the property and placed in a third police car which had been summoned. As he was escorted through the sitting room he shouted abuse at me for calling them and threatened what he would do to me on his return. This did not go down too well with the policemen escorting him and he was dragged away to spend the night in Chipping Norton cells. He was up in court next morning and bound over to keep the peace. He was warned not to make the same mistake again as next time they would not be so lenient. In the meantime, I had a visit from a policewoman armed with all the information about battered wives.

I am not making excuses for Bryan's bad temper and uncontrollable rages but deep down I knew he loved me as much as I loved him and I had accepted that our relationship was never anything else but volatile. There never was a neutral stance in our house, we were either ecstatically happy or arguing like cat and dog. What we must have put the children through does not bear thinking about, but as we cannot turn the clock back and re-enact the scenes with hindsight we have to learn from those experiences and apologise to those who lived in those 'war zones' which we created. I wonder why we do not appreciate what we have until we lose it. Bryan had many faults but underneath he was kind, gentle and generous to all whose lives he touched. When he was

in a good mood I felt protected and safe with him and
I knew he would give me anything within his power
but then he had the 'evil' side which would only rear its'
head when he was stressed out about something. It was
at those times I should have learned to keep my mouth
shut but as always I knew how to 'rattle his cage' and I
always came off worse. I am an intelligent person, you
would think I would learn from past experience when to
keep a still tongue in my head, but no—I always had to
chip in my two pennorth!

On another occasion whilst we were battling with the
Council about our planning application, Bryan fell out
with me over something very trivial. He pushed me across
the kitchen and Kyly jumped in to prevent him getting at
me further. By this time the 'red mist' had descended on
him and without thought he lashed out at Kyly. This was
the only time ever that he had taken out his anger on one
of the children. Shane, her boyfriend at the time, who was
also one of our scaffolders, interfered. He warned Bryan
off and that was all it took. Bryan exploded with temper
as Shane tried to get both Kyly and I, to the safety of his
van. Bryan was one step ahead and demanded the keys as
he said it was a works van and therefore it belonged to
him. I had tried and failed to reach the keys to my Range
Rover so we fled the house with Bryan in hot pursuit.
We ran down the grass verge out of harm's way until he
had a chance to calm down. Bryan, never one to give
up without a fight, was stood on the driveway shouting
abuse. A passing motorist, alarmed by what he saw, rang
the police. By this time we had made our way further
down the verge and were perched on our neighbour's
fence. This was where the police found us and asked what

had happened. In the meantime, Bryan, again in one of his rages, was determined that I would not be able to move the Range Rover even if I could locate the second set of keys. He disappeared down the farmyard and could be heard a few minutes later trundling up in the teleporter we used to load the scaffolding. He drove it to the back of the Range Rover, lowered the forks and then lifted the back right up in the air shouting at me "Now try and drive it!"

The policemen could not believe their eyes and went to try to calm him down. All we could hear was Bryan shouting that "An Englishman's home is his castle" and they were trespassing. They were being told to 'Get out.' They were not amused and tried to get Bryan to co-operate. I am afraid, by this time, Bryan was not in a co-operating mood and found himself once more handcuffed and in the back of a police car. He was still shouting about what he was going to do to me on his return when they arrived in Chipping Norton so I was advised to move out in case on his return he carried out his threats. One of the policemen returned my car to its' normal position before driving off and I packed a bag and went to stay at my daughter's house as a temporary stopgap.

I think Bryan was shocked to find that I had moved out, if but temporarily. He rang me to demand that I return home, but I did not. He refused to let me have my wages and demanded that I return his vehicle, even though I thought he had bought it for me. I knew Bryan couldn't work the office in my absence so Kyly was drafted in to keep things ticking over. While she was working with him she managed to calm the situation enough to hold a meeting between us without any further fireworks. It was the first time that I had ever been able to reason with Bryan and we decided to try again. I am not saying that we never fell out again, that would have been a huge lie, but something happened shortly afterwards that altered the course for us.

It was on the approach to Christmas and Kyly had offered to pay for a set of acrylic nails for me. I was in the habit of biting my nails until they became sore so an opportunity for me to have lovely long nails was welcomed. I went to a local therapist and had them done properly and I was truly delighted with the results. For the first time in years I had lovely talons and was very impressed with how strong they were.
I had had them on about a week when Bryan woke one morning in a particularly argumentative mood. According to him I had got up with the sole intention of annoying him. I had not cooked the bacon to his liking, I had purposely broken his egg and deliberately made him a cup of disgusting coffee. Suddenly he erupted and pushed me back against the kitchen sink with his huge hand around my throat. Where, once upon a time, I would not have fought back, I dragged my acrylics down his face as hard as I could. It was completely unexpected and took him by surprise. He leapt back holding his face and then there was a knock at the door and our neighbouring farm manager walked in. I had never seen such a remarkable change in a man. He smiled and said "Put the kettle on love and make a cup of coffee" The manager commented on the marks down Bryan's face and without thought he explained it away by saying that

a bush had swung round and whipped him. Nothing more was said until the manager left. I was then told to get rid of those nails. I told him those nails were staying, I had now found a weapon of my own/

Funnily enough I never had to use them again as I think at that moment he realised that ' the worm had turned.'Fortunately soon after we managed to get the planning permission we required. It was by no means an easy feat as we had to get a 'farming barrister' involved to fight our corner, but although expensive, he was worth every penny. At last our dream house could be built.

Chapter 71

A Taste of Things to Come

When all had been settled and a builder engaged Bryan was feeling a little less stressed and decided to take us all to the 'Spud' Pub in Woodstock. We had a very enjoyable evening. Everyone was relaxed and happy at the prospect of the building work being started in the not too distant future and we returned home on a happy note. As I approached our property I noticed that there was a car parked across our entrance. I remarked how inconsiderate the driver had been to block the entrance and I meant to tell him so in no uncertain terms.

As I pulled up I noticed cattle out in the yard and several people herding them up. We immediately took charge of the situation and soon the cattle were safely back in their shed, no harm done. We then turned to our 'visitors, for an explanation. A man, his wife and grown up daughter from a nearby village were returning home from a night out, when a man, claiming to be a neighbour, flagged them down and asked for help. He told them that he had noticed our cattle were out and needed help to get them back in before our return. What a nice neighbourly thing to do you might think but the reality was that we did not have any immediate neighbours and certainly none close enough to see cattle on the move. How strange, but we should thank the man in question as we had thanked the man, his wife and daughter before they left to continue their journey home. No matter how hard we searched there was no sign of our 'neighbour.' We asked around in the morning to those who lived in the local vicinity but nobody had heard or seen anything.

This was certainly very odd, almost as odd as the possibility of the cows escaping as they had. If there was one thing above all else about Bryan, he loved his cattle with a passion and always made sure that they were safely penned in whenever he checked them. There was no way they could have got out unless someone had opened the gates. We tried to think why this would happen but had to give up as there was no logical explanation for any of it. We talked about it for a few days and then it faded as a topic of conversation as other, more urgent, more necessary subjects needed discussion.

I had been doing several jobs in the kitchen which meant I was at the window overlooking the A361. I had noticed a white van go past several times as I stood there. It was travelling backwards and forwards from Fulbrook to Shipton under Wychwood. I had too much on my mind at that precise moment as I was also trying to pack a bag for Bryan. He was going to visit his family in Shropshire that afternoon and was, at that moment, checking the cattle up on the field before he left.

Suddenly there was an unexpected knock on the door and lo and behold, the man who had been travelling up and down was stood before my very eyes. He introduced himself as a local builder (although he did not actually give me his name) and asked if this was where SK Scaffolding was based. He looked the part in his 'bib and brace' overalls and flat cap so I told him he was in the right place. Was that why he was travelling up and down? He was obviously trying to find us. I thought it a little strange as he asked for a price list and I told him that every job was priced individually. He explained that he needed a price for a job he had got in Shipton and needed someone to discuss the scaffolding requirements. I explained that Bryan was up the field at the moment but if he could wait a few minutes he would be back in and as long as he had the measurements Bryan would be able to give him a price immediately. He explained that he was in a bit of a hurry and would call back shortly. I had no real reason to doubt his word but the price list request somehow alerted me.

A few minutes later Bryan joined me in the kitchen and I explained about the visit from the builder. Bryan commented that he had seen him go past so many times that he felt he knew him and began to put his hand up as he drove past. Bryan had a cup of coffee and a sandwich but the builder had still not returned. He was impatient to start his journey to Shropshire and decided to wait no longer so he retired to the bathroom to have a wash and shave.

He had no sooner gone upstairs than he was down again clothed only in his socks, pants and vest. He ran through the kitchen and outside shouting obscenities as he did so. I followed him in disbelief, what was he doing? The white van had been discreetly parked behind the tall fir trees and the so-called builder was leaning through the greenery with a telescopic camera, taking pictures of 'who knows what.' Bryan ran out like a screaming banshee yelling at him to explain his actions. Almost in one movement he had withdrawn from the trees, jumped in his vehicle and almost ran Bryan down in his effort to get away. He was heading in the direction of Fulbrook. Bryan shouted for me to get the Range Rover keys as he threw himself into the passenger seat. I grabbed the keys from the hook and leapt into the driver's seat and with gravel flying everywhere took off in hot pursuit. I had only been seconds behind him but he was no longer in my sight as I hurtled along the A361 ignoring all speed restrictions. Suddenly Bryan spotted him to our left up a lane as we sped past and I had to look for somewhere wide enough to spin my car around full circle. Once more we were on his tail but not close enough to read the number plate. He drove like the wind and I tried to catch him up but I was unused to travelling at such high speed and it unnerved me a bit. We chased him through Shipton and I was catching him up when suddenly, out of nowhere, came a white transit van that got between me and the 'builder.' I tried every which way to pass the transit but every time I went to overtake it, it moved across the road to block my way. We manoeuvred like this all the way to Chipping Norton where I finally lost sight of my prey due to the transit driver's antics.

On our return we reported it to the police. They asked if there had been any other incidents recently and we recalled the night of the cattle escaping and the appearance and equally disappearance of our 'neighbourly neighbour.' The police suggested that our property was being 'cased.' As we still had 3 dogs and very seldom all left the property at the same time we did not worry too much and almost pushed it to the back of our minds as more pressing things took precedence. Nothing was to prepare us for the consequence of these occurrences.

As a further precaution we did arrange for local gardeners to remove all the fir trees along the A361 that fronted our property, so as to have a better view of those stopping outside. We then placed huge painted rocks along the verge to discourage day trippers stopping to picnic before hurling their rubbish over our fence into the car park. You would not believe the cheek of some people! Once again life settled down and we got on with the job of farming and scaffolding while we waited for our builder's start date to arrive.

Chapter 72

A New Member in the Family

$\mathcal{I}$n this interim period whilst we were waiting for the building work to start, Bryan would often stop off for his evening meal at "The Masons". I was heavily into Girl Guiding and this meant that quite often I would not be home when he expected to eat so it was easier and more convenient for the local Landlord and his wife to feed him.

On one such occasion my daughter arrived home quite perturbed. She was bursting with news of something and could not wait to get it off her chest. I have to admit I was a little surprised by what she had to say. She had called into the pub on her way past as she had seen her Dad's car parked outside. She had found him cosily having dinner with another woman and jumped to the conclusion that he must be having an affair. I thought it a little strange that Bryan introduced his "other woman" as a lady called 'Cathy' but as much as I knew Bryan was, by nature, a terrible "flirt" I did not think he was stupid enough to have an affair right on our doorstep, so to speak.

Kyly was convinced that something underhanded was going on and I agreed to tackle him about it on his return. Later that evening he arrived home and I asked who his dinner partner had been. He did not seem to be phased or embarrassed by the question but guessed that the "informer" had been Kyly. He laughed at her suggestion and explained that Cathy had moved from London to a cottage in Fulbrook. She was happily married but her husband Gary, due to work commitments, had had to stay in London for the time being. She had introduced herself to Reg the Landlord and he in turn had introduced her to Bryan. As they were both eating alone it seemed only sensible that they both sat at the same table to enable them to talk rather than shout across the bar. I was introduced to his "other woman" on my next visit to "The Masons" and we became firm friends. In fact, Cathy, myself and the Landlord's wife became such good friends that Reg named us "The T-Bags" as we often went out for cream teas throughout the Summer afternoons. When we had exhausted most of the cream tea venues in the surrounding area we then progressed to being "Ladies who Lunch". I have many happy memories of those carefree days when time almost stood still for a short time.

It was after one such Friday night that Bryan decided to have an open BBQ. He told me that he had invited all and sundry to the 'al fresco' meal the following weekend. He decided a pig roast would be the best thing to cater for unknown quantities and I was to do the rest. We organised the pig to be cooked by Bryan's best friend and we set to work organising bales of straw to sit on and table tops made up of scaffold boards. We covered these with colourful tablecloths and draped the bales in various sheets to make them more comfortable to sit on. Food and drink in abundance was bought and plans made as to what dishes were to be served. The day could not have gone better. The sun shone from dawn to dusk. We had a lovely mixture of family, friends and villagers complete with many four legged friends. The kitchen was turned into a bar, the dining / sitting room was where all the food (except the pig roast, which was outside) was laid out and everyone had a great time. Music played in the background but was not intrusive enough to interfere with the many conversations that took place that afternoon. I don't think anybody left later that evening feeling hungry or thirsty. Bryan was in his element entertaining his guests. I, on the other hand, was run ragged, replenishing the food table, collecting both glasses and crockery from the garden and making sure everyone's glass was topped up. We made a great team, Bryan and I, him as the front man and me as the "behind the scenes" worker. It worked really well and when everyone had gone we collapsed in a heap and discussed with pride, our successful day. I am afraid all washing up etc was left until the following day, there is only so much one can complete in a day and what a day it was!

Around this time Steed introduced us to a new girlfriend. He had had several girlfriends previously but I am afraid none of the predecessors seemed to be suitable in his father's and my opinion. This one seemed so different. She was well turned out, confident and well spoken, a far cry from the others in the past. We were suitably impressed. She was Maltese and we found out that she had been married previously to a much older man. Well, we all make mistakes when we are young so we did not hold that against her but accepted her at face value.

Their romance blossomed and they got engaged, I will not say that everything went perfectly because that would be lying. We tried our best to make her welcome but nothing we ever did seemed to be good enough. I remember inviting her several times to Sunday lunch where I would prepare and cook dinner, then the men round the table would retire to the other room for drinks and the women round the table would help wash up and restore my kitchen to some state of normality. I did not ask her to help for the first couple of times she graced our table but as she became more familiar with our Family members I thought I should include her as such. When she got up to leave the table with the men I politely asked her to stay and help wash up. She haughtily stuck up her hand at arm's length and said "Speak to the hand, I do not do washing up" and continued to follow the men into the other room. I was shocked to say the least but I was not going to be 'put down' in my own home. I tried to keep the annoyance I felt out of my tone as I replied, "I am afraid if you don't help today that will be the last meal you eat at my table". I think she was shocked that I had come back at her but I was no one's skivvy and what was good enough for the others was good enough for her no matter who she thought she was. She realised that I meant what I said and succumbed to help if a little unwillingly. I can honestly say our relationship never improved from that day forward. I respected her as my son's wife but we never became firm friends.

On another occasion in the early days I offered her a cup of coffee. She looked down her nose and stated "She hoped it wasn't that disgusting 'instant coffee'". Well, I have to admit that I actually prefer it. I made no bones about it. In the ensuing conversation she told me that her Parents would be visiting her the following week and suggested that we might meet them, maybe she would like to bring them up to the farm during their stay. I was curious to meet the Parents of this stuck up, snobbish little upstart who thought she was so much better than the rest of us. I wondered about her upbringing, she must surely have been born with a silver spoon in her mouth to have such a lofty opinion of herself.

The day of reckoning arrived and her Parents visited us for the first time. I had cleaned the house from top to bottom and baked cakes in order not to let Steed down. His 'prissy' girlfriend had already warned me that her Mother only drank 'proper coffee' so not to insult her by offering her 'instant'. Everything noted and taken stock off I was a little taken back by the car they drove. Our family owned Mercedes, BMWs and top of the range 4 x wheel drives and there they were turning up in a very ordinary family saloon. Please, make no mistake about

me, I am not a snob in any form, but from the way this
girl behaved I was expecting nothing less than a Rolls
Royce or a Bentley, maybe this was their country run
around.

They came in and introductions were duly made. In
true English style I offered them both refreshments.
Bryan whisked her Dad away to partake in something
stronger and I made her Mother a 'proper' coffee. We
exchanged pleasantries and they commented on what a
lovely home we had. Steed and Lorraine accompanied
the two Fathers on the tour of the farm whilst her Mum
and I got to know each other better in their absence.
They seemed a very ordinary pair to throw off such a
daughter. Whilst we were chatting I noticed that she
had not drunk her coffee and was a little shocked to be
asked if I had got any 'instant' coffee as she did not like
'proper' coffee and never drank it. My face showed it all
and she apologised for her rudeness. Well, her daughter
certainly never got her manners from her Mother. I
immediately laughed and told her what Lorraine had
said prior to their visit and went off to make her a cup
of coffee of her choice. She explained that she was not
sure where her daughter got all her high faluting ideas
from as they were just ordinary people living in an
ordinary house in Middlesex. Lorraine had one brother
and had gone to the local comprehensive the same as
all the other children living in the local vicinity. She
had a very ordinary childhood, no frills and certainly
no 'silver spoon'. I asked about her daughter's previous
marriage as I knew my son was smitten with her and I
was wondering why she had 'latched' onto my son. I was
beginning to have my suspicions, my son was a braggart

and flash with his money, he drove a BMW and would
be an obvious target for one such upwardly mobile 'gold
digger'. Time would tell.

At the end of the visit we waved our visitors off and I
must admit I viewed their daughter at this point in a
different light. During their visit they had explained that
their daughter's wedding had wiped them out financially
and if anything came of the romance they would be
unable to do the same again. At least we knew where we
stood with them although we couldn't say the same for
their daughter.

The more she saw we lived a comfortable life the
more the romance blossomed and plans were set in
motion for the big day. Steed had always planned to get
married in Church but of course, Lorraine previously
being married, put paid to this. A compromise was
reached and the marriage took place in the morning at
Fallowfields, an upmarket hotel at Kingston Bagpuize.
This was followed by a Blessing at Burford Church,
complete with Top Hat and Tails and a less than 'virginal'
bride dressed in a formal wedding dress. The wedding
breakfast was back at Fallowfields. This was a very grand
affair, canapés on the lawn, distributed by very smart
waitresses, a formal sit down wedding breakfast complete
with champagne and speeches. Everything a couple
would dream off all paid for by Bryan and I. It would
not have been so bad if the bride had not despised us
but we were doing it all primarily for our son, after all
why should he not have the wedding of his dreams.
We smiled and bore the brunt of the cost, while they
enjoyed all the Pomp of the day and then left for a

honeymoon abroad. It was hard to accept but she was now officially one of the family and we would have to grin and bear it.

The year got no better as the two staffies outside turned on Kandi, the Labrador and resulted in us having to bring Kandi inside the house to live. I had always vowed that the dogs would not be allowed to live in the house but having seen the mess that they left Kandi in after the attack I had no choice. She then became a permanent resident of the house living in the kitchen and utility room only, never entering the sitting room for her own reasons.

It was just before Christmas of that year that we had another domestic animal set back. We came home from a night out to find our daughters cat dragging it's legs in an attempt to get to the back door. The whole of its back end had been damaged and it must have been in a lot of pain. In spite of this we managed to get it into the back of the car, a quick phone call was made to our vet in Hook Norton and we were on our way. The vet thought the cat had either got in amongst the cattle and been kicked or been hit by a passing car. Either way it was not pleasant to see the cat so distressed but she was soon plastered up and we were supplied with a cage to keep her penned in. It was necessary over the next few weeks to keep her in while her bones healed but I don't know who was happiest, her or us when the day came for the plaster cast to be removed and her released from her enforced imprisonment. It was wonderful to have our house back, no cat, no cage and no unpleasant smells.

I am sure the cat felt the same as she roamed the garden rejoicing in her new found freedom. Let's hope she had learned her lesson and in future kept out of the way of passing cars or kicking cows.

Chapter 73

A Holiday to Forget

During Bryan's farming days he never ceased to amaze us all with his veterinary skills. He loved his cattle with a passion and almost knew instantly when something was amiss. He was always on hand when cows were calving and when on several occasions cows pushed their 'beds' out he was on hand to push them back. Although he had an inbuilt knowledge that made him instantly know what to do in an emergency, I think the cows had as much respect for him as he had for them, he could always get closer to them than anyone else when they were stressed for any reason and many a calf would have died if it had not been for his understanding of what was wrong. He was an incredible man.

His talents were not only confined to cattle. His ability
to manipulate and control, extended to officers of the
Customs and Excise. Although Bryan was an intelligent
person he could never understand why he should pay
excessive tax amounts, whether to the Inland Revenue or
to Customs and Excise. I don't think we ever got a return
in on time, Bryan would never see the importance of it.
Inevitably we would get the dreaded knock at the door
and find ourselves confronted with H M Government
Officials demanding huge amounts. Nothing phased
Bryan and on one such occasion I was shopping when a
certain lady arrived with a demand for a VAT payment.
From experience they were usually stern, unsmiling,
unbending morsels specially selected for their lack of
charm. I am not sure how Bryan worked his magic but
on my return I found her sat at my dining room table,
feet up on a cushion drinking wine. He had obviously
worked his charm on her as by the time she left she had
forgotten what she had come for. They seemed to part
on good terms even though no money had changed
hands. I wonder how she explained her lack of funds
to her superiors on her return. Never mind it gave us
a breathing space in order to raise the required funds.
Good old Bryan! The Inland Revenue Officers were
treated no better. The men were not interested in excuses
why we could not pay but they had no more success
with collections than the VAT Officers that plagued us.
Eventually we were visited by a lovely lady who did at
least try to understand. She used to come in, ask if we
could pay anything, sit on the floor and chat for a while
and then leave empty handed. Every month she would
turn up, chat for a while and then leave promising to
see us next month. One day she came showing obvious

signs of being pregnant and we were delighted for her. I later got to know her very well when she enrolled 'that baby' at the age of 7 in my Brownie Unit. Her, and I had many a laugh over the antics of my husband who she said could 'charm the birds from the trees'. It just proves there is always an exception to the rule. Having got at least one child married off I turned my attention to my daughter and her boyfriend Shane. On the surface they seemed to get on fine but Shane was slowly undermining my daughter's confidence.

It was around this time that my sister and I were planning to take a coaching holiday (as I had a fear of flying) and decided to invite Kyly along to give her a break. She was not too keen to go without Shane but we persuaded her that is was a 'girly' holiday and we would have a good time. Our destination was the 'Costa Brava' where the weather was gloriously hot. Our hotel was not too far from the beach which we thought was ideal. On our first visit we were surprised to see youths diving into, what we thought, was ankle deep water. We were, of course, comparing it to our English beaches where the water deepened gradually. We changed into our swimming costumes and made our way down the beach to the water's edge. We were laughing as we crept forward into the sea. All of a sudden we disappeared into a huge hole, or that is what we thought. We disappeared beneath the waves and came up spluttering and gasping for breath. Where had the beach gone? We could not reach the bottom and the tide was dragging us even deeper. I have to admit that it frightened me and no matter how hard I tried I was unable to get back onto the safety of the sand. I stopped panicking and tried to

swim to the shore but every time I found a toe hold
the waves would break over me and they would roll the
stones away from my feet leaving me floundering out
of my depth. I have to admit it was very scary. Now we
could understand why the youths were diving in straight
off the beach. We struggled to get back onto terra-firma
and decided to each buy a lilo so that we could float in
over the top of this chasm beneath our feet. The idea was
perfect but the reality was a different matter altogether.
As much as we tried, almost on every occasion the lilo
was taken by 'the breeze' and we found ourselves rolling
uncontrollably down the edge of the beach in a most
ungainly way. I have to admit that that holiday was not
the most enjoyable and Kyly gave up trying to swim and
concentrated instead on getting a suntan. We tried to
warn her not to lay out in the direct sun but she would
not listen and whilst my sister and I were getting grazed
by the pebbles as we fought desperately for survival, she
went to sleep.

When we finally reached her, having had enough for
that day she looked like a 'lobster'. We carefully woke
her and tried to get her into an upright position. We
could see how burnt she was and on waking she began
to feel sick and started to shiver with cold. Classic signs
of Sunstroke! We helped her back to the hotel where she
went straight to bed. I am afraid the next couple of days
(the last of our holiday) were most unpleasant for her as
she lay recovering from her 'day in the sun'. I am sorry
to say the holiday did not improve for Kyly as on the last
day, feeling a little better, she rang Shane to let him know
what time she would return. She returned from her
phone call in floods of tears, he had 'finished with her'.

What a terrible end to a disastrous holiday. We could not wait to return home.

On our return, Shane and Kyly seemed to sort out their differences and normality resumed between them. They seemed to settle down.

Suddenly things changed when they decided they wanted to live together. Bryan was against this idea but unknown to us they had seen a little house and were hell bent on the idea. Kyly's happiness was very important to Bryan and she soon persuaded her Dad to put down the deposit. Finally they moved into their 'love nest' shortly after her 18th birthday. It worked well for a while but Shane's inability to include her with his friends became a huge problem. The situation began to drain her confidence and she became quite depressed. She began to have suspicions about the reason he was not including her and the rows began.

I hated to see her so unhappy but did not want to interfere but let her know we would support her, whatever she decided to do. Things were very much up and down between them until Valentine's Day, 2000. We thought they had at last settled their differences as Shane cooked Kyly a lovely meal, bought her a Valentine teddy and filled the room with balloons. He was obviously sorry for the way he had been treating her. We sighed with relief, all was well at last.

A week later, everything changed and they split up for good. I think by this time Kyly had realised that Shane would never change whilst he was with her and she decided to do something about it. After one final row she threw all his belongings into the front garden and phoned him to tell him to collect them. She had decided she would be happier living alone in the house. This proved to be untrue and she asked if she could return home as she had decided to put the house in the hands of a letting agent in order to cover the mortgage. It was a very good idea and we were over the moon to have her back home.

Chapter 74

An Ever Increasing Waistline

By this time the building of the new farm house was under way. We had been told that we were to incorporate the old house into the new one and we built round the outside wall which enabled us to continue living in it for several weeks. We knew we would have to move out at some point and we arranged to have a couple of portacabins brought to the farm and set up on the car park. They were complete with running water and electrics. We also arranged for a storage unit to be placed next to the portacabins so we could store everything from the office plus any furniture we may be keeping. The first portacabin, we divided up into two main areas, our sitting room complete with television, and at the other end, our office complete with phone/computer and printer. It was all a bit squashed but we had no choice, it would have to do. The other portacabin consisted of 2 small bedrooms, a toilet with an excuse for a shower and a tiny kitchen, if you could call it that. There was a sink and draining board and enough work surface to place a kettle and make a cup of coffee. There was no cooker and no running hot water. It was certainly not big enough to cook a meal in. I think 'The Masons' did very well out of us during the building of our new house. We worked our way through their entire menu several times, it was either that or have fish and chips or a takeaway. We certainly ate well during those months. We were not the only ones to be eating well. Kandi was putting on so much weight that she could hardly walk, she looked like a land locked seal. I had noticed her putting on weight and had taken her to the vet, who in turn had given me a stern dressing down about the cruelty of letting a dog get so obese. Kandi was put on a strict diet and I was told not to feed her anything else at all. I adhered strictly to the vet's instructions, measuring out her food religiously every day. The following week I attended the follow up appointment convinced there had to be a weight loss. Unbelievably—she had put on more weight. I know the vet didn't believe me but I knew in my heart that I had followed the instructions to the letter. The vet explained that if I had, there was no way her weight could have increased. I must investigate further. Who would have thought it? This dog was so crafty she would do anything for food. At 10 o'clock each morning the builders situated their vans in a circle on the car park so they could eat and still chat to everyone. Kandi, unbeknown to us, lay in the middle of that circle and ate everything that came her way, crusts, fillings, pies, fruit, biscuits, you name it, she devoured it. No wonder she was not losing weight.

I explained to the builders my predicament and after much laughter they promised not to feed her anymore. I was relieved but made sure she did not go out whilst the builders were having their break lest they forget. Once again I turned up for the appointment at the vet convinced she would weigh less even though I had to admit that she didn't look any different. Once again she weighed more. I could not understand it. The vet was cross but as I was paying a small fortune for this diet food I explained I would hardly be coming every week if I was not following the instructions to the letter. I told her about the builders and how I had stopped Kandi's morning jaunts for extra rations and yet she was still gaining weight. I would obviously have to watch her more closely. That week all was revealed. I watched Kandi like a hawk watches it's prey. Every time she went out I discreetly followed her. I then realised what was happening. As soon as she got hungry she would wander off down the farmyard and search out the cattle feed or lamb creep. It did not matter what it was as long as it was edible. No wonder she wasn't losing any weight. I explained the problem to the farm hands and they were very helpful and put all the food in one area and boarded up the front so that she could not gain access. It would be a long time before she lost enough weight to enable her to leap over the boarding. Success at last! Slowly her weight began to decrease and instead of lying in her bowl to eat she began to stand and eat like a normal dog. I felt quite proud that I had at last managed to beat her, although I had to admire her determination. In her new healthier state she outlived all the other dogs, going on, until the ripe old age of 16 years.

Chapter 75

A Spinning Farmhand

During this time the house was progressing well. The outer shell was now up and work was beginning on the interior. Life was getting a little tedious in the portacabins. On cooler nights it became quite chilly but when the weather was hot it was unbearably hot. We couldn't sleep with windows and curtains open as our early morning builders could see straight into our bedrooms. It was just like living in a goldfish bowl, we seemed to be exposed from all angles.

One day we had a visit from 'Mel' our tube straightener. He travelled up from the south coast to straighten our tube and Bryan always enjoyed lengthy chats with him at such times. After several coffees and numerous topics of conversation 'Mel' left Bryan in the office and went down the yard to enlist the help of the two farmhands. He had not been gone long when we heard him shouting as he ran towards the office. We all turned as one as he fell in the door ashen faced and gasping for breath. I thought he was having a heart attack but he shook his head and pointed in the direction of the yard and mouthed 'accident'. The effort of running up the yard had left him speechless, after all, he must have been in his late 60's if not creeping into his 70's. All we could make out was that there had been an accident in the yard involving one of the farmhands. In an emergency both Bryan and Kyly were two of a kind, absolutely useless. I shouted at Kyly to phone an ambulance and she went to pieces when the paramedics suggested if any limbs had been severed they were to be put into plastic bags with lots of ice packed round them. Bryan said he would stand in the road and direct the ambulance in. How helpful, I guess it was me then that had to go and face this accident head on. I grabbed a couple of blankets as I fled down the yard having no idea what I was to find. I had trained in first aid for Girl Guiding so I tried to keep calm. I ran round the corner and was confronted with one of the farm hands covered in blood reeling in the yard. I threw a blanket round his shoulders to keep him warm and led him to a trailer where I sat him down in order to see the damage to his head. I then was able to ask him what had happened. He was wearing a loose fitting woollen jumper which had wrapped itself round the spinning tube, which in turn had tightened so much that it had actually spun him completely off his feet and spun him on the concrete pad smashing his head on the concrete with every rotation. I decided not to touch the gaping wound as the blood was starting to congeal and I was not sure what other damage had been done. I would await the skilled paramedics but just keep talking to him in order that he did not lose consciousness. I suddenly heard the siren as the ambulance came into view up the A361. In the blink of an eye the paramedics had taken control and had the farm hand in the back of the ambulance and were soon on the way to the Oxford Hospital.

Tube Straightening came to a halt that day and after a calming cup of coffee, 'Mel' hooked his machine to the back of his truck and made a hasty retreat. He rang next day to make sure all was well but we did not see 'Mel' for a very long time after that incident. I think it shook him up more than he would admit to. The farmhand was none the worse for the accident and was returned home after treatment to his head. He had a couple of days off and was back working before we knew it. These country men are obviously 'strong in the arm and strong in the head' just as the saying goes.

Bryan and Kyly both admitted to me that they were both useless in the crisis and were genuinely pleased I had been on hand. What a pair!!!

Chapter 76

From The Wrong Side
of The Tracks

It was whilst we were living in the portacabins that we had a visit from our 'friendly' Ministry of Transport man. He used to put the 'fear of God' into us as Bryan seldom took any notice of rules and regulations. Don't get me wrong he always made sure he adhered to all safety regulations as far as the men's safety was concerned and always made sure the vehicles were safe to drive but he was very lapse when it came to renewing licences etc. On this occasion I looked out of the window and saw our Ministry man pull up on the car park. Bryan, as usual, at times like this made a hasty retreat to visit the cows. Kyly and I were left to face the official, totally ignorant of what it might be this time. I smiled as I opened the door and invited him in. He looked extremely serious, as he did most of the time, and quickly came to the point. Could he see our Operators Licence? My heart sank, I knew we had not yet renewed it. I could not let him see that he had me rattled, so I smiled once again and said "of course, I would sort it out for him". I made a thorough search of the limited office area and then declared it must have been put away with most of the paperwork in the other portacabin that we used for storage. He was not to be put off and asked me to go and find it. I agreed and left Kyly in the office making polite conversation. I knew there was no point looking as I knew it was not there so I settled myself into an armchair and had a well earned rest. I was hoping that something more urgent would come up. I stayed there most of the afternoon until Kyly popped her head in to say that he was getting irritated and had I found it yet. Of course I hadn't found it, I returned to the office to inform him that there was so much paperwork to go through that I had only managed to sift through half in the time I had been gone. I apologised most profusely for our stupidity in filing it away when it was such an important document and said I would resume my search until it was found. He said he could not wait any longer but would return in a couple of days. As soon as he left the premises I was onto the local paper to insert the necessary advert as I knew that afternoon was the deadline for printing. That done, I rang the Ministry and in a very contrite voice apologised for my oversight for not renewing the licence and asked if it would be possible to fast track the renewal. We emailed the advert across to them and I paid the renewal fee by credit card. The gentleman I spoke to was incredibly helpful and by the time the 'dreaded visit' was upon us the licence had been renewed and registered. I knew by the expression on his face that the Ministry man was ready to throw the book at us, but we had out manouvred him once again and he hated it. It did make us a little more diligent in the future and we had to make sure that vehicles did not travel over loaded as our Ministry man made it his personal vendetta to bring us to our knees. He obviously knew we did not have a licence but because I insisted that we did, he did not have the audacity to call me a liar to my face. Had living with Bryan turned me into a person who lied without thought? Or was it just a fight for survival? I like to think it was the latter as in general lying does not sit comfortably on my shoulders. Remarkably, when our Ministry man had made his exit, Bryan returned to see what had been the problem and how we had coped? He had been pleased with my performance and results. Maybe, that is where my future lay, on the stage! Before the rebuild of our house had started Bryan had bought me an ultra modern washing machine which had been not so much for domestic use but commercial use. I was 'over the moon' with it as I seemed to have a tremendous amount of washing to do which was far dirtier than most domestic washing. When we moved into the portacabin I stored this 'treasure' away with most of our other belongings and hired a 'domestic' washing machine, to see me over the 'upheaval period'. As the new house progressed towards Christmas I decided to visit the German Christmas Markets with a family friend. On my return Bryan took me into 'The Masons' for our evening meal. There was a young couple in there that couldn't wait to thank me for my kind generosity. Of course, I had no idea what they were gabbling on about so smiled and said that was ok. I made

a mental note to speak to Bryan about it later but my
mind was taken off the topic by my friends, eager to find
out about my excursion to Germany.

On our return journey home I remembered to ask Bryan
what the couple were thanking me for and he looked
a little sheepish. I then exploded on finding out he had
given them my 'washing machine' I had put into storage.
My very expensive, very efficient commercial machine.
He had not just sold it, he had given it away, which
left me having to buy another one. My home coming
was not exactly a happy one. I was furious for days. I
could have asked for it back but that would have meant
showing Bryan up and that was something I never would
have intentionally done. I think he learned his lesson and
never offered anything of mine to anyone in the future.

Kyly during this time had been 'playing the field'.
She was not interested in settling down into a serious
relationship so I found it rather odd when she asked me
to meet her latest friend in a Witney pub. I thought she
must 'quite like' this one and was getting my approval
before taking him home to meet her Dad. I agreed a
time and drove over to the pub in question, it was not a
pub I would normally be seen in and tentatively stepped
through the door. Thankfully there were not many in the
bar as I scanned them quickly to find Kyly. She was sat
in a window seat alongside her friend, which was why I
had not seen them the instant I walked into the bar. Oh,
my God. I am not racist but her friend was 'of a black
hue'! He instantly stood to shake my hand and beamed
a welcoming smile. Kyly, unsure how I would react,
looked a little nervous. I have to admit I was thoroughly

shocked but shook his hand and smiled back. He went to the bar to get me a drink and Kyly thanked me for not over reacting. When he returned to the table and made polite conversation he seemed a perfectly nice lad. He was respectful to both Kyly and myself and I could not fault him. I later found out that he had been adopted by a white family when he was a small child and apart from the colour of his skin, he was no different to any other lad Kyly had been out with. I guess I had seen what I had been bought here to see so after I had finished my drink I made my excuses and left.

Oh, dear. I hope she was not intending to bring this one home knowing how her Father felt about mixed relationships. I was on edge for the next couple of days in case he made a surprise visit. I hoped it would blow over as most of her relationships had done but this was not to be. Kyly asked me if I could broach the subject with her Dad but I knew what his reaction would be.

I waited until he was in a good mood and Kyly had gone out before I dropped the bombshell. I tried to 'sweeten the pill' but he was having none of it. He cursed me for knowing and encouraging her and said she would not live under the same roof as him as long as the relationship continued. I tried my best to smooth things over before Kyly returned but once the 'bomb' had gone off there was no going back. He stormed around the portacabin calling me for everything and winding himself up into a frenzy, so that when she did put in an appearance everything had been decided. He demanded that she hand over her car keys and leave the premises. He had disowned her. She pleaded with me to make him see sense but there was no reasoning with him. He told me if I agreed with her I could go with her. I told her we were not going anywhere, but we would have to wait until he calmed down. It took several hours of him ranting before he calmed down enough to ignore us completely. My argument had been that if we allowed it to continue the chances were that it would break up as quickly as it had started but like always, Bryan liked to be in control. Eventually a dignified silence fell on the portacabin and Kyly and her Dad ignored each other, he kept telling me he had 'washed his hands of her' and he would not be responsible for his actions if the lad had the cheek to call at the farm. We could confidently say that this was never going to happen as the lad was not stupid and as predicted the 'romance' ended almost as quickly as it had started. I sighed with relief. I did not have a problem with the lad himself but I do have friends who had a mixed marriage and know from them how difficult it had been at times. I do still see the lad today, happily married with a child of his own, and he always acknowledges me with the same respect he had always shown me.

I have always tried to instil in my children that it is not what you see on the outside that is important but what people are like within. There is good and bad in all walks of life, no matter what colour or creed, a lesson Bryan never obviously learned from his parents. Once this episode was over normality resumed in the household and car keys were returned to a grateful daughter.

Chapter 77

A Christmas to Remember

The builders worked steadily on throughout the Summer months and into the Autumn. They were given instructions that the house had to be completed for Christmas, as in our anticipation of being in for the Yuletide we had invited friends and family to join us. During the run up to Christmas it had rained hard for several days. The car park, pot holed and uneven from the many heavy deliveries, was awash with rain water that could not escape from the many craters. The day of reckoning came, Christmas Eve. The builders and fitters, true to their word, worked until 4pm to complete the project. Their work was done. Mine was just about to start. We waved a fond farewell to the gangs we had got to know personally and turned our hands to the huge job transforming our new house into a home before tomorrow. At first, Bryan was extremely helpful, moving, with the help of his farm hands, all the larger pieces of furniture. The beds were put together in various bedrooms and the furniture downstairs was situated roughly where it had to go and the television placed in the relevant corner opposite an armchair. The Storage portacabin had now been half emptied. The other half was stacked with boxes containing the rest of our home. Everything had to be moved across, but what was that I could hear? The television had been switched on and there was Bryan comfortably sat in front of it where he declared he was not moving again until it was time for bed. I was at the end of my tether with tiredness and pleaded with him to help me move the rest of our belongings, as unless he did, we would never be ready to entertain our guests on Christmas Day. When Bryan dug his heels in he was immovable and this was one immovable man. I cried with tiredness and threw a tantrum, all to no avail. As so often in our tempestuous relationship, I drew strength from I knew not where and steeled myself to carry on. I would not let him beat me. I would be ready for Christmas Day at all cost. I ignored him completely and walked backwards and forwards across that muddy car park until dusk fell. My one aim was to get everything transferred across before midnight but the piles of boxes were not reducing fast enough.

My legs and feet felt like 'lead' as I traipsed first one way and then back again. It was getting darker and darker by the hour and still Bryan had not moved from that armchair. I think my anger drove me on as I plodded back and forth with my boxes. Some boxes were easy to carry and others felt they would pull my arms out of

their sockets. My deadline of midnight came and went
and as I carried the last few boxes across that potholed
surface, the inevitable happened and I fell face first in
the mud. I lay there exhausted, too tired to lift my head.
Suddenly I felt truly sorry for myself. Cold, wet, tired
beyond belief both mentally and physically, I gave in to
the utter exhaustion I felt and sobbed my heart out. It
was raining hard as I lay unable to move, despair washing
over me. It was time to give up, I will just lay here and
die. Maybe if I die out here Bryan will feel guilty, but I
doubt it. I suddenly remembered that Kyly had gone out
with her friends for the evening and would be returning
quite soon. She would not be expecting her Mother to
be laying prostrate in the car park when she returned and
would therefore swing in over where I am laid. I think
it is time for me to get a grip and return to the house. I
hardly had the energy to extricate myself from the thick
mud that tried to hold me down but forced myself up
and staggered, muddy and dripping into my new kitchen.
I dripped across the length of the kitchen and stood in
the archway to where Bryan was still seated watching
that confounded television. He barely glanced my way as
I explained what had happened but he did grin when he
saw what state I was in. I could have throttled him but he
was too old to change his ways now, I don't know why
I ever expected him to. I quickly changed my attire and
was grateful to see the lights of Kyly's car swing past the
kitchen window. Maybe I would get some help at last?
Kyly came in full of her night out and was hoping to
retire to bed but she could see that I was struggling
and true to form, with her Mother's determination set
to work unpacking the mountain of boxes that I had
retrieved from the storage unit. By 4am the house had

been transformed into a home with preparations for Christmas all in place, the tree and decorations were all in place, the grumpy troll retired to bed and two very tired individuals climbed the 'wooden hill' with great difficulty after a marathon night in more ways than one.

Next morning, Christmas Day, all was forgiven and forgotten. Breakfast was soon eaten and dinner prepared and started as we awaited the arrival of our guests. It was a glorious Christmas, enjoyed by all. There was plenty of everything, guests, presents, drink and food. It was perfect, just as we had planned. All thoughts of yesterday were long gone amidst the smiles and happiness of today. This was a new beginning. We had not been in our new house long when a strange thing happened. Bryan was due home from work, he had been to a meeting earlier in the day and I was preparing the evening meal. Suddenly I heard 'sirens' getting closer and closer and then Bryan spun into the car park followed by several police cars. Before Bryan could emerge from his car the Policemen were out of their cars and surrounding his. The man obviously in charge, was pointing a gun at Bryan and shouting for him to get out of the car with his hands up. I had not realised that Bryan had signed up as an extra in some low budget movie. I ran outside to see what was going on as Bryan had been hauled out and was being searched. The police were looking in his car. Whatever was going on? Bryan always joked about robbing a bank, had he actually taken it upon himself to carry it out? None of this made any sense. Suddenly the heat had gone from the situation and they were all actually laughing. They made their way into the kitchen, where I was asked to make them all a drink. It seemed

that Bryan was driving along the A40 on his way home
when he was mistaken for a 'drug dealer' by police in
an unmarked car. The driver of the unmarked car tried
to get Bryan to stop but he was having none of it as he
did not know who they were and raced off at breakneck
speed. The Police thought he was trying to get away,
which he was, so they had called up for support and
chased him all through Burford and on to the Farm.
Bryan had to show them forms of identification in order
to prove who he was but I could definitely vouch for
the fact he was not a 'drug dealer'. I could vouch for the
fact the only thing he was addicted to was 'Old Holborn'
but I guess that was not the drugs they were looking
for. We all parted on good terms but for a short time it
was like something from 'Police, Camera, Action'. The
police had even asked for aerial support they were so
convinced they had the right man. I am so glad I am not
married to a criminal, I don't think I could stand all that
excitement every time he came home from work. We
had not been in our new house long when something
sad happened. I went out to feed the dogs one morning
when I noticed that something was wrong with Kimnel.
I immediately scooped her up and rushed her to the vet
where I was told she had had a stroke. It had affected her
all down one side and I spent hours massaging her limbs
after our visit to the vet hoping that she might recover.
Unfortunately there was no improvement and we were
advised to have her 'put down'. I took her to the surgery
where she lay in my arms as the vet administered the
drug and I broke my heart. We buried her beside one of
the trees on the farm, a fitting place for our little brindle
Kimnel.

This was not our only death on the farm. There was a serious outbreak of foot and mouth in Gloucestershire and farmers in Oxfordshire were holding their breath that it didn't spread across to our county. Everyone in farming circles, were very aware of the threat to their animals and Bryan was no exception.

We had disinfectant at all openings to the farm and any vehicles entering or leaving were methodically sprayed. On one occasion, during this time, Bryan noticed one of his bulls had gone lame on one foot. He had checked it but couldn't find any cause for it so he called the vet to have a look at it. The vet took one look and called the Ministry of Agriculture as a precaution. Bryan was horrified as he was sure it was not foot and mouth but once the Ministry is involved you have no choice, the decisions are taken out of your hands. We knew what was coming so we loaded up both scaffold lorries and got them off the premises and asked the farmhands to stay at home. We were correct. The Ministry arrived with reels of tape to isolate us and the bull was killed for testing. Bryan was so angry, the bull was not showing any signs of foot and mouth and neither were any of our other cattle. It did not matter, we were told nobody could leave or visit the premises until further notice. The results from the bull they had killed unnecessarily came back negative. There were no apologies or explanations. The Ministry just left as quickly as they had come and left us to pick up the pieces. Bryan was devastated, his cattle meant more to him than anyone realised. He ranted at our vet but he said he was only following procedures laid down at that time. He, I must say, was very apologetic about the way things had turned out but of course, by then, the deed was done. Bryan moped about for days feeling guilty about calling the vet in the first place but something happened just after this event that took his mind off it completely.

A 'gentleman', and I use the term very loosely, turned up at the farm wishing to speak to Bryan. He told me that he had something Bryan might be interested in. He would give me no more information than that so I went in search of Bryan. I left them to it and went back indoors. Suddenly I heard Bryan shouting and threatening the man. I ran outside to see what had occurred.

The reality of the situation was that this man had turned up with a car boot full of specialised fittings that Bryan had had cast for one particular job. He knew they had gone missing from the site they were used on but he had not reckoned with someone trying to sell him back his own materials. How he kept his hands off the man I do not know but the man left the premises far more quickly than he had arrived with the threat of informing the Police ringing in his ears. Funnily enough he did not argue about leaving without payment, I wonder why?

Chapter 78

Give or Take a Few Years

$\mathcal{I}$t was not all doom and gloom, some good things happened in those early days in our new home. On the Boxing Day after our first successful Christmas in our new home our daughter went into Witney to meet up with friends. A chance meeting with a lad in Nortons was to change her future forever. Fortunately, he was white, smartly dressed and seemed to fit the bill. We were told he was slightly older than her but we didn't find this a problem as Bryan was slightly older than I was. The first time we met him was the night of our Firms Christmas Party which was held at Fallowfields a country hotel, at the end of January. Bryan and I were upstairs getting ready as were most of our guests who were staying the night with us. Poor John, that was his name, had no idea what we looked like and every time guests came downstairs he nervously approached them thinking they were Bryan and I. The poor lad, by the time Bryan and I did put in an appearance he was a nervous wreck. Introductions were eventually made and he made a good first impression. During the evening we noticed our daughter was a little more reserved than normal and wondered if her partner was being a little controlling, we would keep an eye on the situation

Over the next couple of weeks more and more was revealed. We made her new boyfriend welcome and invited him to family meals. During normal conversation he seemed to be ageing by the day. One day when speaking to Kyly he would be such and such an age and the following day when speaking to John he would be a year older. There was no mention of his having had a birthday so her Dad and I were a little confused to say the least. Eventually the truth was revealed when he was filling out an application form for a new job. Bryan noted the date of birth he had used and quickly calculated his true age. We were a little shocked to find out that he was actually 13 years older than our daughter. We had to admit that he carried his years well and certainly did not look his age but at this revelation we did have some concerns. We worried that the age gap would cause all kinds of problems if they did decide to settle down together, but the trouble is you cannot manipulate who people fall in love with. Time would tell. We accepted John into the family as he and Kyly seemed to get on so well and he showed great respect towards Bryan and I. Kyly was not the only one spreading her wings. Our eldest lad Karl had previously split up from his girlfriend with whom he had a son, Oliver. I was very concerned at the time when Karl became a father because I knew from conversations I had had with him that he had shown no interest in wanting children of his own. This issue had been a huge stumbling block between him and a previous long term girlfriend who he had got engaged to. The issue became so relevant that it, amongst other things, had caused the break up of their relationship. I could not understand his change of attitude as the relationship with Oliver's Mother was extremely volatile. Approximately 8 months after Oliver was born they parted company. I kept friends with his mother and was allowed to keep in contact with my Grandson for which I will always be very grateful. Karl surprised me by being an exceptionally good Dad, making sure not only Oliver was looked after but also helping out his ex partner when he could. Karl and his son became very close as they still are today. I was and still am a very proud Nana. Karl inevitably found 'true' love at last with a young lady who already had a young son of her own. I was not sure about this new relationship as I had heard adverse rumours about his new girlfriend. I had never met her so couldn't really form an opinion but was a little wary when it was arranged for Karl to bring her over for Sunday lunch with both of the boys.

I saw them pull up onto the car park and everybody started to get out of the car. Suddenly I heard a scream as one of the young boys had shut his finger in the car door. My thought was only for the little lad and I raced out to see what I could do. Neither Karl nor his new girlfriend reacted well in an emergency, mild as it was, so I took charge, carried the lad into my kitchen and made his finger more comfortable. The awkward silence that there could have been was instantly broken and we hit it off straight away. The romance blossomed and I acquired a new Grandson. I have to admit that Wendy bought out the best in Karl and I saw a remarkable change in his general attitude. He became a different character, more considerate and certainly more approachable. Wendy certainly was good for him and what we liked as a family was that she took Oliver under her wing and without stepping on his Mother's toes, united them all as a family.

My tally of Grandchildren was increasing as by this time my other son had produced my first Granddaughter, Skye. She was olive skinned and dark haired like her Mother and I enjoyed the many times I looked after her in the early days. Oliver and Skye each had their own bedroom at the farmhouse and on a family meal occasion when I was playing with all the children in the garden, Sam looked up at me and said "Oliver and Skye call you Nana, can I call you Nana too?" I was so touched and agreed to be his Nana too. He followed this remark up with "If you are my Nana, does that mean I can have my own bedroom and stay over?" Of course I agreed and to see the look of delight on his little face was a blessing. How lucky was I? My own children, grown up and happy and producing grandchildren for Bryan and I to spoil. Could life get any better?

Chapter 79

A Jolt Out of The Blue

Our hens supplied us with eggs in abundance. On one occasion when I went to collect them, there were far fewer than normal. The hens were enclosed in a large orchard area so I guessed they had decided to lay their eggs elsewhere other than in their nesting box. I would have to search out the eggs while they were still fresh.

It had been a wet and stormy night, and everywhere was awash with excess water lying on the saturated fields. I decided not to go into the orchard to search as we had several rather grumpy old cockerels that would attack you just because you were there. I thought a safer option would be to look through the perimeter fence and see if I could spot the eggs first. I was too busy searching out the eggs to notice how deep the mud was around the water trough used by the cattle. Suddenly with a 'glooping' sound I stumbled forward and left my Hunter boot stuck fast in the mud. My foot came out and I had to grab the fence to stop myself falling headfirst into the mire. Now my other foot was stuck fast and I was too far from the original boot to manoeuvre it back onto my foot. There was nothing left to do but to sink my bare foot into the oozing mud up to my knee. I struggled to retrieve my boot and limped pathetically with the aid of the fence to firmer ground. I could not walk back bare foot so I had no alternative but to put my boot back on. (I would have to hose it out later).

As I passed by the cow's field, they were all at the fence curious as to what I had been doing. I stepped up onto the grass verge to stroke them and once again missed my footing and grabbed the electric fence to steady myself. Wrong move! Electricity shot through me making my hair stand on end. Of course, one foot was immersed in wet mud in the bottom of my boot, why did I not think before I did things? My whole body shuddered as the jolt went through me and threw me off as quickly as I had grabbed it. This was all too much, I burst into tears and limped homewards, wet, muddy and shaking from my encounter with the electric fence. I needed a cuddle and a sympathetic word. I fell in the door and dripped wet mud across the tiled kitchen floor.

Bryan was in his usual place by the fireside, eyes glued to the television. I stood there waiting for a reaction, breaking my heart. Did my hero jump up and comfort his damsel in distress, did he hell! He did what I should have expected him to do, glanced up quickly so as not to miss an instant of his racing and then told me in no uncertain terms how stupid I had been. At that moment a red mist descended before my eyes and I wondered what I had ever seen in that inconsiderate, selfish, unfeeling cretin, I could go on forever but I am sure you have the picture.

I made my way to have a hot shower and try to come to terms with my accidental afternoon. Afterwards, when I thought about how stupid I had been I did have a chuckle and realised that I would have been far safer fighting off a couple of irate cockerels. Never mind one is never too old to learn and I must remember for next time.

Chapter 80

As Changeable as the Weather

*L*ife was never dull with Bryan, the red mark above his nose was particularly glowing at this time and we knew he was due to erupt imminently. One day Kyly went off to Carterton to bank some cheques, when Bryan and I had a difference of opinion in the office. Bryan, never one to discuss a difference, completely lost it and wrecked the office. On her return, Kyly found me defending myself with the office scissors poised to stab him if he came near me. He was completely out of control. Everything had been either hurled across the room or upended on the floor. It looked like a bomb had gone off, and then a rep arrived. Over the years this rep had become a family friend and we were always pleased to see him, this time it was no different. Bryan's temper was instantly gone as John appeared in the doorway. Bryan said, in his normal jovial way, "put the kettle on love, we'll have a drink". He went on further to explain to the bewildered looking John that we were just having a sort out in the office. Nothing more was said and during John's visit Kyly and I used the time to put everything back in its rightful place in the office. Eruption over, our kind of normality resumed.

Most Friday evenings, Bryan found himself in the bar of "The Masons". It was now a very busy pub at weekends. I am not sure whether this had anything to do with Bryans character or not, but very soon the 'Friday Night Club' were all wearing waistcoats of varying designs, Dolphins, Cattle, Dogs, Fishing, Polar Bears, there was an array of colourful waistcoats worn every Friday night. I am not sure who started it but they were all worn with pride. Bryan even declared that Friday Night was Music Night, even though no jukebox or disco had ever found its way into the pub, as far as I knew. I think this may have had something to do with the fact that when Bryan had had just a little too much to drink he would break out into song, if you could technically call it that. As Bryan was deaf he never could sing in tune and never learned the correct words to any songs. How he could ever call it "Music night" is beyond me. It was on one such Friday night that Bryan found out that Reg and Marsha were closing the pub for a week, while they went on holiday. I had not accompanied him on this particular Friday and was tucked up in bed sound asleep. On his return he disturbed me when he got into bed and started to tell me conversations that had taken place throughout the evening. I was still half asleep and was only fleetingly listening to his rambling. Was I hearing correctly? Had I heard him say something about inviting all and sundry from the pub to our house for a drink. I dozed back off to sleep before I could confirm my fears.

Next morning, fresh and ready to face the new day, I confronted Bryan across the breakfast table. Had I heard correctly? He confirmed that when Reg and Marsha declared the pub was shutting for a week he had offered the use of our house for the Friday night revellers.

I was to find out in the next breath that it was not only for drinks that the revellers had been invited but to eat as well. Everyone had been invited for a meal as well as drinks. How many was I to cater for? He had left it as an open invitation for anyone who wished to come. That was Bryan, he never made anything easy, but was generous to a fault. I did not mind catering for the family I could easily cope with that but an open ended invitation to the village. That was a different matter. Bryan was extremely enthusiastic and continued to invite neighbours, employees plus friends, as well as most of Fulbrook. There was no stopping him. So, I took a deep breath and decided what would be the easiest option to cook. I decided to cook vast amounts of beef bouginon and mash potato and to follow that up with a variety of sweets. Having unknown quantities of people to cater for made it a little difficult but I did my best and the Friday night was a great success. The food could not have turned out better and Bryan had made sure that our bar was well stocked. Everyone had a great time and nobody wanted to leave but I was very grateful that Reg and Marsh had only gone away for a week as I am sure if they had of been away any longer I would have had to do a repeat performance.

Chapter 81

Uninvited Visitors

One morning as we were having our first cup of coffee, a farmhand enquired where we had put our forklift. As we had not used it since the previous day he was told it was where he had left it. He went off looking bemused saying he couldn't find it. We didn't take too much notice until he returned to tell us that during the night we had been broken into. It seemed that under cover of darkness, we had in fact, been robbed. Two articulated lorries had been placed in a neighbouring field out of sight behind a 'burial barrow' and scaffold fittings had been ferried across to them by use of possible pickup trucks and our forklift. The intruders had had the cheek to bring with them a mattress to sit on to sort the good fittings from the bad and had left that behind. They had not come onto the property past the house where they might have been heard but had entered our neighbour's property, cutting through onto our fields halfway down their long drive. The intruders then moved cattle into a nearby field giving them easier access to our yard. We had only just received a delivery from a supplier so there were plenty of fittings available and they had taken the lot. We were stunned. We had heard nothing. The Police were informed and they reckoned there must have been at least 30 men involved to have moved the amount of gear in the time available to them. It was nerve wracking to think, that that many men, could have been on your property and be totally unaware. Our only saving grace was that we didn't hear them as the Police told Bryan if he had approached the yard that night he would certainly have been seriously hurt, if not killed, it had been a serious heist by determined people, well planned and well executed. It unnerved us both and every night following that robbery we did a reconnoitre of our perimeter, checking gates and fences, keeping an eye out for unfamiliar vehicles and always armed with our shotgun. It took us a long time to settle down again but eventually we stopped doing our nightly ritual and it became more random, but never did we ever leave our guard down again. We locked everything away, machines were never left with keys and all security measures that we were advised to put into place were done. We just had to hope that all we had done was enough to deter any other uninvited nocturnal visitors.

Life on the farm was a series of up and downs, bad things happened and then good things followed to lift our spirits. Kyly and John's romance had blossomed and now there was talk of an engagement. John knew only too well that in order to marry Kyly he would have to do the right thing and formally ask her Dad. Bryan was a bounder in some ways and did not make it easy for him. On the day in question when John had decided to pluck up enough courage to ask, Bryan was sat in his usual place aware of what was coming. I was in the kitchen with both Kyly and John and tried to give him words of encouragement before he did the deed. It took him several attempts before he actually took 'the bull by the horns' and asked permission to marry our daughter. They were very happy together and our initial worries about him being controlling were far from true. We were more than happy for them to get married as we felt that John would certainly do his best, to look after our very precious daughter.

We now had something very special to focus on. Every detail of this forthcoming event had to be perfect. We would plan a perfect day for a perfect daughter.

Chapter 82

In Mind of Keystone Kops

This particular day was just like any other. I was working in the house and Bryan had gone to move some cattle in Fulbrook. Suddenly the kitchen door flew open and Bryan staggered in, his face an ashen grey. He was gasping for air and looked dreadful. What had happened? He had looked perfectly normal when he left?

I helped him into his armchair and realised something was terribly wrong. He was clutching his chest and unable to breathe properly. I got him off the chair, leaned him against it and pulled up his knees as I had been taught at first aid. I was convinced he was having a heart attack. I then dialled 999 for an ambulance. Fortunately, there was a lay-by just up the road where an ambulance

would quite often be parked up. Today was our lucky
day. It drove onto the property almost as I put the phone
down. The paramedics immediately took charge, gave
him oxygen, helped him into the ambulance and assured
me he would be fine. I followed the ambulance to the
JR Hospital arriving just as Bryan was being hooked
up to a heart machine in A & E. I sighed with relief, he
looked a little better and his heart seemed to be beating
a steady rhythm. We were told it was not a heart attack
after all but x-rays were to be done to find out the cause.
He was to be admitted. The children arrived worried
to see their Dad looking poorly. He normally was such
a hale and hearty man who never succumbed to illness.
We were told that he had been given something to make
him sleep and as they were not sure when he would be
x-rayed or moved up to a ward they advised us to return
home and ring up in the morning for news. Although
worried I was pleased to see that he was breathing
easier and left feeling the worst was over. The following
morning, after a restless nights sleep, I rang for an update.
I was told he had been moved to a ward and had had his
x-rays. They were awaiting the results. I asked if I could
visit and arranged to go straight there. I informed the
children and agreed to meet them at the hospital. When
we arrived the x-ray results had just arrived and had been
placed above Bryan's bed. A doctor was with him and
explained to us that what we could see on the x-ray was
fluid on his lung. Bryan still looked poorly and had not
returned to his normal colour. I had an uneasy feeling
and followed the doctor out when he left.

I have to admit that I am neither a doctor nor a nurse,
I have had no medical training what so ever except my

first aid courses I attend every 3 years, but that x-ray did not look good to me. I politely asked the doctor if there was any possibility that what had shown up on the x-ray, could be cancer, every persons dread. He looked down his nose at me with disgust. He questioned my medical background and categorically denied there was any trace of cancer in his lungs and stalked off. Somehow I was not reassured. After a couple of days Bryan was discharged with antibiotics to cure his' fluid on the lungs.' I made sure he took all the tablets but he did not seem to improve. He was not one for going to the doctors but I made him go and attended with him. Stronger antibiotics were prescribed and he took yet another course. Still there was little improvement. He was still breathless, had little energy and was not his usual boisterous self. We were all worried about him. How long does it take for the fluid to disperse? Something was not right.

Alongside the weeks of Bryan not feeling healthy the wedding plans were being put in place. The date had been set for 6th July, Kylys 21st Birthday and they had decided to get married in Burford Church. Fulbrook Church would not have been big enough to cater for all the guests that we were planning on inviting. The reception was to be held in a Marquee on the farm and caterers brought in to serve a roast dinner. A disco from London was booked, a steel band to welcome our guests and a firework display that had to be seen to be believed. Every detail planned to perfection even down to the horse and carriage which Kyly had always wanted. Bryan was caught up in the excitement of it all and it raised his spirits. He was not improving during this time but did not want a fuss and involved himself as much as he physically could, making sure everything was exactly as Kyly wanted. Ever since she had been born he had lived for this day, the day he would walk his daughter down the aisle, a proud Dad indeed.

I was still very concerned about Bryan's health and was not satisfied with the way things were going. I asked his doctor if we could get a second opinion, after all we had private medical insurance, why not use it?

The appointment was made and a couple of days later we attended the Churchill Hospital. We explained what had happened to the Consultant and he arranged for new x-rays to be done that day. When the results had come through we were ushered into his office. He did not beat about the bush, grim faced he said 'I am sorry to have to inform you that you have lung cancer'. The x-rays were above his head on the wall. I looked in horror at those x-rays which looked the same as the ones I had seen weeks earlier in May. Why had this not been detected then? I seethed with anger at the unfairness of it all. Bryan sat and took it in his stride. I wonder if he had had his own suspicions. We looked at each other and tears welled up in my eyes and he held my hands as if to give me support. That was Bryan, a nightmare to live with but always there when I needed him. How dreadful was this, I should be supporting him not the other way round. Suddenly from the depths of despair I heard the consultant saying that they could do something for Bryan. He explained that it was only one lung that was affected so they could remove that and he could live with just one lung. He explained further that Bryan now was going to have a body scan to make sure it had not spread.

Whilst that was being done I sat in the waiting room in a state of shock praying that nothing else would be found. Bryan returned and was told he had cancer in his throat and it had just slightly attacked his liver. Could this day get any worse?!?! Once again the consultant gave us hope as he said he could remove both, neither had taken a hold and could easily be removed. Shell shocked, but now with a glimmer of hope, we returned home to break the news to the children. They were distraught but we explained that the following week Bryan was to start his course of chemotherapy which would keep it in check until they could arrange the operation. There was hope and something positive to look forward to. I tried hard to be strong for everybody, always looking on the bright side and made sure everybody stayed positive. Behind the scenes I was falling apart unable to contemplate a future without my man, if all did not go as planned. Positive, I had to remain positive. The fight was only just beginning and united we could fight anything, we had proved it many times before. I would concentrate on the wedding which was looming up in the next three weeks.

Final plans were put into place and it all began to materialise when the Marquee was erected in the field which had been specially mown for the occasion. Our local landscape gardener had offered to supply all the bay trees and flowers for the entrance and arrangements were made for them to be put in place on the morning of the wedding. Everything was falling into place.

A couple of days after the Marquee had been erected and the generators had been delivered we had a visit from the CID. An informer had supplied them with information that once again we were to be robbed. That is all we needed on top of everything else. They asked if they could set a trap for our unwanted visitors and we readily agreed. The following evening under cover of darkness car loads of policemen arrived to position themselves around the farm. If they were supposed to be doing it unobtrusively they went about it the wrong way. As they got out of their cars they all switched on their extremely powerful torches and it resembled the Edinburgh Tattoo. The night sky was alight with all the powerful beams. I would imagine every robber for miles had been made aware of their presence. An order was barked and the torches, as one, were switched off and the men dispersed to their various look out points. Several other officers were sent to lay in the field in case the intruders came in by way of the road that ran along the fields farthest from the house. Certain officers had radios which when used broke the silence of the night like gunfire. They were told to switch them off. You could tell a lot of thought and planning had gone into this operation. My son, who had been sitting alongside the CID on our upstairs landing, remarked that he had seen the same white van drive past the property several times, slowing as it went by. Nobody else with their trained eyes seemed to have noticed it but obviously, as it had reduced speed further down the road, it had dropped off its passengers, who were now making their way up the field where the policemen lay. One of the policemen obviously hot in his jacket had taken if off, and hung it on one of the generators, before taking his place in the field.

This jacket was spotted by one of the intruders and taken as a 'trophy.' The robbers were alerted to the trap and made their way back to the waiting van by means of the side fence. By the time the Police realised what had happened it was too late, most had made a clean getaway. It threw the plans into disarray, shouts went up, torches were switched on and everybody seemed to be milling about aimlessly. My son looked across to the concrete road which went from our scaffold yard to the main road and noticed someone walking along it with a tiny beamed torch directed at the ground. He pointed it out to the CID, that it was most probably one of the gang as all the Police had been supplied with huge beamed torches. Too late, the white van pulled up, our intruder leapt in and away it went towards Shipton under Wychwood. How could it all have gone so wrong? We did find out later that the van had been picked up as it entered Chipping Norton but all they could charge them with was the theft of the Policeman's jacket as the perpetrator was wearing it at the time. It would be hilarious if these were not the same people we are relying on to keep us from harm, let us hope that they were just having a bad night!

Chapter 83

A Terrible Secret

During the following week I noticed several strange things about Bryan's behaviour. He was still able to come into the office to work, he said it helped him stay focused, and anything that kept his mind of the Big C was OK by me. We tried to keep everything as normal as possible. Now that he understood, what he was suffering from, he was ready to fight it head on and I was with him all the way. During the course of our normal day, people would ring to speak to him, these were people that he had known for over 20 years, but he would seem confused and not recognise their name. At other times he would have a drink and not quite put the cup on the table square causing it to fall and smash or he would topple over having not seated himself properly on the chair. He had never done anything previously like

this before and it worried me. I couldn't wait for our
return appointment in order for him to start his course
of treatment.

The day arrived and prior to the treatment Bryan saw
the consultant and very proudly was telling him about
the forthcoming wedding which was just over a week
away, he was full of it. I am not sure who was more
excited Kyly or Bryan. We were asked if there had been
any significant changes to which Bryan replied no. I
was not so sure and mentioned things that had been
worrying me. The Consultant looked concerned and
told Bryan he was to have a head scan to rule out any
other possibilities. We were told that the chemotherapy
would have to be delayed until they had the results of
this scan. The head scan was done and we were told
to return for the results in a couple of days. We left to
return home but when we reached Eynsham my phone
rang and my daughter said the consultant was trying
to get hold of us urgently. I decided to wait until I got
home to return his call. It was either good news or bad
and I needed to be in my home in order to deal with
it. I rang the moment I got in and nothing could have
prepared me for the bombshell he was about to drop on
me. He apologised for telling me over the phone but said
I needed to know as soon as possible. He asked when
the wedding Bryan had been talking about was to take
place, I tentatively told him just about a week away. He
then went on to tell me that Bryan had 4 tumours in his
brain and would not live to see the wedding. I cannot
put into words what I felt at that moment, shock, horror,
disbelief. My heart stopped momentarily, and the world
stopped turning. It could not be right, it was so unfair. I

stopped in the house long enough to explain to Bryan
and the children about the tumours in his head, omitting
to tell them of the life span that they had given him, and
I raced out to argue my point with God. I know the
vicar at Burford very well and always tried to live my life
with Christian ideals. I could not believe how God had
let me down, I had prayed so hard for Bryan's recovery.
This was utter betrayal and neither of us deserved this. I
screeched to a halt outside the vicarage and hammered
on the door like someone possessed. Richard, my vicar,
was so understanding, as I poured out all my anger and
frustration on him. I called Jesus, God and everything
religious, every name I could muster. I almost think for
a few moments I became possessed by the devil, my
tongue was so evil. When my fears were spent and I had
nothing left to vent, Richard calmly talked me through
it, He told me my belief, although dented a little at the
moment, would give me strength to see it through. I
came away from there feeling a strength I never knew I
had and he was correct, my belief did help me through
the darkest days. I was still angry, but now I had to make
sure I had the strength for all of us, to give Bryan the
support he deserved and to make sure Kyly had the
wedding of her dreams. I would keep that terrible secret
to myself, after all, only we as a family knew the strength
of character that Bryan possessed. We would show those
doctors a thing or two!

The consultant arranged for Bryan to have a course
of steroids but explained to me that they would only
keep him going for a few days and when they stopped
working that would be the end. My idea was that where
there is life there is hope and I had never known a

stronger personality that Bryan. I was convinced that together we would beat it.

His driving licence had been revoked and it was explained to him that he could no longer drive his car. This did not stop Bryan. On one occasion when he had been outside discussing the wedding plans with Kyly, she came in but he did not follow her. Worried that something might have happened, Kyly and I ran back outside to see where he was. We might have guessed—there he was disappearing in the distance riding on his 'little red tractor!' Was there no stopping this man? On his return from visiting our neighbours he informed us with a grin that they had only mentioned his car, nobody had said he couldn't drive his tractor.

The wedding was fast approaching and I could visibly see Bryan losing weight, I prayed so hard in those days on the run up to the wedding. Surely God could not be that cruel? I was even more worried than I let on as when Kyly was approaching 5 years old, Bryan was working up in the Shetlands. I had a phone call to say that he had had a mild heart attack, had been in hospital and was now on his way home to recuperate. I was shocked as he was only in his late 30's. Due to a difference of opinion over God Parents we had not had Kyly christened as a baby. This incident had obviously scared Bryan and he asked me to arrange the christening and to dress her as a bride as he did not think he would live to see her married. I did as he asked and she looked beautiful on the day. She had a christening party at the Shillingford Bridge Hotel at Crowmarsh that resembled a wedding reception with a cake any bride would have been proud of. This thought kept racing through my mind as the wedding got closer.

On the Thursday, before the wedding I noticed a marked difference in Bryan. He slept more, he was not quite so alert and when he was awake his reactions were slower. I refused to think the obvious, concentrate less on the negative and more on the positive. I was worried that his top hat and tails would not fit him as he had been measured before he had lost all his weight, but he was sure everything would fit ok. Who was I to argue? Friday morning came and I thanked God he was still with us, he was chatting about the wedding and fretting about the clothes he had bought before he had become ill. He thought he had forgotten to buy new shoes and then it was a yellow shirt. I think in general he was getting more and more confused but he was excited about the wedding and that was all that mattered. I spent the day in-between looking after Bryan, planting flowers in the flower beds to match the bridesmaids dresses, cleaning the house and checking on all that could be checked in preparation before the big day. I could see Bryan almost deteriorating before my eyes, but I would not give in. He had to live to see tomorrow.

Friday night I hardly had any sleep at all, if I couldn't hear him breathing I would panic and watch for the rise and fall of his chest, as slight as it was. I prayed so hard that night that nothing would happen it would be such a cruel blow to all concerned.

Chapter 84

My Prayers Are Answered

Saturday morning came in a blaze of sunshine and I was up early as there was so much to do. I got Bryan up, thanking God a million times, and got him showered and dressed. It was a very slow process as he had hardly any co-ordination and was still a big man even with his weight loss to manoeuvre. He didn't want any breakfast but I managed to get him to take his tablets and then turned my attention to the florist delivering the bouquets of flowers, the makeup lady turning up, the caterers plus food all arriving and amidst this Bryan decided that he wanted a trip into Burford. Now considering the fact that it was a struggle to get him in and out of the vehicles he was now walking at less than a snails pace and I had a million things to sort out, this really was not the time to be visiting Burford. I asked him why and he said he needed shoes and a yellow shirt he thought he had forgotten to get both, I knew his mind was playing tricks and went and got his new shoes and shirt to show him. Those were not the ones he wanted so after a battle to get him into the 4 x wheel drive we made our trip into Burford. I took him first to the shoe shop where he chose the same pair of shoes he had originally chosen, the ones I had shown him at home, and then off to buy the shirt. We saw guests and ushers drinking on the High Street as we shuffled along in Bryan's quest to get a yellow shirt. Un fortunately there was not one to be had in Burford.

As we made our way home with the clock ticking away, bridesmaids and pageboys had arrived in our absence and the house was a hive of activity. My patience was stretched to breaking point as Bryan could not understand why we needed to hurry. By this time it was obvious to all that he was almost unaware of what was going on. The steroids were no longer doing their job. I left him sitting in the kitchen whilst I got myself ready in my finery. I dressed Oliver my Grandson, who was the pageboy and tried to co-ordinate everything else that was happening around me. My son helped get his father dressed but of course his top hat and tails were far too big, he had lost so much weight. It was too late to do anything now, but with the help of a pair of braces to help hold up his trousers, we did the best we could. The main thing was that he was there on the day, nothing else mattered. The photographer arrived to take the pre wedding photos and Bryan was helped out into the garden to stand beside the bride. The family photos were taken as quickly as possible as Bryan could

not stand for long. He rested in the kitchen until it was
time to accompany Kyly on her ride to the Church. We
wondered if the ride in the horse and carriage would be
too much for him and had a car travel behind in case it
was needed Thankfully it wasn't needed but Kyly was
a little upset that he slept all the way to the Church,
missing the crowds along the way who had turned out to
see her pass by.

I had arrived at the Church with the bridesmaids as
neither Skye, nor Oliver, were very old and I was needed
to look after them. Neither of the youngsters knew the 3
bridesmaids who were friends of Kylys so it was decided
that I would travel with them. It was an agonising wait
at the Church, it seemed to take forever before the horse
and carriage came into sight, but as soon as I set my eyes
on it I sighed with relief. There was a huge crowd outside
the Church, after all, we were well known in Burford and
many of those waiting to see the bride were coming to
the evening reception later. Kyly and Bryan were helped
down from the coach but Bryan was looking somewhat
bewildered and Kyly had to take his arm and guide him
carefully towards the Church's side door. As I left to take
my place inside the Church he was stood proudly by the
side of our daughter, ready to walk her down the aisle
something he had dreamed of doing from the day she
was born. The music started up, the doors opened and
there they both were on the most important day of their
lives. Our daughter looking beautiful and radiant in her
long white gown and her father proudly walking beside
her, still wearing his top hat. I'm not sure who the tears
were for, our beautiful daughter or my very determined
husband but it didn't matter it was a glorious moment
and one I was so grateful to see. The vicar had kindly

placed a chair for Bryan to sit in to give Kyly away as the walk down the aisle had completely tired him out. The service was wonderful and everything went according to plan. Bryan sat in a chair in the Church grounds while photos were taken and as long as he was sat down he seemed to brighten up. He seemed to be enjoying himself now as more and more people spoke to him, it was good to see. After the photo session we made our way by car back to the farm to welcome our guests and await the bride and groom who were travelling back in the horse and carriage. It was a glorious day, the sun was shining and the steel band were a welcome sight to greet the guests. Before Bryan had become too ill, he had arranged another surprise for Kyly for her birthday the wedding plans had rather over shadowed the fact that this was also her 21st birthday, but he had not forgotten that fact. He bought her a new car which we had arranged to be left by the side of the Marquee whilst she was away at the Church. We had left a friend at the house to organise the placing of the new car and the collection of her old one as well as to look after the house in our absence, after all it is an excellent time for unwanted visitors to target a house whilst we were all away at the wedding.

We left nothing to chance. I placed a chair outside the Marquee in view of the new car so Bryan could enjoy the moment of surprise and seated him there on our arrival. His spirits were high and he seemed to be enjoying the day the difference in him to a few hours ago was amazing. Suddenly the horse and carriage came into view and everyone gathered around to see the new couple alight outside the entrance to the Marquee. As she climbed down I tried to give her the keys to her new car, she brushed them aside asking why she needed her car keys. She had seen the car on her arrival and thought that someone had cheekily parked there, she had no idea. I whispered in her ear that we had a surprise for her and that she was to follow me. Unsure what I was doing she followed me to the car and hugged me when she saw the beautiful flowers that adorned the bonnet. She said what a lovely thought and I realised that the penny had still not dropped, she thought I was showing her the flowers. I pressed the car keys once more into her hands and said happy birthday, this is your car, your birthday present. The look on her face was a picture as she hugged me again and then ran to thank her Dad who was watching from a distance. She beamed and he beamed and that picture will be etched on my memory forever. The only hitch to the whole day was that Bryan could not stay for the speeches, our sons took him to lie down and rest as the day so far had taken its toll. He was very tired. The guests were amazing, the food was out of this world and the disco encouraged old and young to take to the floor. The whole day was a huge success, followed by a pig roast in the evening. This wonderful day finalised by the most incredible firework display which bought villagers in nearby Shipton and Milton out on to the streets to watch. After Bryan had had a couple of hours sleep he felt well enough to return to the celebrations and sat outside where it was slightly cooler. Believe it or not, he was the last one off the field and never came in until 4am. I was so happy that everything had turned out as planned. Kyly and John had had the wedding of their dreams and Bryan had lived long enough to walk our daughter down the aisle. What a day, I was totally exhausted. I sorted guests out who were sleeping over, put Bryan to bed and thanked God for answering my prayers. What did those doctors know?? Bryan had the constitution of an ox and a tenacity of steel. I was still convinced that he would eventually beat this against all odds. I clung onto this thought as I closed my eyes and drifted off into a deep sleep.

Chapter 85

A Fencing Post Too Far

*K*yly and John had planned a honeymoon in the Maldives but due to her Dad's illness Kyly did not want to go. I persuaded her that her Dad would be horrified to think he was the one standing in the way of a holiday of a lifetime, and so they went.

They rang every day for an update on Bryan's condition. I tried to keep cheerful for their calls but I was watching the man I love deteriorate daily.

I was prepared to do anything that I thought might help and when someone I knew offered to heal Bryan if he attended a 'Church' in Headington I jumped at the opportunity to do something positive. Two lifelong friends came along to help with Bryan and we went in

hopeful that a miracle might occur. It was unlike any
'church' that I had ever attended. First of all, the service
was not held in a conventional church but in a hall with
chairs arranged in rows, not pews. Hymns were sung
from a projector and screen rather than hymn books and
several of the congregation sang in 'tongues,' which I
have to admit I found quite frightening
They waved their hands around Bryan, who did not
have any idea what was going on as they said prayers
for his return to full health. I so wanted it to work but
I have to admit that I had my doubts. I felt uneasy with
these people and felt that they were more like a cult
than a Christian Fellowship. We would not return. We
were given a prayer cloth in an envelope and told that
it could cure pain if applied to the painful area. Bryan
was sceptical as he never believed in anything he could
not see or understand. The envelope was put away in the
cupboard.

Bryan had good days and bad. On the good days he
was chatty and more his normal self and we would have
serious conversations but never touch upon his illness.
On bad days he slept most of the time and couldn't eat.
On these days I made him as comfortable as I could and
left him in peace, popping in at regular intervals to make
sure he was still with us.

One afternoon he woke with a headache. I gave him
paracetamol but it didn't touch it. By early evening
he was screaming with pain and asked me to take him
outside so he could sit amongst his cows. I thought it
a strange request but I struggled to get him out to the
cowshed and found him a box to sit on. Under normal

circumstances Bryan never felt pain so to see him like this was unbearable. I had no idea what to do until I remembered the prayer cloth. I ran indoors and retrieved it from the cupboard. I raced back to the cowshed and placed it on Bryan's head. We had been instructed to pray, if and when we used it, so we prayed with all our might.

Instantly the pain disappeared and Bryan felt a lot better. I am not sure what happened in that cowshed but I witnessed what I can only describe as a miracle. Others may not believe it but seeing is believing and what I witnessed that night was truly miraculous. We returned to the kitchen very grateful that he was now free of pain.

Just after this incident, the surgery arranged for us to have a bag of drugs for Bryan's use. There was everything in it from aspirin to a morphine driver. That bag was later returned to the surgery unopened. Bryan never felt any pain again for which I am very grateful.

On the day that Kyly and John returned home from their honeymoon, I saw the look of horror on Kyly's face when she saw her Dad. He had changed so much in the time they had been away. He had begun to lose his hair which distressed him as he had always been very proud of his thick mop and I persuaded a villager to come in and crop what was left to make it less noticeable. He was now looking very much like a cancer victim. Being with him daily I had not noticed the change in his appearance quite so much.

As Bryan's strength ebbed I had a bed put up in the sitting room to save him struggling with the stairs. I had a baby monitor placed next to the bed so that if he needed me in the night, I would be able to hear him. Some nights I was now having to sit up with him as his sleep was so restless he would almost fall off the bed, tossing and turning. Other nights he would have hallucinations and wake up not knowing where he was. I was absolutely exhausted as I struggled to keep the farm and scaffolding going as well as trying to nurse him. I knew I was reaching breaking point and the nurses that came in daily to check him offered to have him put into a hospice to allow me to rest. I could not do that to him, he loved his home, his Family and his farm and as long as he had breath in his body I would endeavour to look after him as best I could. My sister came to my rescue and agreed to live with us temporarily to help ease the load. She was a great help, making tea and coffee for our numerous visitors and helping to keep my spirit up when tiredness dragged me down and sitting with Bryan when I was needed elsewhere. I will always be grateful to her for being there to support me when I needed her most.

One night when it was my night to sit with him, Bryan surprised me in the middle of the night by swinging his legs over the side of the bed and pretended to be driving a tractor. He called to me to jump on as we had fencing to do. Really, fencing in the middle of the night? He was very convincing so I went along with it. He patted the bed beside him for me to sit next to him on the tractor. He was rocking back and forwards with the motion of the tractor and I did the same. Every now and again he would stop the tractor and tell me to put in a fencing post from the trailer that we were obviously towing. It didn't seem to matter that I didn't move as I was doing a grand job as we moved down the imaginary field. Job complete and we were on our way back home. I was rocking back and forward on the 'tractor' on our return journey when suddenly he looked at me and said "Irene, what the hell are you doing?" I replied that I was travelling back on the tractor after completing the fencing. He looked at me as if I had taken leave of my senses and said, "You are totally mad woman." He swung his legs back into bed and went straight back off to sleep. I was not sure whether I ought to park the tractor up and unload the trailer before I tried to get some sleep or whether my tiredness was solely due to all that fencing I had done in that imaginary field. Bryan now thought he was married to a lunatic—fencing in the middle of the night—Whatever next? This situation did have it's amusing moments.

Every day I saw him get a little worse. He was now really struggling to walk and each day nurses came in to wash him as I could no longer cope with showering him. When he was well he had always joked with me that it was his ambition to have two women in his bed. Pervert, you may think, but I knew Bryan better. He would have run a mile—a terrible flirt he was, but he liked to do the chasing. Anything beyond that and he backed off. On one occasion when these two bonny nurses tried to remove his trousers he found voice enough to shout for me. He was hanging onto his trousers for dear life and no amount of persuasion was going to make him give in. He was declaring in no uncertain terms that there was only one woman getting into his trousers and that was his wife. I reminded him of his ambition and made the two nurses laugh. They discreetly left the room while I completed his ablutions and we had a little chuckle about the situation. Although he was so ill he never lost his sense of humour.

It was heart breaking to see such a strong man brought down to this but I was grateful for every day that he was still with us. He had completely lost his appetite by now and I could not tempt him with anything. One evening whilst a friend of his was visiting he said he fancied some yellow haddock. He said he thought he could eat some fish so as there wasn't anywhere in the surrounding area at that time that sold fresh fish, I drove to Tesco's in Abingdon. I knew they had a fresh fish counter. On my return I boiled it in milk to make it more palatable but by the time I had served it up the feeling had passed and he no longer wanted it. I would have gone to the end of the earth to give him anything he wanted. I knew he would have done the same for me.

The children were incredible during this time and almost ran the scaffolding between them. I could not leave his side for long in case he wanted something. We were all sat around the kitchen table one morning when he made the children laugh by declaring to them that their Mother was the 'Best Wife in the World' and that she had not deserved all the heartache that he had put me through. He was truly sorry for the way he had behaved towards her for most of their married life and I knew that this was coming from his heart. The children unused to this sentimental side of their Father said that it was not right to hear him speak like this and far more normal if he shouted and cursed about her. He would not be moved, he meant what he had been saying and squeezed my hand in acknowledgement.

I felt he was making his peace with me after a lifetime of battles. He rallied a little over the next few days and was visited by the rep I have previously mentioned, that became a family friend. Bryan had felt tired and was laid on his bed when John arrived. I ushered him in and John told him to hurry up and get better so they could go for a pie and a pint, something they had done many times in the past. I knew that John was shocked to see the condition that Bryan was in and he did not stay long so as not to tire him further. As I saw him out, he hugged me and burst into tears. I could hear him saying how unfair life was as he climbed into his car sobbing his heart out. I knew exactly how he felt but I drew in a deep breath and went back in to face Bryan. It was heart breaking to see him, tears rolling down his cheeks as he turned to me and said, "I will never do that, will I?" I had a lump in my throat as I answered him. I had to stay strong and told him not to be so silly, he had felt a little better this week and who knew what next week would bring. I sounded far more convincing than I felt but I dried his eyes and changed the subject. He continued to feel better over the next few days and suggested that he would like to go and visit his cows and as it was harvest time he would like to have a drink with the men. This was far more positive and I began to be hopeful that maybe my continuing prayers were to be answered.

The next morning Kyly went to Oxford to pick up a wheelchair from the Red Cross. Even though Bryan was feeling a little better he still did not have the strength to walk. Our two sons went around the farm making ramps to give them access to all the relevant places their Dad would wish to go. It was a lovely day and Bryan was much brighter. We had had quite a lot of alcohol left over from the wedding, particularly bottles of coloured 'wkd'. They were not as heavy to drink as the beer we got in for the harvesters so Bryan found that easier to drink. He had a lovely time with all the lads. He was a proper man's man and was in his element. He was gone for several hours. Our sons had taken him round to see all his cattle, something he had not been able to do for several weeks. He'd been able to have a laugh with the lads in the yard and came in looking happier than we had seen him looking for a very long time.

Once back indoors he said he felt really tired but that was to be expected after his exploits of the day. Everyone's spirits were lifted to see him having a good time and I joked with him that after drinking all those coloured drinks he would be 'weeing' a rainbow.

Neither Teresa nor I had eaten properly for days and I decided that once I had got Bryan into bed we would pop down to the Masons for a quick meal. I phoned Marsha to book our meal so that they would be ready when we arrived as I did not want to be away too long. We asked one of the farmhands 'Jack' (real name Stewart) to help us get Bryan into bed as manoeuvring him from the wheel chair onto the bed was no mean feat. We wheeled him into the sitting room and between the three of us, managed to lift him in a way that I am not sure Health and Safety would recommend. We all fell onto the bed laughing, resembling players in a game of 'twister.' I got Bryan undressed and comfortable and then left him in 'Jack's' charge. He was asleep before we left the house.

As promised, our meals were ready when we arrived
and they were eaten in record time. Somehow it did not
seem right to be away from Bryan so we thanked Reg
and Marsha and returned to the house. 'Jack' was at his
station, reading beside the slumbering patient. He said
that Bryan had not stirred and was sleeping comfortably.
I was not surprised after the day he'd had. All the
disturbed nights had finally caught up with me and I felt
totally drained. We were not expecting any upheavals
in the night so Teresa said she would keep an eye on
Bryan whilst I got a good night's sleep. I was so grateful
and climbed the stairs eager to get my weary head on
that pillow. I had just got warm and was drifting off into
'dreamland' when I was awakened by Teresa, frantically
calling to me as she clambered up the stairs. She said
that Bryan was making a 'funny noise' and I instinctively
knew that the end was near. I had heard that the 'death
rattle' was an unmistakable sound and knew without
hearing it myself that that was what Teresa had heard. I
raced to be at his side and held his hand. Teresa began to
ring the Family to summon them to his bedside and one
by one they arrived. She even contacted Bryan's daughter
from a previous marriage that lived in Bicester.

Bryan had become restless, mumbling to someone only
he could see. His eyes were rolling in his head and I
found that quite frightening so I put my hand over his
eyes to shield the sight from those around his bed. Teresa
phoned the Doctor but I was sure nothing else could
be done. Bryan waited until all the children, including
his daughter from Bicester and his brother, who lived
in nearby Carterton, were all present. He seemed to be

fighting the inevitable and I remember shouting at him to give in, he had fought long enough.

I am not sure if he heard me or not, but he finally breathed his last and passed over. If he did hear me it would have been the very first time that he ever did what I told him to do, but of course, now we will never know.

The room was filled with sadness but I immediately opened the window to set his soul free. Bryan had always been a bit of a free spirit and now his freedom would know no bounds. When all the others had left the room I sat with him for a while and told him that I was so pleased that his last day on earth had been such fun. I thought about how others had told me that before death patients often rallied and wondered why I had not been more prepared. My only answer to that was that I always believed in hope eternal and that where there was life, there was hope and I never gave in. I closed the curtains, kissed his still body, and left the room.

Chapter 86

Life After Death in More Ways than One

I found it hard to cry. There were too many people to look after, so much to do and so many to inform. I was carried along on a tide of activity but the strangest thing of all was the feeling that I had not lost Bryan after all. So many strange things happened immediately after his death that I felt he was still there giving me sign after sign that he was still around.

I should explain further. In life, Bryan never believed in life after death, he always argued with me that once you were dead, you were dead and there was nothing else. He knew this was the opposite of my beliefs. I had always believed there was more to this life than you could actually see, I have always believed that there is something beyond death. This is my own belief and I do not wish to foist my opinions on any others. The very first strange happening occurred the following morning when I went into the sitting room to open the curtains I had closed the previous night. As I pulled the curtains apart I gasped at the sight of the lawn. Never in all the time we had lived on the farm had we ever had a single 'poppy' grow on that lawn. The sight that confronted me was a lawn completely covered in 'red poppies'. I don't just mean a few scattered blooms but thousands and thousands of them with not an inch between them, the likes of which we had never seen before. Red poppies were Bryan's favourite flower. Very odd!!!

There was a bit of a tussle after Bryan's death as his doctor had been on holiday and a locum had to attend. As the locum did not know Bryan personally he was not allowed to sign the death certificate. Under these circumstances, the norm is for the undertaker to take the body to the Chapel of Rest until the signature can be obtained. I refused to let this happen as I knew Bryan would have hated it. His place was at the farm and that is where he would remain until his burial. I was aware that there were certain procedures that the undertaker needed to do but Bryan was to be away no longer than necessary, I owed him that. I argued with the Doctor at the surgery and had to really dig my heels in before we were allowed to get the necessary documentation from the Coroner in Oxford. Later in the day, following his death, the undertaker called and the necessary arrangements made. Bryan was taken by them and returned to the farm early that evening. I had him in an open coffin, laid on trestles in the sitting room where he had passed away. Many may think this macabre but I needed him close by, so I could talk to him, play his records and come to term with my loss.

Every morning I would get up, go into the sitting room, open the curtains and say 'Good Morning' to him. I would tell him what the weather was like and each day I would single out two poppies from the lawn, one for him and one for me, and place them in a tiny vase I'd placed between his legs. One morning I couldn't find two poppies perfect enough and searched the whole lawn. My search took me to the furthest tree on the edge of the lawn where I was astonished to find not only two perfect poppies but a baby pigeon. I looked up into the leaves of the young sapling but could not see any nest that it could have fallen out of. The pigeon had no feathers and was nestled at the foot of the sapling. I found this rather odd as baby pigeons are rarely seen and I had never seen one before except many, many years ago when Didcot Power Station was being built. Bryan had been working on this project when we met and found a baby pigeon on site. He brought it home from work one evening and asked me to look after it and to teach it to fly. I have to admit I do not particularly like feathered beings but the alternative was to let it die and I could not let that happen without putting up a fight so I took on the challenge. After several weeks of sitting it on a fence and shaking a tin of food for it to swoop onto, it finally grew feathers and took off for pastures new. This baby pigeon was about the same size as the one Bryan had placed in my care. I felt sure this was another sign I had been lead to. It never seemed to move and was still there on the morning of the funeral. I used to visit it daily and talk to it and I called it Bryan. I was amazed that a fox had not found it as there were plenty of those round and about the fields. On the morning of the funeral I went to speak to it for the last time as I expected it to be gone on my return. Strangely enough that is exactly what happened. On my return I looked to see if it was still there but there was no sign of it. Its job was done. I felt it was another sign. Every day I played Bryan's favourite records at high volume. It was just as well we had no close neighbours as Jim Reeves and Peters and Lee could be heard blaring out across the fields for the whole week between death and funeral.

One other incident during this week convinced us all that Bryan was very much around. A young female farmer from a neighbouring farm, who greatly admired Bryan, burnt my kitchen table on one of her visits to share a 'roll up' with him. She often called and on this occasion had managed to buy herself some tailor made cigarettes. Whilst smoking her cigarette she had been distracted and had left it in the ashtray where it had burnt away and fallen onto the table. I had been out at the time but noticed the burn immediately on my return. Bryan had smoked ever since I had met him but his roll ups were more often out than lit and apart from when the hot ash fell down the front of his shirt and burnt holes in it, I had never known him burn furniture. He explained what had happened and I had no reason not to believe him. He asked me not to mention it as it had been an accident and she had felt awful. I never mentioned it ever again. On hearing of Bryan's death she was really upset and brought over a huge bunch of lilies and asked our permission to fix them to the fence outside the back door. It was a hot sunny day without a trace of breeze and she placed them on the fence accordingly. She also had a candle which she asked if she could light in memory of Bryan. We agreed and she lit it. We were sat around the kitchen table and asked her to join us for a coffee. During the conversation she brought up the incident of the burnt table and blamed Bryan for burning it, the candle instantly went out and no matter how hard she tried to relight it, that candle never burned again. We all thought that was Bryan's way of telling us that she was lying. Bryan was never one to admit he was wrong but I was comforted by the thought that by a series of signs he showed me that my beliefs had some credence.

My rituals throughout that week continued giving me comfort and then the day of the funeral was upon us. We had chosen Burford Church for the service due to the number of people we knew would attend and Fulbrook Church for the internment where we chose a plot right opposite the door of the Masons so he could still be part of the Friday Night Club.

We rose as normal and I took the vase from between Bryan's legs in preparation of what was to come. We each put something special in the coffin and prepared ourselves for Bryan's final journey. I put on his favourite records as I had done every day since his death but none of those records would play. I got everyone to check the record player but there seemed to be nothing wrong, except the records would not play. After the funeral when we returned to the house they played perfectly, very strange indeed.

When Bryan had been returned to the farm after his death the undertakers had crossed his hands across his chest in the usual way. That was not Bryan and we changed it to him rolling a cigarette. That was far more in keeping. He had loved his roll ups and we tucked a pouch of tobacco in his pocket for the journey. That was how he would have wanted it. The coffin lid was screwed down and Bryan was ready for his last journey. I cannot remember the journey itself, all I could think was that Bryan was leaving his farm for the last time. We arrived at the Church and there was just a sea of sad faces. There were scaffolders, young ones and those long retired who had worked alongside Bryan over the years, all looking distraught. Inside the church I had never seen it so full, there was not a place to be had. Faces from all walks of life had come to pay their respects. He had touched so many lives along the way and it was uplifting to see so many 'rough tough' men sobbing uncontrollably. Bryan may not have been perfect by any means but a legend he certainly was.

I was, and still am, so proud to have been chosen by Bryan to be his wife. He was not an easy man to live with by any means but I know in my heart that he loved us all dearly and was the rock that supported us all. We will always love and miss him and thank him for making us the people we are today.

Bryan was a huge influence in my life and someone I could never forget but time waits for no one and life goes on. As this chapter closes, there are more opening up on the horizon. I can now go forward and face whatever life throws at me as I have been taught well.

After Bryan's funeral I was swept along on a wave of various activities organised by my friends in Fulbrook. I had invitations to breakfast, lunches and formal dinners and everything else including trips to the theatre and pantomimes. It did not give me any time to mourn my loss, there was always something to be doing. I had to get off the charitable bandwagon as I found I was no longer living in my house. I had worn a path from my back door to my bed, almost the only part of my house I used except of course, the shower. Cleanliness is next to Godliness and I had already fallen out with my Maker. I had to, at least, keep clean even if I had lost my way a little.

I returned to a kind of normality and got on with my life but nothing could have prepared me for the twists and turns my life was to take. I was to have a very serious wake up call as I realised that Bryan's dream of leaving this world owing the Tax Man £1,000,000.00, was to become my reality. Surprisingly, a close family member, would rob me of almost everything Bryan and I had worked all our lives for, leaving me homeless and penniless. Beyond that trauma a whirlwind romance with a total stranger that left me married to an alcoholic and following on from that disastrous relationship, was a period of Internet dating. There were encounters with various scam merchants, preying on vulnerable women. I became acquainted with a lady from Dartford who was also primed by one of these despicable men and we formed a team, a bit like Inspector Gadget and his sidekick and worked throughout a whole summer period to rid the internet of as many of these pariahs as we could. We became very successful at drawing them out and had a great laugh at their expense. Whilst we were operational we were informing the police at Kidlington of all the details we could glean from them, their greed clouding their judgement. Out of adversity, a new and lasting friendship was formed with my counterpart in Dartford and we still keep in touch. It would have been a full time job but I had a whole new life to be getting on with and many more adventures to be had.

It is very strange how we pick ourselves up and go forward again. I have learned a lot along the way. I have some wonderful memories and some not so good, but my sense of humour has seen me through some tough times and when I look back, there is not a lot I would like to change. The ups and downs and the traumas I have faced have made me a stronger, more resilient person and for that I will be eternally grateful.

As Charlie Chaplin quoted:—Life is a tragedy when seen in close up but a comedy in long shot. I couldn't have put it better myself.

Lightning Source UK Ltd.
Milton Keynes UK
UKOW040242011112

201512UK00001B/1/P